Ruby Doris and her son Kenneth Toure Robinson.

Soon We Will Not Cry

Soon We Will Not Cry

The Liberation of
Ruby Doris Smith Robinson

CYNTHIA GRIGGS FLEMING

ROWMAN & LITTLEFIELD PULISHERS, INC.
Lanham • Boulder • New York • Oxford

ROWMAN & LITTLEFIELD PUBLISHERS, INC.

Published in the United States of America
by Rowman & Littlefield Publishers, Inc.
4720 Boston Way, Lanham, Maryland 20706

12 Hid's Copse Road
Cumnor Hill, Oxford OX2 9JJ, England

British Library Cataloguing in Publication Information Available

Library of Congress Cataloging-in-Publication Data

Fleming, Cynthia Griggs, 1949–
   Soon we will not cry: The liberation of Ruby Doris Smith Robinson /
Cynthia Griggs Fleming.
      p. cm.
   Includes bibliographical references and index.
   ISBN 0-8476-8971-9 (alk. paper)
   1. Robinson, Ruby Doris Smith, 1941–1967.   2. Afro-American women
civil rights workers—Biography.   3. Civil rights workers—United
States—Biography.   4. Student Nonviolent Coordinating Committee
(U.S.)—Biography.   5. Afro-Americans—Civil rights—History—20th
century.   6. United States—Race Relations.   I. Title.
E185.97.R676F58   1998
323'.092—dc21
[B]   97-31362
                                                                    CIP

ISBN 0-8476-8971-9 (cloth : alk paper)

Printed in the United States

⊗ ™ The paper used in this publication meets the minimum requirements of American
National Standard for Information Sciences—Permanence of Paper for Printed Library
Materials, ANSI Z39.48–1984.

To my mother, Marguerite Griggs,
and
to the memory of my father, Yancey Griggs,
and my sister, Carolyn Griggs Sallee

Contents

Acknowledgments

꿁

THERE ARE A LOT OF PEOPLE—TOO NUMEROUS TO NAME—WHO HELPED me during my eight-year journey to learn about Ruby Doris Smith Robinson. However, there are some people who were particularly helpful, and they deserve special recognition. First of all, many former members of the Student Nonviolent Coordinating Committee and the Atlanta Committee on Appeal for Human Rights generously gave their time and shared their precious memories of Ruby with me. Without them I would have been unable to examine the full scope of Ruby's activist career. Ruby's family, on the other hand, revealed a different side of her personality. Members of the Smith family welcomed me into their homes—even fed me on occasion—during my countless research trips to Atlanta. Their reminiscences helped me to understand Ruby the daughter, sister, wife and mother. In addition, Brenda Banks, the archivist at Spelman College, was very helpful.

I also owe a debt of gratitude to the Duke–UNC Center for Research on Women. During the 1990–91 academic year I was a fellow at the center. Out of that experience came the first outline for *The Liberation of Ruby Doris Smith Robinson.* Furthermore, I am particularly indebted to Fay Bellamy for permitting me to use her poem "Soon We Will Not Cry," and to Dorothy Zellner for allowing me to end the book with her "Poem for Ruby Doris Robinson."

Finally, there are two people here in Knoxville, Tennessee, who are critical to the existence of this work. One of them, Avon Rollins, is a former SNCC member who convinced me to begin research on Ruby's life. When I first met Avon he asked me if I knew any graduate students who wanted to write a thesis or dissertation on, as he put it, "this dynamic sister who was in SNCC." I thanked him for his suggestion, but made it clear that I did not know anyone who would be interested. I quickly forgot all about that conversation, but Avon did not. From then on whenever I saw him he would ask me the same question. Finally, one day after I assured him for the twentieth time that I did not know any interested graduate students, Avon asked me, "why don't you write Ruby's biography?" Momentarily flustered, I quickly informed him that I was a nineteenth-century specialist, so I did not do twentieth-century history. That explanation did not persuade Avon. For the next two years whenever he saw me, Avon tried to convince me to begin researching Ruby's life. His tenacity would have warmed Ruby's heart. Obviously, Avon could never forget her.

While Avon Rollins motivated me to start this project, Angelia Roach is the person who made it possible for me to complete it. Angelia has typed this manuscript more times than she cares to count. But she has patiently navigated through all the revisions and different versions. Somehow, through it all she has been able to keep the manuscript on schedule and keep her sense of humor.

Special thanks to Steve Wrinn for his encouragement and vision.

To all of these people, and many others I did not name, I want to say, thank you.

A Note on Names

SEVERAL FORMER SNCC MEMBERS HAVE CHANGED THEIR NAMES IN THE years since their involvement in the civil rights movement. For purposes of consistency and historical accuracy, I have referred to these people by the names they used when they joined SNCC. They include Stokely Carmichael, now Kwame Ture; Curtis Hayes, now Curtis Muhammad; Willie Ricks, now Mucasa; Gwen Robinson, now Zohara Simmons; Mildred Page Forman, now Mildred Page.

CHAPTER ONE

Soon We Will Not Cry

*I guess what I'm trying to write about is
the pain I feel at this moment. Can one
write about pain? What I'm also attempting
to ask is, How does one get used to it?*

*How many people will have to die before we
can make it a two-way street? I'm afraid of
war, never having known it, but I'm even
more afraid of how many of our people have
to die.*

*I would much rather us die fighting to defend
ourselves, since we die all the time anyway.*

*I want to cry but am not able to do so.
With each death we cry a little less.
Soon, we will not cry at all.*

FAY BELLAMY

FAY BELLAMY WAS A SNCC VETERAN WHO WAS PARTICULARLY ACTIVE IN
the Selma, Alabama, campaign. She had seen a number of committed and
courageous civil rights workers die for the cause, and she had grown weary
of the pain that seized her every time she heard about yet another funeral.
Jimmie Lee Jackson, Jonathan Daniels, Herbert Lee, James Reeb, Medgar
Evers, Viola Liuzzo: the list of those who had died for the cause was long,

and their names and faces filled Bellamy's head. These images haunted her and moved her to write the poem "Soon We Will Not Cry."[1] Many other young civil rights workers were similarly affected by the carnage around them. Yet, regardless of how many deaths they witnessed, the pain never diminished and the level of despair deepened with every loss.

On 8 October 1967, three staff members of the Student Nonviolent Coordinating Committee (SNCC) composed a letter to their membership to inform them of still another death. "It is with pain that we inform you," they wrote, "that our sister, Ruby Doris Smith Robinson, passed away Saturday night, October 7."[2] SNCC members were saddened, even devastated, to learn that another of their members was gone. They expected a large crowd at the following Saturday's funeral at the West Mitchell C. M. E. Church in Atlanta, Georgia. Ruby Doris Smith Robinson had been an important power in SNCC, and her death had occurred during a particularly tumultuous time for the civil rights movement and the country.

Just the year before, SNCC members had first articulated the "black power" cry. As representatives from SNCC, the Congress of Racial Equality (CORE), the Southern Christian Leadership Conference (SCLC), and the National Association for the Advancement of Colored People (NAACP) marched across Mississippi in June of 1966, one of SNCC's advance people, Willie Ricks, had begun exhorting crowds by raising the cry "black power for black people." This phrase provided an outlet for the increasing frustration many felt because of the slow pace of change. Despite the building excitement that Ricks's black power cry generated among crowds of frustrated black Mississippians, the news media largely ignored his activities because he was not very well known. It was only later when nationally prominent black militant Stokely Carmichael, who walked along with the main group of marchers a day behind Ricks, raised the black power cry that the news media introduced this phrase to the rest of the country.

This historic introduction occurred when the marchers arrived in Greenwood on 16 June and Carmichael was arrested for attempting to defy a police order. The marchers were hot and weary, and the local people who turned out to cheer them were frustrated and tired of waiting for their lives to change. The marchers and the local people milled around in the hot June sunshine; many began to perspire as their collective resentment grew and their level of discomfort rose. Why had local authorities arrested Carmichael, they demanded to know. After all, they reasoned, they were just trying to hold a peaceful assembly. It seemed that the white folks were determined to interfere with every aspect of their lives. As the crowd became increas-

2

ingly restless, Carmichael suddenly appeared after being bailed out of jail. A hush fell over the gathering as they waited expectantly.

Carmichael spoke slowly and deliberately at first, but then his words came out faster and the level of his voice rose, building to a dramatic crescendo. In a clear lilting voice that was heavy with emotion with just a hint of his Trinidadian accent, Carmichael told the waiting rally: "This is the twenty-seventh time I have been arrested. I ain't going to jail no more." "What we gonna start saying now," he cried, "is black power."[3] The crowd roared back, "Black Power!" Ruby Doris was there to join in the cry, as was James Forman, who explains: "We wanted black people in all parts of the United States to hear the slogan, to be stirred by it, to adopt it. It was a spontaneous move on our part, with nothing false about it. We felt, we knew, we could see that 'black power' was a slogan of the masses."[4] After the Mississippi march, the press routinely associated Ruby Doris with the black power supporters in SNCC. Undoubtedly, many of the mourners at Ruby Doris's funeral could still visualize her shouting "black power" in Greenwood and wearing her hair in an Afro. She had been one of the first women in the organization to wear her hair in its natural state in public.

In that crowded Atlanta church, many recalled how passionately committed Ruby had been to SNCC, how invaluable her commitment and talent were to the organization. It was hard for many to believe that she had died at twenty-five, leaving behind not only her SNCC colleagues but also her husband, Clifford, and her son, Kenneth Toure Robinson. She had been married for three years, a mother for only two, and her black nationalist politics had permeated even these private areas; Ruby Doris had named her son for Sekou Toure, president of the then newly independent West African nation of Guinea.

Despite her youth, Ruby Doris had been famous. Consequently, her family received countless expressions of sympathy from all over the country and all over the world. For example, Whitney Young, head of the National Urban League, sent a telegram expressing the deep regret he and his wife, Margaret, felt at "the ending of such a young and beautiful life."[5] And a telegram came to Ruby's husband from Guinea's president, Sekou Toure, whom Ruby Doris had met several years earlier during a trip to Guinea: "[We] have learned with great sorrow [about the] cruel and premature loss of your honorable spouse. [We] pray for her and may the earth be light on her."[6]

Because many people wished to express their sympathy in person, mourners poured into the West Mitchell C. M. E. Church from everywhere. The church was a red brick structure that could provide seating for about 250 people. The rows of plain wooden pews inside the church were divided into four sections by the three aisles that started at the back of the church and ended near a wooden pulpit in the front. Behind the pulpit was a choir loft, but it was empty. The music for Ruby's funeral was provided by a pianist, and a soloist sang one selection just before the eulogy. Ruby's casket in the front of the church was surrounded by a large number of floral arrangements. The pale lavender, deep yellow, rich red, and bright blue flowers were in direct contrast to the somber dark hues of the garments worn by many of the mourners.

Ruby lay there among all those flowers looking very small, and a little fragile because she had lost so much weight as she suffered through the illness that would eventually steal her life. Some of those who filed past her casket were struck by the irony of her weight loss when they recalled how concerned Ruby had always been about controlling her weight. She was dressed simply in a pale-pink chiffon gown with a matching corsage. A single strand of pearls adorned her neck. Her hair, which she had proudly worn in an Afro from time to time during her activist days, had thinned considerably during her long illness, so it was simply brushed back away from her face. As the mourners looked at her one last time, she seemed serene. But many could imagine her facial expression changing in an instant to one of anger when she was confronting those who had not taken care of their responsibility. It seemed that they could even hear her voice—that authoritative, rich alto voice—alternately issuing orders, chastising a shirker, or even laughing good naturedly.

Then it all died away as the service began. Soothing strains of music from the piano soloist wafted through the air accompanied by anguished sounds of weeping. Sunlight streamed through the stained-glass windows, making the tears glisten on the faces of the mourners. Many of those assembled in the church that day had marched, served jail time, and plotted strategy alongside Ruby Doris. For example, Julian Bond had known Ruby since she first joined the movement. A student at Morehouse College while Ruby Doris was studying at Spelman, Bond began his activist career in the Atlanta Student Movement, but he soon joined SNCC and became communications director.[7] A short time later, with the blessing of many SNCC colleagues, he ran successfully for a seat in the Georgia legislature. The sights and sounds of Ruby's funeral receded briefly as Bond visualized Ruby marching and holding a picket sign. He could still remember the tremendous zeal that Ruby Doris had brought to demonstrations. Bond smiled when he recalled how she had never quite seemed the typical Spelman student; she had displayed no interest in the social activities that attracted so many Spelman undergraduates.[8]

Another of the mourners, John Lewis, also remembered Ruby when she was a Spelman student. He was a student at American Baptist Theological Seminary in Nashville, Tennessee, at the time, and he was one of the first to become involved in local sit-ins. He soon moved beyond the Nashville movement to the national arena and the chairmanship of SNCC, which he guided through some difficult early periods. Through it all, Lewis knew Ruby Doris as an energetic activist. He particularly remembered her courage, her calm demeanor, and her kindness on the freedom rides. She had tried very hard to calm the other freedom riders with words of support, and she had often provided him with encouragement too, as he attempted to administer SNCC.[9] As Lewis sat on the hard wooden pew sandwiched between two other mourners, it almost seemed that he could feel her hand patting him on the shoulder, and hear her calm voice reassuring him as she had so many times before.

Joyce Ladner knew things could never be the same without Ruby Doris. Ladner, a native Mississippian who would later go on to pursue a graduate degree in sociology, had joined SNCC while a student at Tougaloo College. Even then, Ruby Doris was legendary. Ruby was young, black, and female; and she was a leader. Her presence was an inspiration to many activists, but it was particularly meaningful to Ladner and other young women activists. Ruby Doris, however, had been much more than an activist role model to Ladner; she had been a friend. As Ladner sat in the midst of all those other mourners, she felt dazed and empty. Ruby's passing left a painful void in her life that was impossible to fill. "There really wasn't much you could say," she would later note.[10]

Meanwhile, as SNCC colleague Dottie Zellner listened to the eulogy, she realized she was losing control. Zellner tried to restrain the flood of tears that threatened to break through her composure, but she failed. Afterward, she would painfully recall the annoyance some SNCC colleagues expressed at her show of emotion.[11]

Cleveland Sellers was another of the mourners at the West Mitchell C. M. E. Church. Sellers, a fiery young militant, had joined the student movement while enrolled at Howard University and had moved on to SNCC with Stokely Carmichael, also from Howard. When Carmichael had been elected SNCC's chairman in 1966, Sellers had become program secretary and Ruby Doris executive secretary. At times Ruby had been at odds with Sellers and Carmichael; Sellers remembered their skirmishes as he smelled the almost too sweet smell of all the flowers and heard the sounds of weeping around him. Sellers had respected and admired Ruby's commitment to the movement. As he put it, "[She was] one of the persons who inspired me to make the movement my life . . . . I had loved her."[12]

James Forman was also among the mourners. Though Forman had joined SNCC in its earliest days and had become the organization's first executive secretary, he was quite different from the idealistic young college students who constituted much of the early SNCC staff. He was a working man, a family man, and a military veteran. Ruby Doris had begun her administrative career as Forman's assistant, and had soon become invaluable in that position. Under his tutelage, she had developed an administrative philosophy compatible with his and had become a major source of support for him. Forman could not concentrate on the service because he was angry about Ruby's death. There had been too many deaths already. He knew that she was one of the few genuine revolutionaries in the movement and that they could ill afford to lose her.[13] Forman's anger grew as he listened to the minister preach a traditional black Christian funeral complete with biblical references and words of heavenly comfort for the family. Forman wanted to be polite and respectful; he did not want to make a scene. But part of him was crying out, "This is wrong." He was seized by a powerful restlessness.

Eldridge Cleaver attended the funeral as well. While he had never been directly associated with Ruby Doris, he knew she was an important soldier in the cause. By the time of her death, Cleaver, who was an officer in the Black Panther Party, had come to be associated with the most militant form of revolutionary black nationalism. Because of the party's ideology, both it and Cleaver became special targets of media and government scrutiny, giving an enormous symbolic significance to his presence at Ruby Doris's funeral.

An opposing, yet equally famous, black activist was forced to mourn outside because so many people made the trip to Atlanta for Ruby Doris Smith Robinson's funeral that the church could not accommodate them all. This activist, Ron Karenga, and his bodyguard were part of a large crowd outside the church. Though Karenga had never worked directly with Ruby Doris, he was widely recognized as the foremost architect of an ideology of cultural black nationalism to which Ruby subscribed. He had created a festival based on traditional African principles, Kwanzaa, which served as the centerpiece of his ideology; he believed that such cultural symbols held the key to African-American liberation and advancement.[14] By the time of Ruby's funeral, a great deal of friction had developed between Ron Karenga and Eldridge Cleaver that would lead to some nasty confrontations. The presence of both men at her funeral clearly indicates the breadth of Ruby's appeal among disparate segments of the activist community.

As scores of activist mourners listened to the service and contemplated the meaning of Ruby Doris's life within the movement for black liberation, others remembered Ruby Doris quite differently. Mrs. Inez Hill, a neighbor and friend of the family, could still picture her as a little girl, "streaking across the corner from [Ruby's] house to [hers] . . ."[15] Ruby Doris's brother, Willie, recalled both how exasperating and how kind his older sister could be. He could still hear her voice when she gave him unsolicited advice and reminded him that she was his older sister. But he could also see the look on her face the day she had surprised him with a very special gift: the set of weights he needed to help him train to win an athletic scholarship to Morris Brown College.[16] Ruby Doris's older sister, Mary Ann, would never forget the many times Ruby Doris had raided her closet and worn her clothes to school; but Mary Ann also remembered the excitement and determination on Ruby Doris's face when she had talked about going to jail for the movement.[17] Such happy memories only sharpened the pain and grief that family members felt. Many sobbed openly as they were jolted back to the present by the sight of Ruby's small, fragile body in the casket in front of them.

Ruby Doris's younger sister, Catherine, had been her constant companion during the last months of her life while she suffered through the agony of her terminal condition. As painful memories of Ruby's last days flooded Catherine's mind, a sense of emptiness threatened to engulf her, and a dull, pulsating ache began to spread throughout her body. The pain became sharper and more focused; it unleashed a torrent of tears that dissolved what was left of Catherine's self-control. The mourners' anguished cries all around her seemed to mingle with the minister's assurances of an afterlife to produce a deafening roar that was more than Catherine could stand. She fled the sanctuary. Within a few minutes, she was followed by an equally distraught Mary Ann. The sisters shared a private moment away from the rest of the mourners that seemed to comfort them. After a short time, they were able to reenter the sanctuary and sit through the end of the service.

Catherine, with the blessing of the Smith family, had taken the lead in planning Ruby's service. It was a very traditional southern black funeral, and it was an exceedingly emotional one. Reverend O. M. Sims read a passage of scripture, Reverend B. B. Carter offered a prayer, and West Mitchell's pastor, Reverend E. H. Hicks, preached the eulogy. Reverend Hicks had not known Ruby Doris well, but his words were inspired by the weight of black southern Christian tradition. In an emotional voice that alternately rose to a roar and fell to a whisper, Hicks offered the mourners comforting assurances of a just God and a peaceful afterlife that struck a responsive chord in many.

While Ruby's family and friends were able to find some comfort in the minister's assurances, her movement colleagues were not. So many of these young activists were seething with a terrible anger because of all the deaths they had seen. They did not want heavenly assurances; they wanted earthly explanations. A eulogy full of biblical allusions only seemed to exacerbate their frustration. Willie Ricks remembers the dissatisfaction expressed by many: "The funeral was, uh, not a typical SNCC funeral. . . . Her family had a lot to do with it. So, you had the preacher . . . and just the whole thing. . . . We wasn't satisfied with that."[18]

Many of Ruby's movement colleagues were convinced that because of her importance to SNCC and the civil rights movement, she should be accorded a proper SNCC funeral, that is, one that emphasized her relationship to the civil rights movement. It would be a way for movement colleagues to say good-bye and would also inspire the mourners to continue the struggle.

Because of this need to address movement concerns, James Forman stood up and spoke to the mourners. In a voice that cracked under the weight of his emotion and betrayed his weariness, Forman told the audience that Ruby Doris Smith Robinson was a martyr to the movement. He claimed her as part of the SNCC family. Ruby's SNCC colleagues wholeheartedly agreed. As Willie Ricks puts it, "We had lost one of our own."[19] Death had taken Ruby Doris from them, and they wanted to stake their claim on her memory.

The Smith family had other ideas, however. Mary Ann remembers that friction had developed between her family and members of SNCC even before the funeral. Some of Ruby's SNCC colleagues had talked about cremation, while the family clearly wanted a traditional burial. In the end, the family's wishes had prevailed, but the Smith family had included a few movement people in the service. For example, some of the active and honorary pallbearers listed on the funeral program were movement people. In fact, Dr. Martin Luther King, Jr., was listed on the program as an honorary pallbearer. But for the most part, the service was dominated by friends and family members who were not connected to the movement. As the Smith family tried to claim Ruby's memory, they carefully selected a photograph for the funeral program that portrayed the Ruby Doris they had known.[20] SNCC staff member Dottie Zellner remembers how shocked she was to see it: "Her hair was straightened in the picture, and she hadn't worn it that way in years."[21] The photo reminded Zellner of one from a high school yearbook.

After the funeral, SNCC mourners who were dissatisfied with the tone of the service reassembled at Ruby Doris's house. They had to say good-bye to her in their own way. They talked about Ruby Doris, about SNCC, and about themselves. "I remember all of us getting together," recalls Ricks. "It was a SNCC gathering, it was us."[22] If their disappointment with the funeral was keen, it was not without cause. Political funerals had become a routine part of the civil rights movement by this time. They were often the occasion for moving eulogies that helped activists cope with the sadness which struck especially hard when young people were consumed by the violent forces opposed to the movement. James Chaney, Andrew Goodman, and Michael Schwerner had been brutally killed in Mississippi during the early days of Freedom Summer in 1964. Sent out to investigate the burning of a black church, they never made it back alive. At Chaney's funeral, Dave Dennis from the Congress of Racial Equality addressed the mourners. Intending only to offer inspirational words of comfort, he ended up making an emotional declaration to a restive audience. "Don't bow down anymore," he exhorted them. "Hold your heads up. I want my freedom now."[23]

The funeral of Jimmie Lee Jackson witnessed an even more stirring speech. During a civil rights protest in Selma, Alabama, in 1965, Jackson had attempted to stop a state trooper from assaulting his mother. The trooper shot him in the stomach, and Jackson died two days later. Dr. Martin Luther King, Jr., preached the eulogy. He urged his listeners not to lose hope and encouraged them to work "passionately and unrelentingly to make the American dream a reality." Yet even King could not disguise the anger and frustration he felt at such a senseless and brutal killing. After demanding to know who had killed Jimmie Lee Jackson, he declared that many were responsible: racist politicians, lawless sheriffs, indifferent white ministers, and any passive black person who "stands on the sidelines in the struggle for justice."[24] Passionate and inspirational eulogies such as this had become a standard feature at the funerals of civil rights activists.

In the wake of Ruby's funeral, her SNCC colleagues struggled to come to terms with their loss, but they could not understand it or accept it. Prompted by their shock and grief, some lashed out and made serious charges and angry accusations. West Coast SNCC organizers charged that Ruby Doris had been "destroyed by the tedious day-to-day brutality of jails, organizing, and the work that must be done."[25] Others bitterly asserted that her "severe illness . . . [had] resulted from mistreatment in American jails and hospital segregation in Atlanta. In a subtle and insidious manner, her death [was] a political murder and assassination by white America, as was the death of Brother Malcolm, Marcus Garvey, Nat Turner, and the many other warriors who were eliminated by Uncle Sam."[26] Still others were convinced that the United States government would have been too impatient to use such subtle methods. SNCC staff member Michael Simmons recalls, "At that point SNCC was trying to put her death in some political context—even to the point of suggesting that it was some sort of conspiracy of the government. . . . Forman was trying to suggest . . . that they gave her something [poison]."[27]

9

Conspiracy theories and questions of martyrdom were foreign to the Smith family. As far as they were concerned, Ruby had been their sister, their wife, their daughter. She had been warm and caring, strong and steady, and they would miss her. As they filed out of the church into the bright October sunshine, Ruby's family quietly seated themselves in the waiting limousines for the trip to the cemetery. The brilliant blue of Atlanta's fall sky and the bright blaze of colors adorning the trees were in sharp contrast to the black limousines, the dark clothes worn by the mourners, and the somber expressions on their faces. The procession slowly wound its way through part of Atlanta's black community. A few curious onlookers paused as it passed. Finally, the hearse bearing Ruby's body, followed by the limousines bearing her family, approached the cemetery's front entrance, and the finality of their journey hit Ruby's family with sickening certainty. The procession soon came to a stop where a fresh grave had been dug in the gently rolling ground that was covered with well-manicured grass.

Family members slowly walked the short distance from the waiting cars to the grave site. But the warmth of the October sunshine did not seem to reach them; the brilliance of the day made no difference, for they were able to focus only on her and on each other. William Porter, a SNCC colleague and a very close friend of Ruby Doris's, recalls being quite moved by the family's focus and composure at the grave site:

> I just stood back afterward, and I, uh, I watched her family. And the way that the family held themselves together is that they all had gotten, they must have gotten together some time before that. I think they were either repeating the Lord's Prayer or they were repeating the Twenty-third Psalm . . . and they just stood right over the grave.[28]

Others besides Ruby's family would also miss her on an intensely personal level. One of those was Brenda Jefferson Smith, one of Ruby Doris's closest childhood friends. Brenda felt an overwhelming sense of grief and loss that pushed her close to the brink of hysteria. Unable to control the waves of sadness that washed over her and threatened to drown her, she started screaming and sobbing in her father's car on the way home from the service. She was inconsolable. She recalls, "I had this strange feeling in my head, and I—for a moment I felt like . . . half of me was gone."[29] Avon Rollins, a SNCC project director in Danville, Virginia, also had trouble accepting the finality of Ruby's death. "As I [look] through some of Ruby's old letters, I still cannot bring myself to believe she is gone," he wrote in a letter to members of SNCC.[30]

Joyce Ladner also felt Ruby's loss in very personal terms: "I felt that she'd been cheated somehow. I felt that I'd been cheated by God . . . of the friendship that I shared with her."[31] William Porter felt such a keen sense of loss that he dropped out of movement work for a time. Porter had been a student at Albany State College when in 1961 he decided to attend a SNCC conference in Atlanta. During the conference, Ruby Doris had recruited him into movement work, and she had carefully nurtured him along his way. When she died, Porter felt he could not go on with his work without her. "Ruby had been like a mother to me," he says. "And one thing that I wanted to do was just to get out of the movement."[32] Six months later, his commitment brought him back to the movement. A generation after Ruby Doris had passed away, SNCC freedom singer Matthew Jones, Jr., succinctly expressed the feelings of many: "We haven't known how to relate yet to her death."[33]

While Ruby Doris's absence was a great loss for the black freedom struggle in general and for many people in particular, many were also concerned about its effects on SNCC, since the force of her personality and commitment had contributed so much to the organization. According to one SNCC staffer, "She ran everything."[34] Says another, "She was the boss."[35] The organization's October 1967 newsletter succinctly explained her importance and the impact of her loss:

> Ruby's passing is especially tragic for all those involved in the struggle for human rights and the liberation of black people. During her seven years in the movement, she was the heartbeat of SNCC, as well as one of its most dedicated administrators. Her memory will be a shining light to all who continue the battle to which she dedicated her life.[36]

For so long, it had seemed that their youth would ensure that these young freedom fighters would have the time to leave their mark. Ruby's untimely passing shook the faith of many and left them pondering an uncertain future. As Jim Forman puts it:

> Ruby's illness and eventual death gave me a new sense of urgency. For years I had said that the fact of death was inconsequential for revolutionaries. But now I felt that we must speed up time, we

could not let the years slip by, because you never know how much time you really have.[37]

Even though she was no longer with them, Ruby's movement colleagues would carry her spirit in their hearts. But she was more than just an inspiration or a role model; she was a member of their family. Through their common experiences and dedication, she and the others had formed bonds that rivalled the strength of family ties. This movement family had known Ruby Doris all of her activist life. Its members had seen her raise her fist and shout, "black power," had watched her serve jail time, and had relied on her to organize SNCC activities. Her biological family had, of course, known her even before her activist days; they had watched her excel in school, had seen her march as head majorette in the Price High School marching band, had seen her in her evening gown on the night of her debutante ball. And regardless of the differences in their views, each of Ruby Doris's families had watched her die an excruciating death from cancer.

Though that last year of her life was almost the only vision her two families held in common, each thought they had known her well. Which cherished image was the real Ruby Doris Smith Robinson? If Ruby Doris had been present, she would have claimed that both families saw her correctly. A complex woman, she never saw any contradictions between the parts of herself. Yet how did she move from her typical black middle-class upbringing to the jails and streets and offices of the freedom struggle? How did she transform herself from a college coed at a safe middle-class school into one of the most influential and outspoken women in the civil rights movement?

CHAPTER TWO

Growing Up Black in Atlanta

꒐

RUBY DORIS SMITH WAS BORN ON 25 APRIL 1942 IN ATLANTA, GEOR-gia.[1] America was at war, fighting the Germans and the Japanese, and large numbers of African-American men were participants. Some had volun-teered; some had been drafted. But all were segregated. The segregated mili-tary reflected a segregated American society. By this time, racial tension was at an all-time high.

Twenty-five years earlier, during World War I, black scholar and social activist W. E. B. Du Bois had advised fellow African Americans to set aside their own interests and close ranks behind the American war effort. By the era of World War II, however, black activists were less interested in closing ranks than in using the war atmosphere to pressure the federal government into supporting black rights. A. Phillip Randolph's threatened march on Washington, D.C., in 1941 was just such an attempt. The threat was in-tended to force more equitable treatment of black workers in defense indus-tries. As the nation began gearing up for war, African Americans were generally less likely to be hired, and when they finally were hired, they were usually placed in the most menial and least lucrative positions. Since some of the companies that engaged in these hiring practices were producing war materials for the federal government, the government had become an unwit-ting partner in discrimination against its own citizens. Randolph was con-vinced that the federal government was sensitive about the discriminatory practices of some of its defense contractors and that it would not want the publicity his march would generate. He was right. In exchange for the can-cellation of the march, President Franklin Roosevelt issued Executive Order 8802, outlawing racial discrimination in defense industries.[2]

But economic inequity was just part of a general pattern of unfairness that characterized this nation's treatment of its black citizens during World War II. In fact, the widespread nature of these inequities fueled a wartime black discontent that sometimes erupted in violent confrontation. One such incident occurred in Detroit, Michigan, in June of 1943. Detroit had been the destination of many hopeful southern migrants, including some members of the Smith family, through much of the early twentieth century. These southerners were lured by the promise of good jobs in Detroit's burgeoning auto industry. During the early part of the century, auto pioneer Henry Ford had revolutionized the industry by introducing the moving assembly line in his Highland Park, Michigan, plant. This innovation allowed auto makers to produce cars more quickly and cheaply, and it created thousands of jobs. Members of the Smith family, along with many black and white southerners who had barely been able to make a living wage in their home states, eagerly rushed to fill these jobs. While the wages represented a welcome change from their previous economic status, conditions in the factories were less than ideal. Monotony quickly set in as workers stood in the same spot for hours on end, performing the same task over and over on the car skeletons that moved along the assembly line. At the same time, the workers' senses were assaulted by pungent smells and sharp noises that seemed to echo all over these cavernous plants.

Despite the problems, many working-class Detroiters were proud to be associated with an industry that had such an impact on their country. These were Detroit's glory years, when stunning innovations in automotive design were regularly introduced and incorporated into American cars. Detroit was a city that clearly felt its own importance, and many of its working-class citizens proudly identified with this feeling. But things changed when World War II started. The city's manufacturing capacity was quickly converted to the production of war materials; Detroiters who had been working in the auto plants were now producing weaponry. They were still as proud of their city as they had ever been, but this pride was now accompanied by a patriotic fervor stimulated by the war.

The irony of this situation was not lost on black Detroiters. As they worked to produce the implements of a war that would make the world safe for democracy, many wondered about democracy in their country in general and in their city in particular. For years, black Detroiters had regularly experienced discrimination and de facto segregation. By 1943, many of them were increasingly willing to voice their criticisms of racial inequality. In this tense atmosphere, on a warm June day, a fistfight broke out between a black man and a white man on a city street. The violence rapidly spread through the city as Detroit's neighborhoods were engulfed by the fires of racial hatred. Before order was restored thirty hours later, twenty-five black and nine white residents were dead, several hundred thousand dollars' worth of property had been destroyed, and President Roosevelt had sent federal troops into the city.[3]

The frustration that had provoked such episodes as the Detroit riot and Randolph's threatened march was part of a general restlessness and discontent affecting dark-skinned people all over the world. It was clear that colonialism's days were numbered in Africa and that legal segregation's grip on the American South was threatened as well. This was the world into which Ruby Doris Smith was born.

The most prominent organization attacking segregation in the United States at that time was the National Association for the Advancement of Colored People. In the 1930s, 1940s, and 1950s, NAACP attorneys successfully challenged segregation in various arenas. The *Sweat* case, the *McLauren* case, and *Brown v. Board of Education* all struck at the root of public school segregation. *Smith v. Allwright* challenged segregation in political life. In *Powell v. Alabama* and *Brown v. Mississippi*, NAACP attorneys turned their attention to black vulnerability in the criminal justice system. Slowly, it seemed, the laws were beginning to change.

Despite such positive developments, serious problems remained. African Americans continued to face profound and suffocating oppression that strangled the life out of their dreams. Conditions for black people in Ruby Doris's home state of Georgia were no exception. The majority of Georgia's African-American citizens still resided in rural areas, largely because the Southeast in general and Georgia in particular were very slow to develop their manufacturing capacities. The state's continued dependence on agriculture resulted in a limited economy that afforded most black residents few options. When manufacturing did expand, the discriminatory pattern in labor and social relations that had characterized plantation agriculture extended to this area as well. Consequently, black Georgians were almost completely barred from jobs in the expanding cotton mill industry, but some were employed in lumber and cottonseed-oil mills, as well as fertilizer and brick factories.[4]

Even when black Georgians were able to secure manufacturing jobs, they remained trapped in menial, dangerous, and low-paying positions with little hope for advancement. "The result of this process," writes Numan Bartley in *The Creation of Modern Georgia*, "was to concentrate blacks in 'nigger work,' which by standard definition meant the jobs that were the lowest paying, the hardest, and the dirtiest." Because their husbands were unable to make a living wage, many African-American women were forced to enter the labor force. They, too, were trapped in menial positions—mostly as maids, cooks, and washerwomen.[5]

Such a dismal occupational outlook was further complicated by a virulent and often violent racial atmosphere pervading Georgia's urban and rural areas. Any assertive act by an African American was viewed askance; many white people were convinced that such acts constituted a direct threat to their cherished system of segregation. In such an atmosphere, white violence against black Georgians was common, and lynchings were acceptable. Between 1889 and 1930, a period of only forty-one years, more than 450 lynchings occurred in the state.[6]

Their economic well-being tenuous, their physical well-being insecure, some black Georgians chose migration to improve their circumstances. Some left to seek factory jobs in the industrial cities of the North, while others sought opportunities in cities closer to home. Among those who migrated in search of better economic opportunities were Ruby Doris's parents. Her mother, Alice Banks, had been born in Barnesville, Georgia, in 1912. The community of Barnesville, which is located approximately twenty-five miles north of Macon, offered very few economic options for its residents. Like the vast majority of their neighbors, the Banks family worked the land. One hot day seemed to melt into another as Alice and her family sweated and strained out in the fields planting, tending, and harvesting their crops. When Alice and her brothers and sisters dared to look into their future, they saw only a depressing and frightening vision of a succession of long, hot, dusty days that never ended. Like so many others, the Banks family rented their land and usually borrowed the resources they needed to plant their crop at the beginning of each season. Regardless of how hard they worked, it seemed that the value of their crop never equaled the amount of their debt. Alice's younger sister, Ruby Banks O'Neal (for whom Ruby Doris was eventually named), succinctly explains the family's plight: "You always come out in the hole with these people."[7]

When Alice was only eight years old, she and her family experienced a personal tragedy: her mother died of tuberculosis. As Mrs. Banks, who was a skilled seamstress, prepared for her death, she used the last of her strength to make new dresses for Ruby and Alice to wear to her funeral. The Banks children were profoundly affected by the memory of their dying mother sacrificing to provide for her children. That memory followed the young Alice into adulthood, through her own marriage, and into the relationships with her own children. Their father later remarried, and the children were raised by a stepmother.[8]

As the years passed, the family's economic prospects did not improve. The Banks children never expected any of life's luxuries because they were often forced to do without many of life's necessities. Even though such grinding poverty undoubtedly made an indelible impression on the Banks children, they did not completely lose hope. Inextricably bound up with that hope was a faith in the power of education to transform their lives. But their opportunities to secure an education were severely limited, since only a poorly equipped, segregated school was locally available. Furthermore, the Banks family was so poor that they were sometimes unable to provide the children with adequate clothing so they could attend even this poor school. Mrs. O'Neal remembers having to drop out of school twice: "We was running around there, I remember [I] didn't have a dress to wear."[9]

These dismal educational and occupational prospects convinced some members of the Banks family to move to Atlanta. Alice's older sister, Annie, was one of the first to make the shift. A short time later, in 1928, sixteen-year-old Alice decided to join her. While trying to get established, Alice lived with Annie and then with her uncle Will, her father's brother. Atlanta was very different from Barnesville. To young Alice Banks the city seemed to be a pulsating, breathing, living entity. Everywhere she looked, Alice saw busy people dashing to and fro; there seemed to be so many people; they seemed so sophisticated; and their clothes were so fancy. Atlanta offered many things to do, but young Alice Banks from Barnesville was not tempted; she was too busy trying to get the education and training she had been denied in her home town. She enrolled in the Apex Beauty School. Upon completing her course of study, she began working as a beautician, sending money home whenever she could. At nineteen, determined to complete her formal education, Alice took classes at Atlanta's Booker T. Washington High School. Some years later when Alice walked across the stage to receive her high school diploma, she almost felt like she was walking on air. For a split second the school auditorium disappeared and all the proud friends and relatives were gone. Alice felt the hot Georgia sun on her back, the sting of sweat in her eyes, and the painful isolation of Barnesville. But this flashback vanished just as quickly as it had appeared, and Alice's feelings of pride and hope returned. On the heels of her success, by late 1936 Alice was able to convince two of her sisters, including Ruby [Banks] O'Neal, and her brother to move to Atlanta.[10]

During this same period, J. T. Smith, Ruby Doris's father, migrated to Atlanta from the rural Georgia community of Ashburn when he was about fifteen years old. His mother, who died at the age of forty, was one of the few African Americans in the Ashburn area to graduate from high school, and one of even fewer to own a car. Like the Banks family, the Smiths worked the land and could never make a profit. Motivated by similar hope and determination, many of the Smiths left Ashburn. They chose various destinations, including Detroit and Atlanta.

When J. T. Smith left home on foot, he had few financial resources and no job prospects, but this did not worry him. The young and eager J. T. barely noticed the natural beauty of the many pine trees and hardwoods, or the vivid color and sweet scent of the wildflowers, that he passed during his trek through the rural Georgia countryside; he was too intent on following the road out of Ashburn and into his future. As he walked along the dusty back-roads, there was one disturbing concern that did intrude on J. T.'s consciousness from time to time, however. He realized that he was especially vulnerable to racially motivated attacks once he left that part of the state where he and his family were known by local white residents. Incidents of racial violence were quite common in Georgia during this era, and J. T. clearly recognized his vulnerability as he walked through rural Georgia. But even this dangerous prospect could not quell J. T.'s excitement and anticipation as he walked farther and farther away from the stifling atmosphere of Ashburn. He would be careful, but he would not be deterred.

During his journey, he encountered a white doctor who offered him living quarters and a salary to perform a variety of tasks around his office. Smith gratefully accepted. After working for the doctor for a time, though, Smith decided to move on. He held a series of positions as he continued his journey toward Atlanta. Smith was a hard-working young man who was very determined and fiercely independent. He had known for a long time that he wanted to be his own boss, and he never lost sight of his determination to establish his own business. J. T. knew that Atlanta was the place for him, with its large black population and its thriving black business district. He knew he could make his mark there.

The sight that greeted J. T. Smith when he finally arrived in Atlanta did not disappoint him. There was a vibrant and prosperous black business section unlike any Smith had ever seen before. As J. T. settled into his new home, his head was spinning with excitement and brimming with plans. During the next few years, he used the varied work experience he had gained on his journey to Atlanta to establish a series of small businesses.[11] The only thing that diverted this restless and determined young businessman's attention from his fledgling enterprises during these early years was the young Alice Banks. Shortly after they met, they were married in 1939. Alice quickly found a house that she liked in Atlanta's black Summerhill neighborhood, and she and J. T. purchased it. It was a large house that had both a beauty shop and a grocery store attached to it. Ruby Doris Smith grew up in this family home at 794 Fraser Street in Summerhill—the oldest black community in the city. Mary Ann Wilson, Ruby Doris's older sister, called Summerhill a mosaic. Solid middle-class professionals and businessmen lived in comfortable houses interspersed among the dwellings of working-class and very poor people.[12] The reality of housing segregation was responsible for the creation of similarly varied black neighborhoods in many American cities. During Summerhill's earliest days, it could be a difficult place to live, with more than its share of problems. One resident recalled:

> Of course, there were some who had nice bathrooms and good toilets, . . . but where we lived on Fraser Street, they didn't have that. You had to go out to the outhouse, had a big old tub that the effusions from your body ran [into,] and about once a week the citizens would get a big old tub to empty the slop in. And sometimes when they came down the place would stink so bad.[13]

Sanitation problems were not Summerhill's only worry. In some areas of the neighborhood, decidedly unwholesome activities flourished. On weekends, there was often "carousing, corn whiskey, drinking, fussing and fighting" among some of the residents. Such activities sometimes had tragic consequences. "In 1951 almost 100 people died or went totally blind from drinking 'rot gut' corn whiskey on one Friday night."[14] Community members generally had to cope with these problems themselves since Atlanta police were reluctant to intervene. "They didn't want to spend a lot of time on Fraser Street where everybody was black. . . . They wouldn't go there except when they were called, and then they had no enthusiasm for what they were doing. They'd rather go patrol on Cherokee, where [the residents] were white, see."[15]

Despite the problems, there was a positive side to life in Summerhill. For example, the Smith children took part in a local club's fund raiser that was known as a "tour around the world." Participants would visit certain designated houses in the neighborhood. Each house represented a different country, and the family living there was responsible for preparing food from that country. The delicious smells of exotic dishes floated out into the street, tempting neighbors who were happily caught up in the festive occasion. Eager children dashed from house to house sampling the foreign delicacies, while the adults used the opportunity to socialize. Neighbors felt secure in the cozy atmosphere that such social occasions generated. Mary Ann recalls how various community institutions contributed to that atmosphere: "It was a very intricate . . . bringing together . . . a social life from the school, the neighborhood parks, the churches . . . and just everything intermingled there."[16]

In the midst of this close-knit community, Ruby Doris Smith and her brothers and sisters suffered the usual triumphs and traumas of childhood. Alice and J. T. Smith had a total of seven children. Mary Ann was the oldest. Next came Ruby Doris, followed by Catherine, John, Bobby, Willie, and Gregory. Even though the Smiths did not have a lot of money, J. T. and Alice were able to provide a comfortable living for their seven children. Just as important as the income they provided was the example they set: the source of their income depended on black patronage rather than white support. Alice operated the beauty shop attached to their home, while J. T. supervised the store on the other side of the house and tried his hand at a sucession of other small businesses.[17] J. T. had shown his entrepreneurial spirit when he was just a young boy growing up in Ashburn, Georgia. At age fourteen, he had managed to persuade a white property owner to allow him to use his building on the weekends. J. T. sold fried fish and cold drinks in the building to local black residents. His little "weekend restaurant" was so successful that he was able to pay rent to the white property owner and still make a profit.

After the young J. T. arrived in Atlanta, one of his first businesses was a dry-cleaning establishment. He was still involved in this business when he met the young Alice Banks. Sometime later, J. T. became the manager of a local black baseball team. When Mary Ann was six, he managed a gospel group. Mary Ann remembers traveling to churches with her father and his gospel group when she was very young. She also remembers that when she was about twelve she used to wait on customers in a used furniture store her farther owned. The store was located in the warehouse district near downtown Atlanta for a time; and then it was moved to the south side of the city. J. T. also owned an appliance store, and operated a restaurant. Mary Ann has fond and delicious memories of the barbecue her father would regularly bring home from his restaurant. During this same era J. T. bought a taxi cab, and he and his brother started their own cab company.[18] As if this were not enough, the Smiths sometimes took in boarders, who were often relatives or close family friends. Later, when Mary Ann was in high school in the late 1950s, J. T. Smith became a Baptist minister; he eventually established his own church. By the early 1960s he had started a moving business and purchased a red moving van. His sons worked with him in the business.[19]

J. T. Smith's business enterprises were part of a rich and restless striving by a generation of black Atlantans who had no desire to get trapped in the vicious cycle of menial, dangerous, and poorly paid work that ensnared so many. Opportunities for ambitious black men in Atlanta were limited. Even when modest industrial progress came to the city, few African Americans were hired to fill these new factory jobs. On the contrary, it seemed that on those rare occasions when factory owners were willing to employ a few black workers, their white labor force expressed unequivocal opposition. The circumstances at Fulton Bag Mill illustrate this reality. In 1897, when the company hired twenty black spinners, the white workers walked out in protest.[20]

In many instances, those companies that had hired black workers fired them and employed white men in their places. Atlanta's Sanitary Department fired all of its black truck drivers and replaced them with less experienced white men whom it paid forty dollars a month more. Private companies routinely followed the city's lead. For example, in the decade between 1919 and 1929, the Hormel Company, the Swift Company, Cudahy Packing Company, Wilson and Company, and the White Provision Company all replaced their experienced black drivers with white employees. Furthermore, black truck drivers were not the only ones subjected to this practice. The Georgia Baptist Hospital replaced all of its black employees with whites. The Jacob Drug Company followed suit and discharged all the black messengers at its 120 stores.[21]

One of the few areas of the Atlanta economy that did employ significant numbers of black men in the early twentieth century was the railroad. Black men were routinely hired as porters, or red caps, to carry luggage for passengers. As one of them remembered: "[We] didn't have a salary then. . . . We was only working for tips. During the time of 1937, I believe, the redcap porters went to Mr. Randolph, and they formed a union. And after they became organized, the first salary was given to the redcaps here." African-American men also filled other positions with the railroad. Some were hired as brakemen; many, as firemen. By 1924, there were over ten thousand black railroad workers in Georgia. At the start of World War I, some 80 percent of the firemen were black. Firing the engines with coal was a dirty, strenuous, and uncomfortable job. But while white men who were hired in more modest positions had a reasonable expectation of advancement, black men knew better. As one explained: "At that time they couldn't promote a colored man out there . . . and he stayed what they hired him. If they hired him a laborer, he was a laborer."[22]

Because of such limited economic opportunities, scores of ambitious black Atlantans like J. T. Smith created a dizzying array of enterprises that showcased their talents and provided goods, services, and entertainment to Atlanta's burgeoning black population. For example, one of those enterprises was the Atlanta Black Crackers baseball team. While the Black Crackers usually had to struggle to turn a profit, there were times when their struggle paid off. Most often that happened when they played one of the black independent teams. Gabby Kemp, a former Black Cracker, explains: "They were a drawing card when they came to your town or when you went barnstorming with them . . . and they drew so many people that the ballplayers got paid handsomely."[23]

At the same time as Atlanta's black small businessmen operated a variety of enterprises wherever there were black residents, a nationally famous concentration of businesses, located on Auburn Avenue near downtown Atlanta, came to be known as "Sweet Auburn." This group of successful black businesses proved to be a powerful symbol for all black Atlantans. Auburn was lined by tidy establishments, most of them brick, with neatly printed signs that announced each one's name. The owners took pride in how their businesses looked, and black Atlanta residents noticed and appreciated this. During business hours, the street was often filled with black men and women sporting their latest finery as they strolled through the heart of their business district. One black Atlanta resident remembers: "I stayed on the safe side. I would go to Sweet Auburn Avenue. That was my street, Sweet Auburn. I just enjoyed Auburn Avenue. It was a beautiful street."[24]

At the same time, Auburn Avenue businesses provided black shoppers with an alternative to the white, segregated, and often hostile environment downtown. A black resident explains: "There are plenty of people . . . who have never been to pay a light bill or a water bill anywhere other than Yates and Milton drugstore (in the black business district). The bills were paid there. The post office and your Christmas shopping and all—you see, they brought as much business down there that kept you out of having to take the slurs and all of downtown."[25] Thus, black Atlantans who lived in other parts of the city, like the Smith family in Summerhill, often preferred to conduct much of their business on Auburn Avenue. In response to customers' demands, a variety of businesses flourished there. By the early twentieth century, "Sweet Auburn" had sixty-four black-owned firms and seven black professional offices.[26]

These businesses offered a wide variety of goods and services to their customers, and some of them even achieved national prominence. For example, when the black-owned Citizens Trust Bank joined the Federal Reserve in 1936, it became the first black bank in the country to do so. The existence of such a healthy and prominent black financial institution in Atlanta helped facilitate the growth of other black businesses. L. D. Milton, president of Citizens Trust, explains his bank's importance: "The bank was a powerful negotiator for Negro businesses in the city of Atlanta . . . and helped these businesses to grow and expand. Oh, there were gracious plenty of businesses started." Another of Atlanta's unique black businesses was the *Atlanta Daily World*, founded in 1928 as a weekly. In 1932, it had the distinction of becoming the country's first black daily newspaper. Alongside the prominent businesses were scores of small struggling enterprises. One Auburn Avenue entrepreneur describes the mind-set that was shared by many small businessmen: "Back in those days I didn't start no big business, I just started from a shoestring. My first business I had on Auburn Avenue was just a little place, little hole in the wall. That's where I started from. Then I spreaded [sic] out, got in a bigger business. Most all of them started that way, on shoestrings. A man started on a small basis and grew, took what they made and put it back into the business."[27]

Men were not the only ones who owned businesses on Auburn Avenue. Black women owned a variety of businesses too, including beauty shops, restaurants, and even a funeral home. Yet this was not the typical black female experience in Atlanta. The majority of the city's black working women were in some form of domestic service. In 1930, just two years after Alice Banks migrated to Atlanta, 90 percent of all black women in the labor force were domestic workers. As one domestic worker recalls, those women suffered from chronic job insecurity:

> You had to walk a chalk line. And if you talked back in those days, you was an uppity nigger, you was sassy, and you was fired and put out. And where would you go, you didn't have nobody you could call back to get any reference. They could lie on you quicker than anybody could lie on you.[28]

Not only did these women fear job insecurity, but they were also vulnerable to sexual harassment by white men in the household. Dorothy Bolden, who started working as a maid in Atlanta in the 1920s when she was nine years old and went on to organize the National Domestic Workers Union in 1968, bitterly describes that vulnerability:

> They had the advantage over you, you was locked into a system that we didn't create, but they created. And nobody knows how ugly that system was. It was always attempts made on black women from white men, always. Sometimes he had a knack for patting you on the back, not on the back but on your behind, and telling you that you was a nice-looking black gal and this type of thing. And I resented that.[29]

Clearly, the system of domestic service that trapped the vast majority of black Atlanta women who worked outside the home was very hard on them in a variety of ways. At the same time, however, its negative impact reached beyond the workers and into their families. One of those workers sadly explained, "I've lived through two generations rearing white children but I never had time for my own child."[30]

Despite the dismal occupational picture confronting the majority of Atlanta's African-American women, most black Atlantans continued to focus on the progressive commercial and educational features of their city, and they remained optimistic about their chances for upward mobility in this city of the New South. But their optimism was tempered by one striking similarity between the rural Georgia counties that many of them had just left and their progressive new home: an adversarial relationship with local law enforcement. Herbert Jenkins, a veteran policeman who would later serve as Atlanta's police chief during the student sit-in movement, has identified the root cause of this uneasy relationship: "Well, I can almost say that at one time most of the members of the [Atlanta] Police Department were members of the Ku Klux Klan . . . and there were officers in the Klan that were also officers in the Atlanta Police Department." Klan influence did not stop at the city limits; it reached into the surrounding county. According to Fulton County attorney Harold Sheats: "Everybody in the courthouse belonged to the Klan. . . . Virtually every judge down there, the prosecuting officers belonged to the Klan. The mayor of East Point [an adjoining community] did."[31]

Periodically, Klan members, with the cooperation and support of the Atlanta police, ventured into the black community to remind its residents of racial realities. Chief Jenkins has recounted the details of one of those incidents:

> I remember on one occasion I had orders from police headquarters to be at Peachtree and Baker Street at eight o'clock that night to lead a Klan parade. . . . And there must have been fifty cars in the parade, and of course I knew many of the people in there, the drivers and the others, and they were in uniform. They wanted to parade down Peachtree Street by the Capitol, go down Capitol Avenue to Georgia Avenue, down Georgia Avenue to Fraser Street [the street where Alice and J. T. Smith lived], which was right in the heart of the black community, and then come back through and disband. And the police escorted them and helped them through. And it was pure and simple an attempt to intimidate black people.[32]

At times, such sinister visits stimulated fear, but not always. Black Atlantan Horace Sinclair witnessed a particularly illustrative incident in the 1930s. One day he and several others stood on a sidewalk and watched a Klan procession. As the parade slowly advanced, the Klansmen's white robes billowed out behind them in the evening breeze. The whiteness of those robes provided a stark contrast to the sea of colors adorning the crowd of black Atlantans witnessing the parade. Many of the spectators felt dread mixed with the excitement of danger, and there was also an unarticulated anger that was almost palpable. That anger held the crowd transfixed so that they did not retreat as the procession approached; it showed in many of their faces. Grim white faces stared out from under tall, pointed white hats aiming to strike fear in that sea of black humanity and wondering why it would not retreat. When a young boy standing with Sinclair and his friends remarked, "I reckon I'd do almost anything to get me enough money to go to that dance tonight," one of the men in the group replied, "Well, if you get me one of them hoods . . . off one of them Ku Klux, we'll see that you go on up there in grand style." None of the men took the boy seriously. Turning back to watch the march, they were amazed to see him boldly run up to one of the Klansmen and yank on his hood. "It was tied around [the Klansman's] neck like a bonnet, and like to pulled him out of that jeep. But he got that hood." Klan members were too stunned to retaliate.[33]

Through the late 1930s and on into the 1940s, such acts of resistance against segregation and its symbols occurred with increasing frequency. Many of these acts were individual and spontaneous. Others were organized and collective. One example of community effort was the black voter registration drive of 1946. In the wake of the 1944 *Smith v. Allwright* decision outlawing the white primary, Atlanta's black citizens organized a massive voter registration drive. Atlanta University professor Clarence Bacote recalls: "The effort lasted for fifty-one days . . . We were able to increase the registration of blacks in Fulton County from 7,000 to 24,750. And that's when we were going to be recognized." A short time later, black Atlantans used their newly acquired political clout to pressure the city into hiring its first black policeman. One man vividly remembers the public reaction to the city's decision: "The first time these black police came out on the street in their uniforms from the Butler Y . . . Negroes popped out of the ground. Some of them sang, 'Thank God Almighty, I'm free at last.' "[34]

In this optimistic and progressive atmosphere the Smith children came of age in the forties and fifties. During the early years of their marriage, both Alice and J. T. Smith kept in touch with their family members living in rural communities. The Banks family had a family reunion—they called it homecoming—every summer on the grounds of a Barnesville church. While the adults met inside the church, the children played outside. J. T. often brought food from his store in Atlanta to sell, and when she was old enough Mary Ann helped her father sell the food. Alice and J. T. also took their children to visit J. T.'s family in Ashburn, but these visits were fewer and more sporadic than the regular visits to Barnesville. More often J. T.'s family members came to the Smith's house in Atlanta. On one such visit, one of J. T.'s brothers introduced the family to hot tamales. He showed Alice how to make them, and from then on they became a regular part of the family's diet.

In the midst of these warm family connections, Ruby Doris's brothers and sisters recall, she developed into a very outgoing, self-confident, and tenacious child. Mary Ann insists that even when Ruby Doris was quite young, "whatever her opinion was, you would hear it." Ruby Doris was physically agile. She also had a "decent alto voice."[35] These qualities undoubtedly proved helpful when Mary Ann, Ruby, and some of their neighborhood friends decided to put on a show that included dances and a skit. They made costumes and sold tickets for five cents each. It proved to be a less than spectacular success, however, when only a couple of people came. But the children performed anyway. Aside from their brief foray into show business, the Smith sisters amused themselves with pastimes typical for youngsters of their generation. One of their favorites was skating. When they skated up and down the streets with the wind in their faces and the warm Atlanta sunshine on their backs, the Smith girls knew they were in the sheltering arms of their neighborhood. Neighbors looked out for each others' children as if they were family. And, in a sense, they were all members of an extended family. This gave all the Smith children a feeling of belonging, of security and connection; they knew their place in a comforting way, not in a limiting way.

Although Mary Ann and Ruby Doris liked to play with Coca-Cola bottles—they put "hair" on the bottles, which they would comb and style, and they dressed the bottles in skirts—[36] they also had real dolls. Usually, younger sister Catherine recalls, each of the children received one toy (often a doll) and some clothes for Christmas.[37] Their father always brought home a huge Christmas tree that filled the house with the wonderful clean scent of pine, and the rest of the family really enjoyed decorating it with brightly colored glass bulbs, strings of Christmas lights, and lots of tinsel. Under the tree Mrs. Smith carefully placed brightly wrapped packages for Ruby and her brothers and sisters to attack on Christmas morning. Even after the children tore open their presents, a sense of excitement still permeated the household as everyone prepared to receive the friends and family who would come by for a visit during the day. The whole house was filled with the mouth-watering smells of Alice's home-baked delicacies. Mary Ann remembers that there was always so much food around on Christmas that they would "snack and eat and cook" all day long.[38] Feelings of happiness, security, and stability enveloped the Smith house on Fraser Street during this most important occasion of the year.

The Smith family also carefully observed Easter. Alice Smith made sure that each of her children received a completely new outfit, a treat that Mary Ann, Catherine, and Ruby were particularly fond of shopping for. Alice also had each girl's hair freshly straightened and styled for Easter Sunday. After the Smith children returned from the church service where they proudly sported their new outfits, they each received an Easter basket with lots of brightly colored straw that barely concealed candy eggs and chocolate bunnies.

Throughout the rest of the year there were many other occasions when the family spent time together. Often close friends or extended family members would go with the Smiths on picnics to local parks. One day at Lake Alatoona, right outside of Atlanta, after everyone had eaten, J. T. decided to take his family for a boat ride on the lake. Alice decided not to go, but all the children, including Ruby Doris, joined him. The Smith children had very little boating experience. Upon leaving the shore, Mary Ann was suddenly struck by the realization that she did not know how to swim. It was at this moment that she thought, "surely we [were] going to die. . . . we were scared." All the children laughed about their fear later—when they were back on land.[39]

Although during the week their hectic schedules usually prevented the Smiths from eating together, Sunday dinners were special. On Sunday they almost always dined on Alice Smith's crispy fried chicken. Ruby Doris was particularly fond of the breast, but she had to get to the table early to have any. Whoever reached the table first staked a claim on his or her favorite piece. After they had settled the chicken question, family members passed around Alice's fresh green beans, lettuce and tomatoes, and dessert of jello and fruit cocktail. Sometimes they had homemade ice cream. Ruby Doris and her brothers and sisters took turns with the crank on the ice cream freezer. It seemed to take forever, and the Smith children could barely contain their impatience as they kept turning the crank and imagining the rich, creamy taste.

Even after Ruby and her two sisters became teenagers, their mother continued to do all the cooking. She never asked her daughters to help because she wanted to make sure they had enough time to concentrate on their studies and participate in extracurricular activities. Mary Ann recalls that her mother paid for the ballet lessons she badly wanted, even though finding the money for such extras was not easy. As long as Mary Ann continued to show interest, Mrs. Smith continued to pay. She also financed piano lessons for all three of her daughters. While the Smith girls enjoyed their piano lessons, none of them was interested in becoming an accomplished pianist. In fact, some days when the girls sat in front of the piano seeing their own images in its polished surface, they would rather be playing with their friends or listening to another kind of music. But they would sigh and begin to practice, because they knew that their mother wanted these lessons for them and they understood how hard she worked to make it possible. Alice Smith insisted on the piano lessons not because she expected any of her daughters to became virtuosos, but because she wanted them to be well rounded and cultured. She never requested or received any help from her husband in providing these extras.[40]

Alice Smith was not the only Summerhill mother who was determined to provide her daughters with the means to participate in extracurricular activities. On the contrary, many others were optimistic about their daughters' chances for upward mobility, and they were willing to do whatever they could to prepare them for eventual success. Brenda Jefferson Smith, one of Ruby Doris's best friends through grade school and high school, remembers how hard her mother worked to provide her with such extras. During her high school years, Brenda participated in a number of beauty pageants that often proved to be quite costly. Somehow Brenda's mother always seemed to find the necessary resources. At the time, Brenda took all of this for granted and just assumed she was middle class. However, years later when she reflected on how low her mother's wages were, Brenda wondered, "how did she afford all those evening gowns?"[41]

All through these early years, Brenda and Ruby Doris shared numerous adventures. In many ways, their personalities were quite dissimilar, but they seemed to complement each other. Ruby was bold, brash, and blunt, while Brenda was painfully shy and very insecure. Brenda's feelings of insecurity were prompted largely by her battle with a learning disability that plagued her throughout her school career. No matter how bad things seemed, however, her friend Ruby Doris was always there to provide support and understanding. Brenda remarks: "You know, the kids made me feel bad, because I had a learning disability . . . and I didn't read good . . . but I kept trying, and [Ruby] was always there. . . . She always tried to help me."[42] Ruby had a sense of fairness and a sympathy for the underdog that were an important part of the essence of her personality. That is why Brenda's vulnerability triggered a nurturing response. In fact, Ruby's brothers and sisters were also the recipients of her nurturing and support on numerous occasions. Later on, movement colleagues would greatly appreciate Ruby's nurturing and support when they became weary and discouraged.

Throughout their teenage years, Ruby and Brenda remained extremely close. Ruby was always ready to help Brenda with any problem that might arise. Once Brenda left her lunch in a classroom while the two girls were rehearsing for a school play. When she returned for it, someone had already eaten it. The same thing happened the day after. On the third day, Brenda's stomach fluttered with nervous anticipation as she slowly opened the door and walked to the desk where she had left her lunch. Once again, it was gone. Brenda's stomach growled angrily at the prospect of another long hungry afternoon. At this point, Brenda consulted Ruby Doris, who immediately devised a plan. The next day, Ruby sprinkled a liberal amount of hot sauce on Brenda's sandwich, and then Brenda left her lunch in the customary place. That was the last lunch that disappeared.[43]

The close relationship that Ruby and Brenda shared in school extended beyond the classroom. When they were younger, they were both tomboys. They liked to play at Brenda's house because she had a large yard with a crabapple tree that grew next to the kitchen window. The tree's bark had a rough, solid feel beneath their hands as the girls climbed its branches; in the spring, its delicate blossoms gave off a distinctive sweet scent. When the two friends tired of outdoor activities, they used to hang around Alice Smith's beauty shop. The girls knew most of the women who came to get their hair straightened and styled, and they enjoyed listening to the women's lighthearted banter. Ruby and Brenda giggled at the familiar phrase, "chile did you hear," which prefaced each new revelation about the latest romances and neighborhood developments. Occasionally, the conversation turned to more serious issues like the topic of race. But, regardless of the topic of conversation, Ruby and Brenda felt at home in the warm familiarity of Alice Smith's beauty shop amid the pungent odor and the distinctive sizzle of frying hair.

When Ruby and Brenda grew older they joined with other neighborhood girls to establish a social club. They named their group the Voznesenski's Social Club because they wanted something different. Everyone was required to pay dues and attend meetings regularly. The major topic of conversation at many of those meetings? Boys! Ruby Doris and Brenda also enjoyed listening to popular rhythm-and-blues hits of their day. Black rhythm-and-blues singers crooned in silken tones about love, life, and black realities. Their songs embraced the value system of the black audiences they entertained; this was before the era of crossover music, so the influences on these artists from the larger white society were minimal. The songs had a rhythmic and definite beat that invited listeners to dance. As Ruby and Brenda sang along with their favorite artists and snapped their fingers to the beat, they practiced their dancing in Brenda's kitchen. The girls were often treated to a variety of delicious aromas as they performed line dances like the madison and the stroll. They also did the bop and the cha-cha with only the crabapple tree outside the window as an audience.[44]

When the two friends went to Ruby Doris's house, they had to find other ways to amuse themselves, since Mr. Smith refused to allow dancing in his house. J. T. Smith was a very strict man who carefully monitored his children's activities. The family had only one radio, and Mr. Smith kept it in his bedroom. He did not permit the children to listen to it, although they could watch television. Willie remembers the rules for television viewing in the Smith household:

> All we had was a television, okay, and then the rule we had started, we had started a rule around the house about the television. The first one in there [the room] was the one that controlled the television. And if you get up and go out, you lose your control. You had to watch whatever the one who'd been sitting there the longest . . . whatever he watched.[45]

Anyway, Ruby Doris's involvement in a dizzying array of extracurricular activities left her little time to watch television, and once she entered high school she was busier than ever.

Their freshman year, Ruby and Brenda attended David T. Howard High School. Then, when the new Luther Judson Price High School was completed, they transferred there. Through it all, Ruby Doris continued to nurture and support Brenda. She even persuaded Brenda to run for campus queen, though Brenda was more than a little reluctant at first. Ruby and another Price student organized and managed Brenda's campaign. Because Brenda was still plagued by shyness, Ruby accompanied her to various classes and made speeches in her behalf. Every time Ruby and Brenda prepared to enter another classroom, Ruby paused to speak a few reassuring words to her candidate before striding purposefully into the room. She was greeted by neat rows of desks where polite students were seated with their notebooks open and their pens poised to take notes. Standing next to a nervous Brenda who was trying very hard to appear calm, Ruby went to work on her audience. Her pitch was short, and her quick mind provided her with just the right words she needed to persuade her fellow students. After she finished, Ruby politely thanked the teacher and ushered her nervous candidate out of the room. All the hard work paid off when Brenda was elected first runner-up to Miss Price High School.

Brenda and Ruby Doris were members of the yearbook staff, the tennis team, the basketball team, and the track team. Ruby Doris was also a member of the student government association, and she sang in the choir. While Brenda played in the band, Ruby Doris was a majorette. When the band went on road trips, the two friends were able to spend time together because the majorettes were usually asked to come along. Brenda remembers that Ruby Doris was often forgetful about certain mundane details: "She would lose everything—her purse, her books. . . ."[46] Because Brenda had a talent for organizing practical details, she was generally the one who kept Ruby Doris prepared for these trips.

In many respects, Ruby Doris was a normal teenager. According to Catherine, Ruby's taste in clothes was typical of her generation. She favored wide skirts, wide belts, and sweaters. "She had very expensive tastes. Very! She wore nothing cheap. She couldn't stand cheap clothes, and cheap shoes she would not put on her feet." Ruby Doris wanted to be sure that her clothes flattered her figure. She had large shapely legs, large hips, and a very small waist. Although quite concerned about her appearance, Ruby Doris did not want to take the time to coordinate her outfits for school in advance. Catherine remembers: "She never made any preparations for what she was going to wear the next day. When she got up she went straight to my closet—my end of the closet."[47] Ruby Doris would wait until Catherine left the house and then dress in one of Catherine's outfits. Mary Ann experienced similar raids on her wardrobe:

> I always every weekend would get all my clothes ready for school. Everything I needed for the whole week—try to have it organized. Ruby Doris would do none of that. But she would piddle along at home, and this happened, I mean, consistently. I'd go to school, she'd always come late. And I'd see Ruby Doris coming down the hall, and she'd have on all my clothes. And I'd just cry. There was nothing I could do about it.[48]

Ruby Doris was not any more willing to make scholastic preparations than she was to coordinate her clothing. Catherine never remembers seeing Ruby Doris study for any of her classes. Mary Ann agrees and insists that schoolwork came very easily to Ruby. Even though she was two years younger than Mary Ann, Ruby was only one grade behind her in high school. Because scholastic achievement was so easy for her, Ruby had trouble understanding why others had difficulty with their schoolwork. When Ruby Doris saw all the effort Catherine was putting into her homework, "she would just shake her head and say, 'You know, I just wouldn't go through all those changes. I would go to bed if I couldn't get it by now.' "[49] Ruby Doris's advice to her younger sister is completely consistent with her "Last Will and Testament" that was published in the 1958 *Wildcat*—the Price High School yearbook from Ruby Doris's senior year. On a page that contained many other senior wills Ruby Doris wrote: "I, Ruby Doris Smith, will to Sherry Gresham my leader's majorette uniform, and to my sister, Catherine, the ability to make the honor roll."[50] Ruby Doris had an inquisitive mind, and she was a voracious reader. Yet even though she achieved academic success—she consistently made the honor roll—there were times when she found the regimentation of high school life dull and annoying. Her Aunt Ruby recalls that when one of Ruby Doris's teachers questioned whether or not she was paying attention in classs, she admitted she was not because "it wasn't interesting."[51]

But Ruby was not always bored. Black teachers at Price High School worked very hard to engage and inspire their students. They saw their mission as going far beyond the intellectual enlightenment of their students. They were convinced that they must prepare these black youngsters for racial uplift. The strong conviction and sense of mission exhibited by Price High teachers was part of a long-standing commitment to education that is deeply embedded in the African-American value system. As historian Vincent Franklin put it, "To be educated and literate had an important cultural significance to Afro-Americans and was highly valued because of its association with advancement, self-determination, and freedom."[52] Because teachers saw themselves as the instruments of this important work, they challenged and pushed their students. In the words of Mary Ann:

> I mean the schools we were in gave a kind of support. . . . There were teachers who cared about you. [At Price High School] every black child was told to be the best you can be. . . . So if you had it in you, they were going to help you get there.[53]

Furthermore, the education that Ruby and other black youngsters of her generation received was firmly anchored in Christian moral ethics. Consequently, the personal achievement and racial uplift that were the twin goals of black education were intertwined with the insistence on adherence to Christian ethics as a prerequisite to achieving these goals. Vincent Franklin explains the genesis of this educational and ethical connection: "Afro-American families not only preserved and passed on cultural values supporting education and social advancement, but also taught their children to read and write as part of the parental responsibility for the 'Christian education' of the younger generation."[54] The connection between education, racial uplift, and Christian ethics made perfect sense to a young Ruby Doris who had grown up surrounded by acceptance of these values in her family and her neighborhood. Thus, her high school experience provided powerful reinforcement of a value system that had always been part of Ruby's life.

As Ruby Doris matured during her high school years, her relationships with her younger brothers were quite close but also complex. In such a large family, the usual squabbles happened periodically. Bobby recalls a disagreement that he and Ruby Doris had: "We had a little confrontation one time. And . . . I was talking to her, and . . . before I knew anything, Ruby . . . kneed me in my stomach and knocked all the air out of me and it was over."[55] Despite the arguments, however, the Smith children always helped and supported each other. For example, when Bobby had trouble in his ninth-grade English class, the person who took the time to help him was his sister, Ruby Doris.

Ruby Doris Smith and her sisters and brothers lived a comfortable life in their separate black world. They had strong adult support, and they had their own churches, schools, and social activities. No matter how insulated they were, though, the reality of racism and segregation still managed to intrude into their lives from time to time. Black youngsters of this generation reacted in a variety of ways to America's ugly racial reality. Mary Ann was aware of segregation, but "everything was so separate you just didn't think about it."[56] Willie's response complemented Mary Ann's: "You basically accept what you have to accept and then you move on from there." Bobby remembers that one of the injustices they had to accept was segregated schooling. During that era, the vast majority of white public school students attended neighborhood schools. That was not true for African Americans. Race, rather than proximity, routinely determined the black student's fate. Whereas a white elementary school stood on the corner of Little Street and Capitol Avenue, only one block from the Smith house, the Smith children attended E.P. Johnson, ten blocks away. In reflecting on the absurdity of this situation, Bobby recalls: "We never thought about it because it was just . . . like we inherited it. So it was just like something that we came into."[57]

Even though segregation was always with them, the Smith family never quite got used to it. They confronted it in different ways on different occasions. One day, Mary Ann boarded a bus on her way home from school. Since usually only black passengers rode this route, most sat wherever they chose. Consequently, without even thinking, Mary Ann sat down right behind the driver. But on this particular day there was a white woman sitting behind her, and when Mary Ann realized this, she jumped up and moved behind the woman. Mary Ann was stunned by her own reaction; she realized that something was terribly wrong.[58]

Segregation also made a deep impression on Ruby Doris. When she was just a young girl, she experienced segregation in a very personal way on the day she and Catherine went to a drugstore on the corner of Capitol and Georgia Avenue. It was a warm Georgia afternoon. The sisters had decided that they wanted an ice cream cone. As they passed the tidy, familiar houses on their way to the drugstore, they could almost taste the cold, sweet ice cream. The girls enthusiastically burst through the store's front door and headed straight to the soda fountain. Their enthusiasm quickly cooled, however, when they saw what the sullen white clerk did:

> This particular time we went in there . . . I remember [Ruby Doris] wanted a cone. So they pulled the cone down. 'Cause, you know, they didn't really want us to come in there. She waited till they fixed it and got ready for her to pay and everything, and they handed it to her. She said, "Oh, you can keep that one, I won't be eating that one." And so they didn't know what she was talking about, you know. And they were just standing there [and they said] "Well, you ordered this." And she said, "But you're not going to put your hands on my cone." She knew that when whites came in they used a tissue to pull the cone down and when blacks came in they would use their hands.[59]

This was not the only time Ruby Doris encountered the reality of American racism. As she later observed: "I was conscious of my blackness. Every young Negro growing up in the South has thoughts about the racial situation." This racial consciousness affected her actions toward white people: "I didn't recognize their existence and they didn't recognize mine. . . . My only involvement was in throwing rocks at them."[60]

Ruby Doris's brothers also had direct dealings with nearby white residents. Willie regularly patronized a neighborhood store. There were two routes he could take to the store: one through a white neighborhood and the other through his own black neighborhood. He often defiantly chose to walk through the white neighborhood. As forbidden, alien territory in his own backyard, it exerted an irresistible attraction for a curious young boy. But a black boy's curiosity could get him in trouble:

> I was coming back from the store, and I was determined that I was going to go through [the white neighborhood]. 'Cause I could have turned back. I saw the whites. I saw them. You know how when you see a gang and you know that they're sort of up to something, and I was determined that I was going to go through there. And I remember—it was probably about five or six boys, white boys probably my age and up, okay, and [so what I did]; they had firecrackers. And they were sort of plotting to throw some on me. So I went sort of like I was going to go at them, straight through. Then I [remember] backing off just a little bit seeing what was happening . . . then I ran around, crossed the street, and they tried to run behind me, but I was just gone.[61]

On another occasion, the Smith brothers struck back at a locally segregated target: Chenny Stadium. The stadium was so close to their home that when white high schools played football there, the Smith brothers could hear the cheers of the crowd. After a game the white spectators would drive by the Smith house honking their horns and calling out to each other. It was frustrating to the Smith boys to know that they were excluded from sporting events staged right in their own neighborhood. Willie reveals how they vented their frustration against the segregated system that the stadium represented:

> John was the most devilish, and so he possibly was the ringleader. Along in that time it probably was John—between John and Bobby's idea—to put tacks out [in the street]. They probably had me to put the tacks out. So that really put me involved. Gregory was probably too young to even be a part of it. But we watched from the back window as the cars came by and actually got their tires sort of flattened. . . . But [one] man came by and cursed. . . . And he came out and he started looking around and we got real quiet because we were afraid he was going to look up and see us in the window. So we got on the floor. We didn't say anything else.[62]

While the Smith brothers feared discovery by white motorists, they were probably more afraid of their father's reaction. " 'Cause if Daddy had ever found out that we put those tacks . . . we would not have made it to today."[63]

In the midst of this atmosphere, Ruby Doris began to give increasing thought to racial issues. Like most of her high school classmates, she was keenly aware of such racial milestones as *Brown v. Board of Education*. She read about Rosa Parks's action and the resulting and successful Montgomery bus boycott. She witnessed the white South's defiance when black students attempted to integrate Little Rock's Central High School. She was undoubtedly moved by the white South's brutality as evidenced by the lynching of Emmett Till. Despite the evidence of racism and southern intransigence all around her, Ruby Doris and other young African Americans like her thought they had reason for hope. They were cold war babies who had cut their teeth on the anti-communist, pro-democracy rhetoric so characteristic of the 1950s. This was a time of unprecedented patriotism when America defined its goodness in opposition to the evil totalitarian governments in communist countries. The vast majority of black and white Americans believed that their constitution and their system of government were the best in the world. Although African Americans in the South clearly recognized that state and local governments were the enemies of their people, they maintained their faith in the power of a moral federal government.

An incident from Ruby's childhood underscores the patriotism that she felt. One evening Mary Ann and Ruby Doris watched television until the last program of the day ended and the station played the national anthem. Without even thinking the girls quickly stood up. They remained standing respectfully until "The Star-Spangled Banner" ended. Ruby Doris was about thirteen and Mary Ann was fifteen at the time.[64] This patriotic young Ruby Doris Smith was a very serious girl. The fledgling civil rights movement that heralded the coming of a new day had deeply affected her conscience. Coupled with her sense of patriotic duty, the feeling of responsibility for racial uplift instilled by her upbringing soon began to push Ruby toward the quiet southern revolution that would come to define her adult life. Catherine remembers,

> One particular conversation we had and she told me, she said, "I know what my life and mission is." And I said, "What is it?" She was a teenager, and she said, "It's to set the black people free," and she said, "I will never rest until it happens." And she said, "I will die for that cause."[65]

As she pondered the future of her country and her own obligations and responsibilities, Ruby faced a difficult personal problem: her strained relationship with her father. J. T. Smith's domineering demeanor periodically caused tense times among family members. In fact, he was so strict that he alienated several of his children. With the exception of Mary Ann and Willie, all the children were forced to leave home, at least for a time, during their formative years. Just before her high school graduation, Ruby Doris left to live with her Aunt Ruby O'Neal. Catherine characterizes the particular difficulty between Ruby Doris and her devout Baptist father this way:

> He was a very domineering-type father. [He] had strong religious beliefs. He wouldn't let her go to dances, parties—couldn't go out on late dates and all this. And very strict about everything.[66]

As she packed her clothes and her most treasured books and keepsakes, Ruby felt excited, but just a bit scared. The thought of moving out of the only home she had ever known gave her a knot in the pit of her stomach. She would miss her brothers and sisters terribly. Her eyes became moist, and a wistful smile played about the corners of her mouth as she remembered the countless times that she had complained about wanting more privacy. She shook herself out of her reverie and resumed packing. Living in her Aunt Ruby's house meant more freedom. Enrolling in Spelman College that fall meant a new beginning.

In one way, Ruby's decision to attend Spelman represented a fulfillment of the expectations of many of those around her, but at the same time, it represented an attempt to assert her own independence and personhood. Members of Ruby's family and community, and indeed African Americans all over the country, viewed Spelman as one of the most prestigious black colleges in the nation. Not surprisingly, Spelman was considered a logical and desirable next step for a bright Summerhill girl like Ruby who came from a family and community that had middle-class aspirations. Consequently, Ruby's attendance at Spelman was greeted with enthusiastic approval by those closest to her.

Yet just previous to this, Mary Ann had chosen Morris Brown College. She had received scholarship offers from both Morris Brown and Spelman. Although most of those closest to her expected her to choose the more prestigious Spelman, Mary Ann insists that none of that mattered to her. She found Morris Brown more attractive because it was coeducational and offered activities she found exciting. In Ruby Doris's case, on the other hand, Mary Ann is convinced that one of the reasons Ruby chose Spelman was that Mary Ann did not. At Price High, Ruby had quickly become known as Mary Ann's little sister. Determined not to follow in her big sister's footsteps again, Ruby struck out on her own and went to Spelman. Furthermore, Ruby undoubtedly looked forward to competing academically with some of the brightest students black America had to offer.[67] Over the next year, she chose another new path to follow: she became involved in civil rights demonstrations. These were all momentous events in the life of a seventeen-year old.

But, in the midst of these new beginnings, Ruby still participated in typical teenage activities. In 1958, during her senior year of high school, she became a debutante. Her debutante ball, sponsored by Sigma Gamma Rho sorority, took place in downtown Atlanta at the Municipal Auditorium on Thursday 2 January 1958, at nine o'clock in the evening.[68] Watched by family and friends the young Ruby Doris Smith, dressed in a white evening gown, marched through a flower arch with her escort. The sweet fragrance of flowers filled the auditorium as the young debutantes danced the first dance with their fathers. Even though Ruby and J. T. still were not communicating, his pride was obvious despite his stern demeanor. Just a few months later, in the spring of that year, Ruby graduated from Price High School. Like all the other girls in her class, she wore a white dress. Most of the girls got a special hairdo for the occasion; many even wore a little make-up for the first time. When their turn came to march across the stage and receive their diplomas, Ruby and the others squared their shoulders and held their heads high. Ruby could feel the warmth and support radiate from the audience filled with family members, friends, and neighbors. All her mother's hard work had truly paid off. The community support, encouragement from school, backing from local churches, and family nurturing had finally come together to produce a self-assured young woman who expected to lead a comfortable, meaningful, middle-class existence.

But even as she basked in the warmth and community approval of her graduation, even as she anticipated her freshman year at Spelman, Ruby Doris was haunted by the quiet civil rights revolution that was already underway. She heard the steady and relentless rhythm of the footsteps of black Montgomery residents. She felt the fear of the Little Rock nine when they faced the mob. She shared their exhilaration and pride when President Eisenhower deployed the 101st Airborne to escort them to school. The struggle was raging all around her, and slowly but inexorably, Ruby Doris would be drawn into it.

CHAPTER THREE

Early Movement Days

SPELMAN COLLEGE, THE SCHOOL RUBY CHOSE TO ATTEND, HAD A LONG and distinguished history. It demanded academic excellence, and it also provided rigorous moral and religious training with a dash of etiquette. Spelman was founded in 1881 by Harriet Giles and Sophia Packard, two northern white missionaries who wanted to provide both practical skills and moral training for young black girls. Early in their endeavor, Giles and Packard recognized the enormous power of their influence:

> These pupils are as clay in the hands of the potter. They strive to live as they see us live. Our responsibility is tremendous. Nothing but the best teachers with the best method can do justice to the work. The hope of the race lies not in their getting knowledge alone but with it a true appreciation of the value of labor and its necessity together with right ideas of Christian living.[1]

The careful teachings of Packard and Giles quickly bore fruit. One Spelman graduate from the class of 1902 discussed her perception of her alma mater's influence.

> Once upon a time it was shamefully asked in the tone of bitter incredulity, "Can a black woman be pure?" "Can the black woman be elevated to culture and piety?" I call for an answer to these cynical, heartless, unchristian and pagan questions: My answer is "Spelman Seminary". . . Spelman Seminary stands for a trained hand in domestic science, for a cultured brain in liberal education, for a pure heart in biblical morality and for a consecrated life in the battle of life for the womanhood of the race. She stands for a redeemed and elevated womanhood for the

Negro race in all the lines that have made for the best things among the best women of any other race.[2]

Sophia Packard and Harriet Giles were only two of many white missionaries who were particularly concerned about black female morality in the late nineteenth century. Most reasoned that black female peculiarities required just the right curriculum. Anna Cohill, a white teacher at Fisk University during this era, expressed a popular contemporary view of black female characteristics and special needs:

> Speaking of the future of the colored women these days, what choices she will make is [sic] a question of breathless interest. How to help her make the choice wisely and in time is the problem upon which we are at work. The door to greater evil is wide open at her feet. The tempter can no longer command but he can allure with deadly certainty because *inherited tendencies* and customs of the past aid in gaining easy victory. . . . The foundation of a strong moral nature must be laid first of all as the basis of true womanhood. [Emphasis added][3]

The pervasiveness of such a negative view of black female character prompted many who established black schools in the wake of the Civil War to include rigorous and rigid rules and regulations governing black female behavior in their student conduct codes. On most of these campuses, including Spelman, the faculty and administration carefully scrutinized the behavior, demeanor, social life, religious views, and academic goals of their female students. Even though contemporary white female college students were restricted by similar rules and regulations, the basic assumptions in these two cases were quite different. On the one hand, administrators in white institutions were convinced that their female students already possessed superior morals and that strict student conduct codes would help *safeguard* the virtue of those women students. On the other hand, administrators in black schools sought to provide an environment where black women could learn to become virtuous. One scholar of the black female educational experience unequivocally confirmed this view:

> The one role of her past that did come up in discussion concerning the Negro woman's new role carried not only the stigma of being a Negro but also a new sense of inferiority in being a woman. . . . Authorities prescribed a rigid moralistic curriculum.

... Many of the Negro women's rules and regulations may possibly have been predicated on reasons relating to her foremother's role as sex slave. Over night she was to so live that by her ideal behavior, the sins of her foremothers might be blotted out. Her education in many instances appears to have been based on a philosophy which implied that she was weak and immoral and that at best she should be made fit to rear her children and keep house for her husband.[4]

In order to understand the genesis of these negative assumptions that shaped the treatment of black women students, it is first necessary to place them within the broader context of assumptions about black people in general.

After 1865, when African Americans emerged from their experience as slaves, they were still viewed as an immoral and degraded group of people. In the first years of freedom, many white people were convinced that black degradation was a legacy of the slave experience. Later, toward the end of the nineteenth century when social Darwinism became popular, increasing numbers of white Americans stopped blaming the environment and started blaming the victims. Black character flaws were innate, they reasoned. This new conclusion sparked a lively interest in studying and classifying the races constituting the human family. White physicians regularly measured skulls and facial angles and speculated about brain capacity and sexual prowess. Invariably, these new classifications ranked Africans at the bottom of the heap of all the races on earth.

In fact, according to a number of studies, black people were so poorly developed that their extinction was imminent and inevitable. Only the protective institution of slavery had allowed them to survive this long, many reasoned. A number of nineteenth-century white physicians insisted that "the American negro [would] never become firmly established in the right methods of living before disease and death . . . thinned his ranks and there [was] no race problem." Still others thought that the reason black people would become extinct was that the race was "in danger of being destroyed by insanity."[5]

White physicians in the late nineteenth century speculated about a variety of black character traits, but in the sexually repressive atmosphere of Victorian America, they invariably focused particular attention on sexual behavior. One physician asserted:

When all inhibitions of a high order have been removed by sexual excitement, I fail to see any difference from a physical standpoint between the sexual furor of the negro and that which prevails among the lower animals in certain instances and at certain periods . . . namely, that the furor sexualis in the negro resembles similar sexual attacks in the bull and the elephant, and the running amuck of the Malay race.[6]

Since it was the nature of black men to behave with such sexual abandon, some scientists argued, "morality was a joke among Negro society."[7]

These physicians maintained that black men were immoral because they were anatomically different from white men: they had larger penises. This physical peculiarity made the black man exhibit "stallion-like passion," and it provoked him "to run any risk and brave any peril for the gratification of his frenetic lust."[8] Every bit as important as this distortion of black male sexuality, though, is the companion distortion of black female sexuality. If black males were such lascivious and lustful creatures, common sense dictated that the women of the race must be promiscuous and depraved too. In fact, some nineteenth-century physicians even argued that black women possessed anatomical peculiarities that separated them from their white sisters:

> One of the characters of the Ethiopian race consists in the length of the penis compared with that of the Caucasian race. This dimension coincides with the length of the uterine canal in the Ethiopian female, and both have their cause in the form of the pelvis in the Negro race. There results from this physical disposition, that the union of the Caucasian man with an Ethiopian woman is easy and without any inconvenience for the latter. The case is different in the union of the Ethiopian man with a Caucasian woman, who suffers in the act, the neck of the uterus is pressed against the sacrum, so that the act of reproduction is not merely painful, but frequently non-productive.[9]

In this one neat passage, the author elevated white women, placed them out of reach of black men, and justified the rape of black women by white men.

According to some of these physicians, differences in reproductive systems were so pronounced that black female genitals showed less resemblance to those of white women than to those of "the female anthropoid ape, hepale [sic], lemur and other pithecoid animals."[10] This belief takes on added significance when viewed against the backdrop of Victorian notions of women's roles. By the late nineteenth century white women were thought to be morally superior to their men. They were assigned the task of instilling moral virtue in the children and making the home a safe haven from the corrupting and unwholesome influences of the outside world. Because of their virtue, the continued moral well-being of the white race was assured.

Conversely, conventional wisdom dictated that the moral depravity of black women sealed the fate of their entire race; since African Americans could never expect to progress beyond their semibarbarous state without a virtuous female influence. Given the popularity of this negative notion, the virtue of black women was attacked frequently, vigorously, and publicly. One particularly virulent attack was written in 1895 by Jno. W. Jacks, a newspaper editor, Sunday school superintendent, and son of a slaveholder:

> Out of some 200 [Negroes] in the vicinity it is doubtful if there are a dozen virtuous women or that number who are not daily thieving from the white people. To illustrate how they regard virtue in a woman: one of them, a negro woman, was asked who a certain negro who had lately moved into the neighborhood was. She turned up her nose and said, "the negroes will have nothing to do with 'dat nigger', she won't let any man except her husband sleep with her, and we don't sociate with her."[11]

Late-nineteenth-century black women reacted angrily to such efforts to impugn their character and morality. To defend themselves against these scurrilous attacks, they often found it necessary to discuss the realities of their lives. One of the most unpleasant of those realities was rooted in black female vulnerability to white male advances. Because of their economic circumstances, most black women worked for white employers—often in the homes of those employers which provided a perfect opportunity for white men to make sexual advances. Countless women testified about the prevalence and unpleasantness of these advances. Unfortunately, most of these women had little recourse. Nineteenth-century African-American leader Alexander Crummell perceptively summed up the circumstances:

> Of the fifteen thousand colored school teachers in the South, more than half are colored young women, educated since emancipation. But even these girls, as well as their more ignorant sisters in rude huts, are followed and tempted and insulted by the ruffianly element of Southern society, who think that black men have no rights which white men should regard, and black women no virtue which white men should respect.[12]

African Americans in general, and the women in particular, eagerly sought to discredit white men's unflattering and dangerous notions of their morality. Late-nineteenth-century black women reformers regularly preached to their working-class sisters the gospel of racial uplift through the cultivation of black female virtue. Clearly, these middle-class women wanted to polish the tarnished image that was indiscriminately projected onto all black women.

Throughout the late nineteenth century and on into the twentieth, this pervasive negative view of their moral state continued to shape the treatment received by women of African descent. It particularly influenced the administrators of black educational institutions, who continued to emphasize the development of black female virtue. At the same time, these administrators worked to raise their academic standards and modernize their curricula. Because of this dual emphasis on moral *and* intellectual development, black colleges and universities had an enormous impact on the communities they served. This was certainly true of Morris Brown, Clark, Spelman, Morehouse, and Atlanta University—the five black higher educational institutions functioning in Atlanta.

While all these schools were private and church affiliated, each was unique. In the decades after the Civil War, white northern missionaries established four of the five: Spelman, Morehouse, Clark, and Atlanta University. Morris Brown was the only one established by an African-American denomination, the African Methodist Episcopal Church. Hence, white board members, administrators, and faculty were important participants in the development of the former four schools well into the twentieth century. One Spelman graduate describes the power of this presence on her campus:

> Most of the teachers were New England people, and I can remember the names of some because they were historic. My art teacher was Miss Rose Standish, a direct descendent of Miles Standish. Two sisters there, the Dickinson sisters, were great-nieces of Emily Dickinson. It gave you quite a sense of history. I felt they were marvelously dedicated women.[13]

Another important difference between Morris Brown and the other four schools was funding. While all five schools suffered from problems associated with insufficient funds, Morris Brown was the poorest; Spelman and Morehouse, the best endowed. Former Morris Brown student Julia Fountain Coles recalls that her alma mater became known as the "soap wrapper school . . . because people used to sell soap and things like that to raise money to keep

Moris Brown going. We didn't have any rich foundations, any rich uncles and angels and so forth."[14]

African Americans in Atlanta and all over the country attached a great deal of significance to these differences in funding and origin; so much so that by the early twentieth century, Spelman and Morehouse were viewed not only as the most prestigious among Atlanta's black colleges, but also as two of the best black schools in the nation. Because of their growing reputations, these two schools routinely attracted black sons and daughters of privilege. But in early-twentieth-century America, it seemed that quite often a disproportionate number of those African Americans with large incomes also possessed light skin. This circumstance had a powerful impact on the perception of the prevalence of light skin among members of the Spelman and Morehouse student bodies. Indeed, in some quarters, those schools came to be viewed as exclusive clubs that required a substantial bank account, proper family connections, and light skin for membership. Spelman and Morehouse were not the only schools affected by this reality:

> Cliquish social circles and biased admissions policies were also common at many of the historic Black colleges and universities established in the nineteenth century, including Wilberforce in Ohio (1856), Howard in Washington, D.C. (1867), Fisk University in Nashville (1866), Atlanta University in Georgia (1865), Morgan in Baltimore (1867), Hampton Institute . . . in Virginia (1868), and Spelman Women's College in Atlanta (1881). At some of the most prestigious schools, including Spelman, applicants were allegedly required to pass a color test before being admitted.[15]

When Mary Ann, Ruby Doris's older sister, was trying to decide which school to attend, she was aware of the connection between prestige, money, light skin, and Spelman College. However, none of this had any influence on her choice of schools. The warmth and nurturing influences of her family, her neighborhood, and her high school combined to give Mary Ann such a positive self-image that she simply "did not make the connection" between such artifical distinctions and her own experience.[16]

Regardless of people's perceptions, however, all five of Atlanta's black colleges concentrated much of their energies on providing a quality education to the best and the brightest students that black America had to offer. Not surprisingly, many of the city's and the nation's outstanding black leaders and achievers matriculated at these schools. Professor E. A. Jones of Atlanta

University summed it up: "The intellectual, commercial, and social life of this community has felt the impact of the combined efforts of these institutions."[17] The faculty and administrators felt the same sense of mission that motivated many of Ruby's teachers at Price High School. These educators knew that their student bodies included some of the best black minds in the country; they were excited about the chance to mold, shape, and inspire these young people who would be the future instruments of racial uplift.

Their commitment to their students' well-being prompted the faculty and administrators at Atlanta's black colleges to try to provide a measure of protection from the most injurious effects of segregation. They understood only too well how coping with a segregated system day after day could break their students' spirits and steal their optimism. These dedicated professionals wanted to show their young charges that there was another way. Professor Clarence Bacote notes, "Atlanta University was an oasis. . . . You could live here, at any of these schools, and not suffer the injustices that the person who had to make his living in the city did. You didn't have to face Jim Crow, you had your own group right out here." As these colleges attempted to insulate students from segregation, they also sought to introduce them to integration. School administrators provided their students with invaluable examples of an alternative to segregation when they regularly invited local white residents to school activities, where the seating was always integrated. B. R. Brazeal, a dean at Morehouse College, insisted: "None of our activities would be opened on a segregated basis. We would give a Shakespearean play nearly every year and it was attended by whites. Our football games were attended by whites in those days. I remember once I was at the gate during a football game and several whites came out and bought tickets and said, 'Where shall we go?' I said, 'Well, go anywhere you wish to, the whole place is open. Just go on in.' "[18]

Through this positive atmosphere, school officials tried to inspire their students to look beyond segregation. Benjamin Mays, the president of Morehouse College, advised his students against submitting to the indignities of segregation: "I did not want them to go up in the 'buzzard roost' to see anybody's show, to see any theatrical performance. And I made it very strong. I said, 'Even if God Almighty came to preach at a white church I wouldn't go to hear him.' " As they pondered such advice, students were afforded practical opportunities to discuss their views with local white students. As early as the 1920s, an interracial group of students, mostly affiliated with campus religious organizations, began meeting to discuss racial issues. When students from two white institutions—Emory University and Agnes Scott College—expressed an interest in discussing race with their black counterparts, some were surprised, including Morehouse's Dean Brazeal: "I didn't know we would find many people—whites—who would take a stand in behalf of Negroes."[19] Like the other Atlanta schools, Spelman College urged students to participate in these challenging activities.

But at the same time, Spelman's faculty and administrators refused to abandon their focus on transforming students into proper and virtuous middle-class ladies. Because of its unswerving commitment to this part of its mission, the college still tried to regulate students' activities even as late as the 1950s. Lana Taylor Sims and Norma June Davis, two of Ruby Doris's classmates who later became involved in the Atlanta student movement, describe this restrictive atmosphere: Students were told how to dress, who to see, how to act. "We had to wear stockings; we couldn't wear socks. You couldn't go without something on your feet. You couldn't go bare legged." Spelman was determined that students should act like "ladies." "The whole overlay was of giving girls an education and some social graces." And one of the tests for proper ladylike behavior was a genteel tea that the wife of Spelman's president held every year. "Mrs. Manley had this welcoming tea, and you must be able to negotiate this whole deal with the tea cups and the little sandwiches and your white gloves."[20]

It seemed that virtually nothing in the students' lives was left to chance—or to their own control. Gwen Robinson, another Spelman student who was a contemporary of Ruby Doris's, recalls that even their choice of male associates was closely scrutinized. When students attended a school function, their choice of an escort had to be approved by the institution. Robinson is convinced that part of the reason for this requirement was rooted in Spelman's attempt to discourage its students from dating anyone but a Morehouse man.[21] After all, proper middle-class ladies had to have appropriate mates.

But by the 1950s, the students who enrolled in Spelman had far different expectations from earlier generations. They were coming of age in an America where legal segregation was successfully being challenged. The new medium of television personalized these challenges, broadcasting into America's living rooms vivid images of the determined black citizens of Montgomery, the angry white mob in Little Rock, and the nine brave black children who faced that mob. Such images challenged these young women, haunted them, and provoked them to action. In addition, this was a very difficult time for the faculty and administrators at Spelman. Their school had always provided a sheltering and nurturing atmosphere for the bright young innocents entrusted to their care. But this new generation of students was different. They were restless, they were assertive, and they chafed under anybody's restrictions or control—whether it was the limiting restrictions of segregation or the nurturing restrictions of their own institution. It was a confusing time for faculty and administrators. Clearly, their priorities and relationships would have to be redefined.

Ruby Doris was one of the new breed of students. Reverend Albert Brinson, a student at Morehouse when Ruby attended Spelman, observes: "She was a Spelman woman . . . but she was not the quintessential Spelman woman. . . . She was not the ladylike kind." On the contrary, Brinson insists, Ruby exhibited one characteristic in particular that was most unladylike: "she was rather aggressive."[22] Norma June Davis unequivocally agrees: "[Ruby] seemed so atypical of Spelman, I mean at that point in time. It was amazing that she was even there. She didn't look like a Spelmanite, she didn't dress like a Spelmanite, and she didn't act like one."[23]

Despite the change in its student body, Spelman continued to try to make "ladies" out of its students. It concentrated particular attention on their activities outside of the classroom. Spelman women were not allowed to leave campus in the evenings without special permission. Later, when some students became involved in the movement, they were often forced to choose between civil rights rallies and Spelman's rules. Gwen Robinson became so frustrated by the limitations these rules placed on her life that she protested against them in campus demonstrations. Her protests angered Spelman's president Albert Manley and prompted him to question her politics. He demanded to know if she was a communist.[24] Up to this point, President Manley had expressed his admiration for those Spelman students protesting segregated facilities in the city of Atlanta. Obviously, challenging segregation in the city was one thing, but questioning Spelman's rules and regulations was quite another.

Even though Spelman's missionary legacy and nurturing tendencies could, at times, be quite limiting, the school still managed to provide vigorous intellectual challenge. Much of that challenge was provided by Spelman faculty in their classrooms, but additional intellectual stimulation came from outside speakers. During the late fifties and early sixties, the college regularly hosted a wide variety of guest speakers. In 1957, for example, noted black sociologist E. Franklin Frazier addressed the Spelman student body. Many were undoubtedly shocked by Frazier's scathing denunciation of the black middle class. Frazier insisted that all black people, especially the black middle class, had "thus far failed to meet the challenges of a swiftly changing world." He went on from this attack on the middle class's vision to attack one of its most hallowed institutions: the black college. He insisted that this institution was not adequately preparing its students for the challenges of a competitive American society, and he characterized the content of its curric-ula as "sentimental slop."[25] Many of the well-groomed, middle-class young women in the audience moved restlessly in their seats as Frazier's harsh words stung them. The quiet, dignified serenity of Sister's Chapel provided little comfort to these thoughtful young women as they listened to Frazier chal-lenge many of their most cherished assumptions.

Other speakers provided perspectives that differed markedly from Frazier's. Harlem Renaissance figure Langston Hughes told his Spelman listeners about Africa when he addressed them in 1960. While he talked about the fact of economic exploitation on the continent, he also discussed his feeling of connection with his ancestral homeland. Hughes insisted that during a re-cent trip to Africa, he had gained "a new appreciation for my own racial background, a new love for my ancestry. . . ."[26] Other visitors to the Spelman campus, such as Kenyan nationalist leader Tom Mboya, also encouraged stu-dents to focus on the land of their ancestors. Mboya informed the students about Third-World freedom struggles which he claimed were much more than mere assaults on colonial domination. "Our people in Africa and the people in Asia are involved in a struggle for basic human needs. They are talking in terms of the need for food. Now you can't go to a hungry man, a man whose only demand is that he should have one decent meal a day, and talk to him about the evils of this or that system." Mboya went on to suggest that only after basic human needs were satisfied could people become con-cerned about governmental processes. At the end of his analysis, the Kenyan leader prophetically added, "Each of you will have to face these problems for yourselves."[27] Along with his message, Mboya also provided the basis for concrete contact between Spelman students and Africans. Under his spon-sorship, a group of young Kenyan women became exchange students at Spelman.

Details of the African freedom struggle were undoubtedly inspiring to the young idealistic coeds at Spelman. Through much of the twentieth century, the majority of sub-Saharan Africa's inhabitants had been colonized and ruled by European nations. In the years immediately following World War II, serious cracks in the facade of European domination had begun to appear, and by the 1950s, European nations had started to grant independence to some of their colonies. The British took the lead when they relinquished their claims to their West African colony of Ghana in 1957. During the next few years, the pace of African independence accelerated rapidly as still more colonies were freed. This flurry of nationalist activity kindled the hope and ignited the excitement of Ruby and her classmates. Many experienced a sense of ancestral connection that was spiritually uplifting. They recognized a striking parallel between the African freedom struggle and their own civil rights movement.

Others who addressed Spelman's student body during this period talked more about domestic and regional issues. Martin Luther King, Jr., delivered the college's Founders Day address in the spring of 1960. In that address, entitled "Keep Moving from This Mountain," King advised his audience, "Segregation is a cancer in the body politic which must be removed before our democratic health can be realized." Since the detrimental effects of segregation touched all Americans, not just black people, those who battled segregation were not fighting for black rights only. He argued, "We are struggling to save America in this very important decisive hour of her history." King concluded that it was up to everyone to do as much as they could. His voice reached a dramatic crescendo as he offered this parting advice: "If you can't fly, run; if you can't run, walk; if you can't walk, crawl; but by all means keep moving."[28] The young, charismatic preacher's words raised goose bumps on the arms of many Spelman students in the audience that day. They stirred restlessly in their seats as they thought about life's possibilities.

King's advice was reinforced by Spelman's President Manley. In his charge to the graduates of the class of 1960, Manley surprised many of his listeners with a ringing endorsement of student protest activities: "Then, just as we had settled back and begun to believe that you were indifferent to the great social issues of the day, you surprised us all by engaging in large scale demonstrations." The president went on to applaud the students' vision and courage:

> I want to commend you for demonstrating that college students are not apathetic, but can become involved in great causes when the moment arrives. Twenty, thirty, or forty years from now, I hope you will be able to refer to the present tensions as birth pains out of which a new order was born.[29]

Many of the graduating seniors who listened to Manley's praise felt a thrill of pride. Most were convinced that they were part of a generation that was changing history. But they could not become too complacent for there were regular reminders of the work that remained to be done. One such reminder came from Morehouse's president, Dr. Benjamin Mays, who challenged Atlanta University Center students to intensify their efforts, since, "freedom [would] not be given away." He advised them to act forcefully because "pressure for freedom ha[d] to come from the 'oppressed and not the oppressor.' "[30]

Yet, in the midst of all this supportive advice, some continued to emphasize the importance of traditional roles. Dr. Benjamin Mays's Founders Day address to Spelman students provides an example:

> But over and above business, politics, and the professions, you Spelman women will be called upon to be wives, mothers and homemakers. You will be called upon to be good in all these areas. . . . The husband and father will make exacting demands of you and he will expect certain things of you in spite of your training and degrees.[31]

Thus, Spelman students were receiving mixed signals. The same school officials who took pride in their students' intellectual and activist achievements took equal pride in their student's ladylike demeanor. They insisted that one could always tell a "Spelman girl" because she "walked gracefully, spoke properly, went to church every Sunday, poured tea elegantly, and in general had all the attributes one associates with the finishing school."[32] Even the school's physical appearance helped to project an air of southern gentility. The red brick classroom buildings and residence halls were separated by wide expanses of carefully trimmed grass. A variety of trees, plants, and shrubs, including graceful and distinctly southern magnolia trees, provided a soft and fragrant atmosphere for Spelman's students and faculty. The campus exuded quiet security, its air heavy with one hundred years of history.

Most students did not completely abandon Spelman's notions of proper black womanhood. Yet this did not prevent them from attacking the symbols of segregation in their own backyard. For example, in the late 1950s some Spelman students tested bus segregation. Ruby was not among them. As these young women slowly climbed the bus steps to pay their fares, then walked to the front seat behind the driver, it felt as if they had lead weights attached to their legs. White passengers stared at them in confusion that quickly turned to anger. The silence on the bus was deafening and the hostility palpable. The bus seemed to creep along while these outwardly calm coeds continued to sit in their forbidden seats all the way to their destination. Their quiet resistance sometimes provoked more than hostile stares. Faculty advisor Howard Zinn recalled: "Once a white man pulled a knife from his pocket and waved it at one of my students sitting opposite him in a front seat. She continued to sit there until she came to her stop, then got off."[33]

A few months after this spontaneous Spelman activity, the first student sit-ins in Greensboro, North Carolina, had a profound impact on black college students all over the South, including those at Spelman. Ruby Doris later described her feelings at the time:

> I began to think right away about it happening in Atlanta, but I wasn't ready to act on my own. When the student committee was formed in the Atlanta University Center, I told my older sister, who was on the Student Council at Morris Brown College, to put me on the list. And when two hundred students were selected for the first demonstration, I was among them.[34]

But before they scheduled their first sit-in, Atlanta students took a unique step. At the urging of Dr. Rufus Clement, Atlanta University's president, the students drafted a statement outlining their concerns. Dr. Clement then arranged for Lillian Smith, a noted white southern author, to donate the money necessary to publish it in Atlanta's daily newspapers. The students' statement, "An Appeal for Human Rights," explained the problems that plagued black Atlanta residents, and it promised action: "We must say in all candor that we plan to use every legal and non-violent means at our disposal to secure full citizenship rights as members of this great Democracy."[35] A number of student leaders from the Atlanta University Center signed the appeal, although Ruby did not. Her sister Mary Ann, who was secretary of the student government association at Morris Brown College, signed it even though her school's student body president refused. A short time later, the students decided to form a committee. On 15 March 1960, the new Atlanta Committee on Appeal for Human Rights conducted its first sit-in.

Their early targets were the segregated facilities in government buildings, railroad stations, and the Trailways and Greyhound bus stations.[36] During one of those early demonstrations, when students attempted to eat at a segregated state office building cafeteria a short distance from the Spelman campus, Ruby was among those arrested. Later that spring, the Atlanta Committee on Appeal for Human Rights decided to stage a symbolic march on the Georgia State Capitol on 17 May to commemorate the U.S. Supreme Court ruling in *Brown v. the Board of Education.* Because the *Brown* decision had been announced on that date in 1954, Atlanta students felt that the march would be a "link with the immediate past and with the legal strategies of their elders."[37] The segregated capitol was a particularly potent symbol for many of these students. It served to remind Ruby and the other young Georgians in the group of how little influence they and their ancestors had had in state government. Summerhill, where Ruby had grown up, lay practically in the shadow of Georgia's domed capitol. But as far as Summerhill residents were concerned, the capitol might as well have existed on another planet; even though they paid taxes, they were completely excluded from the business of state government.

That blatant unfairness hardened the resolve of the young protesters, and they needed all the resolve they could muster. As they approached the capitol, its gold dome looked higher, shinier, and more forbidding than ever. Pausing in front of the massive structure, the group seemed to take a collective deep breath. They straightened their backs, looked up one more time at that shiny gold dome, and then proceeded with their solemn commemoration. Ruby and the others felt a sense of empowerment—here at last they were confronting one of the most potent symbols of segregated state power, but they knew that this was just the beginning.

From state government, the students extended their protests to downtown lunch counters and a large public hospital. Although Ruby did not assume a leadership role in the early stages of the Atlanta movement, she did prove to be one of the most faithful participants.

> There was a core group . . . who were there for the hard planning, and Ruby Doris was always there. I mean she was always there. And I'm not even sure whether she was officially on the executive committee or not. But she was the kind of person who would be there if something had to be done. She would get an assignment whether she was on the committee or not.[38]

Also during that spring, many of Atlanta's student demonstrators attended a meeting at Shaw University in Raleigh, North Carolina. The meeting had been called by Ella Baker, the acting executive director of the Southern Christian Leadership Conference. Baker borrowed eight hundred dollars from SCLC to defray meeting costs, and then she sent a note, cosigned by Dr. Martin Luther King, Jr., to all major protest groups. Her note invited the groups to send representatives "TO SHARE experience gained in recent protest demonstrations and TO HELP chart future goals for effective action."[39] At the meeting, the students formed a temporary Student Nonviolent Coordinating Committee, which helped to foster a sense of community among them. The atmosphere on Shaw's campus was electric. Gathered here were leaders from all over, the best and the brightest that black America had to offer. As these young protesters became acquainted with each other and with each other's movements, they grew more convinced than ever that they were on the verge of changing their nation forever by rooting out the evil system of segregation. Commitment and conviction clearly shone on their eager young faces; they could actually feel power coming from each other. At this early point in the movement, students still had an unshakable faith in America's inherent goodness. One observer's description of the mind-set of the Atlanta students could have been applied to their colleagues from other schools as well: "The Atlanta students illustrated the generational distance between the early and the late 1960s. They were 'good Americans' who did not yet question the system."[40]

Throughout that historic weekend, student leaders engaged in vigorous and challenging debates. But the debates were not yet acrimonious; the developing rivalries, not yet serious. There was much that united the students and very little that divided them. During these early optimistic days when the sit-ins were just a few weeks old, young activists shared a profound commitment to nonviolence and Christian ethics. They believed that American society was just and moral and had the capacity to change. Their shared vision of a bright future came from their acceptance of the teachings of their churches, schools, homes, and communities. They were able to maintain that vision in the early years because of their unique innocence. Thanks to the special treatment they had received in their own communities—the special nurturing and encouragement that had been poured into them—these young activists felt like God's chosen people, not God's excluded people. And as God's chosen people, they felt obligated to act because they could make a difference.

Many activists of that generation recall the efforts their families and communities made to protect them. For example, Angela Davis has said that her mother "did not want [her] to think of guns hidden in drawers or the weeping Black woman who had come screaming to [their] door for help . . . but of a future world of harmony and equality."[41] Similarly, Charlayne Hunter-Gault, one of the first black undergraduates at the University of Georgia, explains, "We had been protected and privileged within the confines of our segregated communities." Furthermore, this protection allowed Hunter-Gault's generation to view their society's faults without bitterness, but with determination. As she puts it, "But now that we students had removed the protective covering, we could see in a new light both our past and our future. . . . Now without even ambivalence or shame, we saw ourselves as the heirs to a legacy of struggle, but struggle that was . . . ennobling; struggle that was enabling us to take control of our destiny."[42] Indeed, the breadth of their vision even allowed these idealistic and innocent young black people to look far beyond the issue of race. John Lewis explains: "To me, the whole thing was like I had the feeling that we was involved in something like a crusade in a sense. It was a sense of duty, you had an obligation to do it . . . to redeem the soul of America. . . . It was like going to church."[43] Lewis's Nashville coworker

Diane Nash concluded: "I think we need radical good to combat radical evil. . . . In a word, it is a question of dignity."[44] Casey Hayden adds: "What we were into at that time was the redemptive community. That we were into healing and reconciling. We were not into getting any power."[45]

Even though Ruby did not attend SNCC's founding meeting, she had much in common with the young people there. She shared their background and their point of view; she, too, was convinced of the righteousness of their cause. It was this belief that made Ruby continue to demonstrate in Atlanta throughout the spring of 1960. Even that summer, after most of the Atlanta University Center students had gone home, Ruby continued to organize. Mary Ann, who was also involved, recalls that they did not want to lose the momentum from the spring protests: "It was decided we wanted to maintain some kind of intact organization during the summer so we got an office downtown on Auburn [Avenue.]" The students worked to develop contacts in the community, and they produced and distributed a newsletter, *The Student Movement and You.*[46]

One of their most important goals that summer was to generate support for an economic boycott. Ruby was particularly enthusiastic about this idea. She insisted: "We do not intend to sell our dignity for a few dollars. We do not intend to go downtown and sell ourselves out." During a mass meeting at the South Atlanta Methodist Church she exhorted others "to hold as [their] slogan for the merchants downtown: have integration will shop, have segregation will not." Ruby and the other summer volunteers cultivated support for their boycott, and they continued to picket selected establishments. Among the targets was an A & P grocery store that had a large black clientele but refused to employ African Americans in anything but menial positions. Ruby was one of those dispatched to picket the A & P. On numerous occasions, she was the only person marching around and carrying a picket sign in front of the store.[47]

As Ruby marched back and forth in the hot Atlanta summer sun, she was very uncomfortable. The heat made her sweat, and that made her clothes stick to her. She could feel beads of sweat popping out on her face too; sometimes the sweat ran into her eyes, making them sting. Ruby felt like a limp dishrag. She was acutely aware of how she looked because her appearance had always been important to her. In addition, Ruby experienced a sense of aloneness. All her activist experience up to this point had been part of a group effort. That is what made this solitary demonstration so hard. Ruby thought about how she and her friends had all comforted each other during marches and sit-ins in the past. It is not that they had talked to each other, but each had felt the strength and the commitment flowing from the others, and it had helped to bolster everyone's courage. Walking back and forth in front of the A & P, Ruby ached for that camaraderie. In the midst of her discomfort, though, she discovered a strength deep inside herself, an unshakable commitment to the cause of civil rights that kept her coming back day after day when there was no publicity, no one to march with her and bolster her courage, and almost no recognition of her activity from her own community.

But Ruby did more than picket the A & P that summer. She was also active in kneel-ins that targeted selected churches. Because she fervently believed in the Methodist tradition in which she had been raised, she was shocked by the existence of discrimination in the church. Of course, Ruby completely understood southern racial etiquette; she had grown up southern. But she was idealistic enough to expect Christian moral ethics to soften the heart of even the staunchest segregationists. Ruby was disconcerted when this did not happen. She explained, "When I was refused admission to the Church, I was stunned at first by the reaction of the ushers."[48]

Not only the ushers' reaction but also that of the congregation dismayed her. Though the ushers blocked her entry into the sanctuary, Ruby could glimpse the congregation just beyond them. Some turned to see what was causing the disruption in the vestibule but when they saw her, they quickly whirled back around and resumed their participation in the service as though she were not there. Others stared directly at her with looks of pure hatred. For an instant, Ruby recoiled from these looks. She wanted to scream at them, "But this is the Lord's house!" Instead, she simply refused to leave. She reported, "I pulled up a chair in the lobby and joined in the singing and worship services which I enjoyed immensely." Clearly, her idealism and her faith were too strong to be destroyed by an encounter even as distressing as this one:

> I feel that segregation is basically a moral problem, and for this reason, I feel that Church is the one institution where the problem can be "thrashed out." I think the kneel-in movement is an appeal to the consciences of Christians, who are primarily "good" people. Even if we were not admitted to worship, as was true in my case, I think that the attempt in itself was a success, because the minds and hearts of the people who turned us [a]way were undoubtedly stirred.[49]

When students returned to school in the fall, the Atlanta student movement accelerated the pace of its protests. In October 1960, Mary Ann and

Ruby took part in a large demonstration at the lunch counter in Davison's, a downtown Atlanta department store. During a later demonstration at Woolworth's lunch counter. Mary Ann was horrified when a waitress threw a "Coca-Cola" bottle at Ruby. It just missed the back of her head "by inches." Witnessing that scene really frightened Mary Ann: "I was so astounded. I mean, I just knew she was gone."[50]

When these young activists sat in at downtown lunch counters, they were always careful to act in a dignified manner. They paid special attention to their appearance. The men dressed in suits, or sport coats and dress slacks, and they wore ties. The women wore skirts-and-blouses or dresses, with stockings and pumps. While they sat on the hard, uncomfortable stools hour after hour, the students generally did not speak to each other. Most held their faces in sober expressions. Some brought their textbooks and attempted to study, while others simply stared straight ahead as the time crawled by.

An aura of tension settled over these counters when angry store employees, hostile white onlookers, and determined black students all held their ground. Store managers and lunch-counter employees resented the negative impact the student presence had on their livelihood. For their part, the students, motionless and expectant, could feel the angry eyes of the white mob boring into their backs. They could hear the racial slurs that were intended to wound them. Even worse, they realized that the onlookers might very well inflict physical damage. Because unruly crowds of young white toughs invariably gathered at the site of most sit-ins, Ruby and the others lived with the threat of danger every time they demonstrated. Once when Atlanta student leader Benjamin Brown was sitting in at a lunch counter, a white man came in brandishing a machete. Although the man never attacked the students, his presence was quite menacing. Yet Brown did not feel any fear at the time: "Never thought about it. Honest to goodness, I never thought about it."[51]

Many students in the movement did not have time for fear. As one puts it, "We were driven. We were absolutely driven."[52] Spelman student Lana Taylor Sims showed just how driven so many of them were. When she was sitting in at a lunch counter one day,

> the manager walked up behind her, said something obscene, and grabbed her by the shoulders. [He shouted] "Get the hell out of here, nigger." Lana was not going. I do not know whether she should have collapsed in nonviolent manner. She probably did not know. She put her hands under the counter and held. He was rough and strong. She just held and I looked down at that mo-

ment at her hands . . . brown, strained . . . every muscle holding.
. . . All of a sudden he let go and left. I thought he knew he could
not move that girl—ever.[53]

During the fall of 1960, Ruby Doris became a familiar presence at demonstrations, recognized and appreciated for her tenacity and discipline. Ruby Doris "was often the glue that held everyone together," notes Charlayne Hunter-Gault. "Once during sit-ins in Atlanta, a crowd began tormenting the students, who wanted to scream back. But Ruby Doris walked the line, whispering, 'Don't forget why you're here.' "[54] Norma June Davis agrees: "[Ruby] was willing to take the chance and be on the line, and be out there. And that was unusual at Spelman."[55] Ben Brown remembers Ruby as a "team player" who was "one of those people . . . responsible for rallying the troops."[56]

As Ruby and her colleagues continued to demonstrate, they became increasingly confident that they had the power to effect change. Hundreds of black college students all over the South were similarly affected. Franklin McCain, one of the four freshmen who started the sit-ins in Greensboro, insists, "We had the confidence of a Mack truck." That confidence was based on the students' belief in their own power and in the basic goodness of American society. In the words of Julian Bond:

> We were operating on the theory that here was a problem, you
> expose it to the world, the world says "How Horrible!" and moves
> to correct it. . . . We thought there was even a hidden reservoir
> of support among white Southerners. . . . And we thought that
> the Kennedy Administration was on our side and that, again, all
> you had to do was put your case before them and they would
> straighten out what was wrong.[57]

As their confidence and their actions were rewarded with concrete results, these student activists stood back to survey the changes. They were proud and a little awed. As one put it: "I myself desegregated a lunch counter, not somebody else, not some big man, some powerful man, but little me. I walked the picket line and I sat in and the walls of segregation toppled. Now all people can eat there."[58] Committed student protesters soon found that their movement activities changed their society and irrevocably altered their lives. Participants' views of their region, their nation, and themselves would never be the same again. Observes SNCC Chairman John Lewis: "Being involved tended to free you. You saw segregation, you saw discrimination, and you had to solve the problem, but you saw yourself also as the free man, as the free agent, able to act."[59]

Ruby's view of her involvement complemented Lewis's perceptions. Her protest activities taught her: "No one can imprison your mind. As long as you think free, you are free."[60] Anne Moody, who worked in the movement in Mississippi, underwent a similar evolution of her thinking: "But something happened to me as I got more and more involved in the Movement. It no longer seemed important to prove anything. I had found something outside myself that gave meaning to my life."[61] Spelman's president Albert Manley noticed how movement activities changed student attitudes at his institution. Before the movement, students routinely deferred to authority. "[If] I had wanted [a student] to come see me there would be a bit of [a] tremor." After students began protesting, however, they became much more assertive. "During and after the sixties they would tell me they wanted to see me and I would tremble."[62]

While movement participation changed these students, it also had a profound impact on their parents. Many were alarmed by their children's new commitment. Because these black parents were well acquainted with the brutal nature of southern racism, they were afraid for their children's safety. They understood the anger and frustration that the system of segregation provoked in their children. They even understood their children's determination to fight the system. But many still did not want their sons and daughters to be the ones to risk their futures and their lives—even if the cause was just. Joyce Ladner explains that ambivalence: "My mother was never involved in the civil rights movement. There were a lot of inherent contradictions in my mother . . . because she was terrified of what might happen. . . . She was scared the Klan would come and burn down the house." But this was the same mother who allowed "her fourteen- and fifteen-year-old daughters to attend an NAACP mass meeting in Jackson."[63] Similarly, the Smiths were gravely concerned about their daughters' willingness to risk their futures to protest segregation, but they were still sympathetic to the cause. Mary Ann recalls: "I think they had concerns. I don't think they ever had a desire to tell us not to. They must have felt that whatever part we could play in making the change was worth it."[64] Although Ruby's parents usually kept their concerns to themselves, her mother did express apprehension on at least one occasion. Mrs. Smith told Atlanta Student Movement leader Lonnie King, "You've got both of my girls in this thing and I hope it works out."[65]

As Ruby became more involved in the movement, she rarely told her parents what she was planning. Often the family would find out about her protest activities only after the demonstration had ended. Her younger brother Willie describes how the family's uncertainty felt: "We knew Ruby Doris was out there, but we didn't know exactly when she was going to do something. I think we had times when mother . . . when we prayed for Ruby Doris." Not only was the family uncertain about Ruby's activities, but they were also uncertain about her fate. "When we would hear about anything . . . , she was already in jail."[66] There were at least two reasons for Ruby's reluctance to inform her family. The first was rooted in her personality. From her earliest days, she had always been an intensely private and independent person who did not want to inform anyone of her activities or even ask for their understanding. According to Mary Ann, her parents understood this about Ruby, and accepted it: "They would just sort of discount or just sort of say, 'Well, you know Ruby Doris.' I think they felt so helpless with her. Whatever she's going to do, she's going to do."[67]

The second reason for Ruby's reticence was based on her desire to stay out of the spotlight. She absolutely did not want any personal notoriety. When she was confronted with the prospect of receiving special attention for her protest activities, Ruby Doris complained, "I'm no celebrity and you know it."[68] But despite her best efforts, Ruby did receive recognition, and it had an impact on her family. Her younger brother Bobby recalls how bewildering it all seemed:

> What comes to mind really is that one day when Ruby came back from a march and the A. U. Center [students] came over here on the bus, and I was in the backyard playing. And when they came out [to] really cheer her, she had just gotten out of jail and had served a long sentence and had come back home. And they came over here cheering her—cheering for Ruby. But I didn't understand what was going on, you know. . . . they were just making a lot of noise. . . . And [I] was just like, "What has she done?"[69]

Ruby's colleagues in the movement faced a wide variety of family reactions. For example, fellow Spelman student Norma June Davis had to cope with the reaction of her godmother, the head of Spelman's French Department, who "thought [her movement participation] was somehow unladylike." June's mother's reaction was a great deal stronger. When she received the news that her daughter had been arrested and sent to a work camp, she was so upset she had to be hospitalized and sedated.[70] Joyce Ladner's mother, even though afraid for her safety, "never said don't."[71] In contrast, when Martha Prescod Norman announced that she was going to Mississippi to help black people register to vote, her parents "really, honest to God, be-lieved that [she] had to be out of [her] mind to think that made sense." Martha refused to back down, but her parents would not accept her decision. "It ended up with my parents disowning me for a period of time . . . and I'm an only child."[72] It was a split that lasted for ten or fifteen years.

Gwen Robinson recalls an equally difficult encounter with her family over her decision to become involved in Freedom Summer. When the Spelman administration learned of her intentions, they immediately called her family, who, in turn reacted swiftly and decisively.

> And so I wake up, one morning in my dorm around 6:30 in the moning, and there is my grandmother, my mother, [and] my two uncles. My grandmother's saying, "Gwen." And I'm like, where did these people come from?[73]

Despite this early morning visit, Gwen would not change her mind.

Thus, Ruby and her African-American movement sisters faced various kinds of pressure from family members concerned about their safety and their future. Resisting familial pressure was often difficult, but these young women somehow found the strength deep inside themselves to continue protesting and risk expulsion from school, jailing, beatings, and perhaps worse. Part of this strength came from their belief in the justness of their cause, and in the basic goodness of American society. Strong black female role models also served as a source of strength. Many of these young activists had grown up in close-knit communities where the existence of strong women was considered normal and common. Although Ruby's family cannot remember any particu-lar female role models in her early experience, they insist that the warm, supportive atmosphere in Summerhill encouraged all of them to assert them-selves and do their best.[74]

Other African-American women of SNCC do remember the influence of specific female role models, however. Gwen Robinson was impressed by the courage of her grandmother, the same woman who eventually tried to dis-suade her from working in Freedom Summer. Her grandmother would not allow any white person to give her orders. One episode in particular deeply affected Gwen's consciousness. One night her grandmother heard a noise outside. When she grabbed her shotgun and went out to investigate, she found two white policemen on her front lawn. They had been chasing a black man through the neighborhood. The officers immediately yelled in their most intimidating voice, "Auntie, watch out. Put that gun down!" In response, Gwen's grandmother squared her shoulders, looked them in the eye, and replied in an even, but determined voice, "I'm none of your god-damned auntie."[75] She did not retreat, and she did not lay down her weapon.

Dorie Ladner also had an important female role model: her mother. Do-rie's mother often admonished her and her sister Joyce to think and act independently. "Mother was a very determined person who always told us to work for yourself. Get an education, work for yourself, and don't depend on any man to take care of you." Mrs. Ladner's actions toward white people conveyed a potent message to her daughters. "Mother never allowed any white man to call her auntie, and no white woman to degrade her."[76] Al-though such role models were important for the young African-American women who faced danger in the civil rights movement, the reinforcement and support they gave each other were equally important. Joyce Ladner ex-plains, "We didn't need models from the outside. There was a sense of sister-hood in the struggle between southern black women."[77]

Ruby and other African-American coeds had to confront the question of how their protest activities would affect their academic careers. One or two demonstrations or rallies made little difference. But those who demonstrated day after day and spent time in jail had to consider the effect of long absences on their schoolwork. Families had sacrificed a great deal to send their daugh-ters to college. Many of these young women were the first in their families to have this opportunity. This was certainly true in Ruby Doris's case. Acutely aware of their families' high expectations, these students were haunted by the potential for academic disaster that accompanied the move-ment's demands. Thus, Ruby Doris and all the other student activists had some hard choices to make.

As they pondered their chances for academic success in the context of the movement, a crucial factor was how sympathetic their professors would be. Predictably, there was a wide variety of attitudes among Atlanta University Center faculty. Professor Lois Moreland, a political scientist at Spelman, was identified by many as being among the most supportive. Many of the student protesters in her class regularly communicated their thoughts on the move-ment to her. Ruby was one of those students.

> They were talking to me [Moreland] about what would happen to them on campus. And whether or not they should actually go sit in and miss class. And would there be repercussions. And what should they do if they actually went to jail. And how could they make up the work.[78]

Moreland encouraged the students to continue both their demonstrations and their schoolwork. She insisted that students complete all their classwork regardless of their protest schedules, and she devised methods, such as make-up exams and tutoring, to assist them whenever she could. She recalls that many other Atlanta University Center faculty were not as willing as she was to make allowances for student demonstrators who missed class. Moreland is convinced that this lack of faculty support was largely motivated by fear of the negative impact demonstrations could have on student achievement.[79]

Howard Zinn, a white historian on Spelman's faculty, was quite concerned about student academic achievement, but he still supported student demonstrations. In fact, he actively encouraged his students to protest, and even participated with them on some occasions. In January 1957, he accompanied a group of Spelman students intent on challenging segregated seating in the gallery of the state legislature. Although they sat in the "white" section initially, they were soon forced to move to the "colored" section. Zinn moved with them, causing consternation among the white Georgia legislators.

> The presence of the white teacher (myself) with [the students] in the "colored" section, created much nervousness in the chamber below; the legislators, forgetting about the business at hand (a bill on trout fishing), craned their necks and stared. Not quite sure whether the teacher was a dark white man or a light colored man, they hesitated to order him out.[80]

Dr. Clarence Bacote was another sympathetic Atlanta University Center faculty member. Although Bacote was officially on the Atlanta University faculty, he taught a number of Spelman students, including Ruby Doris Smith. Bacote thought that the depth of Ruby's commitment deserved special consideration:

> When I discovered her sincerity, I decided a young woman like this deserves all the help you can give her. So, what I did was to have conferences with her. I would give special tutoring. Tell her what she missed and suggesting things she should read.[81]

Of course, not all the faculty recognized and supported the students' right to protest. Clark College student and Atlanta Student Movement leader Ben Brown experienced serious difficulty with one of his professors: "There was hostility on the part of some of them—especially my major professor, who was Ed Sweat of South Carolina." When Brown was demonstrating, he missed an exam in Sweat's class. Even though Brown had a B average before that exam, Sweat decided to take drastic action: "He put me out of the class." This created a serious problem since Brown was a senior who needed that class to graduate. Brown was fortunate, however, because Clark's president, Dr. James Brawley, was willing to intercede to have him reinstated in the course. Brown was grateful. "Dr. Brawley was strongly supportive and proud of our involvement . . . quietly."[82]

Ben Brown was not the only student movement participant to incur an instructor's wrath. Spelman student Norma June Davis also had trouble. For the most part, Davis believes, faculty and administrators at Spelman who were not openly supportive at least displayed a sort of "benign support" toward the sit-in participants. But, there were exceptions. One of those exceptions was her German teacher, Professor Axelrod. When she went to see her to discuss an upcoming final exam, Axelrod threw a book at Davis and then sarcastically suggested that they should install bars in the classroom so that she would feel at home. Davis found herself in a predicament similar to Ben Brown's: she was a senior and needed to pass German in order to graduate. The morning of the exam, Davis fortified herself with a cup of white lightnin'. Whether the white lightnin' relaxed her or her preparation paid off, Norma June Davis passed her German final with a grade of D and was able to graduate on time.[83]

To continue both their studies and their protests, students employed a variety of coping strategies. Most soon realized, though, that they would have to seek a new balance between the two. Many began to use jail as their study hall when they were arrested. This worked for a while, but as the pace of movement activities accelerated, participants were forced to reevaluate their priorities. While the majority of these students continued their education as they protested, some concluded, after much painful soul-searching, that their commitment to the movement should take precedence over academic goals—at least for a while. Atlanta student leader Lonnie King, describes the mind-set of students who faced this decision:

> A lot of us, though, actually dropped out so we wouldn't have that kind of burden. It was a conflict trying to score on the exams, and at the same time fight folks downtown. There are some people who dropped out who have never gotten it back together. There are some casualties in the movement.[84]

One who opted to leave school explained:

> Well, we tried. You'd try for a long time to balance school work and this kind of work [protest]. It was something I couldn't bal-

ance. I had to give one up. I gave up the school work. Most people tried. Some people suffered.[85]

Ruby was among those whose commitment to the movement took precedence over school. She dropped out during her junior year in the spring of 1961. This decision signaled a major transition: she was no longer merely a part-time protester; she had become a full-time activist. Ruby would later return and finish her studies at Spelman, but her life would never be the same again.

Even if they managed to earn a college degree, Ruby and her activist colleagues still had serious concerns about the movement's effect on their futures. In the spring of 1961, the *Atlanta Inquirer* reported on one of these concerns: "Many students had raised questions as to whether trespass law or other arrests, jailings, or convictions growing out of sit-in activities would prevent them from securing federal employment." As increasing numbers of students voiced this concern, the *Inquirer*'s editor decided to put the question to Attorney General Robert Kennedy. Kennedy conceded that if a job applicant had a conviction record stemming from civil right activities, it was "one matter which would be considered," but each individual applicant would ultimately be judged on the basis of "character, integrity, and ability to do the job."[86] Such a pronouncement was only partially reassuring. The possibility that students' civil rights activities could affect their career choices and earning potential made the question of whether or not to become involved in the movement a very difficult one. At the same time, however, most recognized that these activities could ultimately expand the career and educational options available to them and to all African Americans. These young people who were poised on the brink of middle-class existence clearly faced a dilemma. One false move and they could jeopardize everything, but if they did not protest vigorously enough, race could still circumscribe their opportunities.

Ruby and the others also had more immediate concerns. One of the most pressing was incarceration. The prospect of spending time in a southern jail was something that African Americans had good reason to fear, since southern law enforcement officials regularly brutalized and terrorized black prisoners. Black female prisoners were vulnerable not only to the same kind of physical abuse suffered by men, but also to sexual abuse. Of her first trip to jail, Ruby's movement coworker Norma June Davis says: "I felt degraded. I felt like I had lost some sense of dignity. I was being fingerprinted; they were taking mug shots of me as if I were a criminal."[87] Such treatment was especially terrifying to a middle-class college coed with no prior experience with the criminal justice system.

The worst was yet to come. When Davis and the other protesters were escorted to their cell, she remembers thinking that it resembled "modern slave quarters." One of the most striking things about it was the absence of any natural light from the outside. The cell had an almost subterranean feel, and the unevenly spaced bright fluorescent lights did little to dispel the gloom. Drab instititional paint, peeling and cracking in many places, covered the cell walls. An unpleasant odor, a mixture of sweat, urine, and stale vomit with just a dash of disinfectant, assaulted the jittery young protesters when they entered their cell. Looking around, Davis spotted two rows of bunk beds. As the group leader, she requested that they all be given beds on the top row. She soon realized that her request probably helped save them from becoming the victims of sexual violence. In a voice trembling with emotion, Davis later explained: "That night . . . I found out we had a white male guard who sat outside the door and had a rifle. And he came in and raped the women at night. And the first night I was there, he came in and raped the woman in the bed under me."[88] As Davis lay there in the dark listening to the brutal sounds of sexual assault beneath her, a formless, suffocating fear battled with her commitment. The next morning, a shaken but determined Davis demanded to see the warden. She threatened to expose conditions inside the prison if reforms were not made. The warden responded by replacing male guards with female ones, and the young activists breathed a little easier.

When these protesters were not in the classroom, on the picket line, or in jail, they tried to find ways to relieve the stress and relax. Most tried hard to establish a proper balance between their social lives and their movement commitments. After all, socializing was a very important part of growing up. Since Ruby and the majority of her movement colleagues ranged in age from eighteen to twenty-one, this was a significant issue for them. In fact, Atlanta's black community provided an abundance of social outlets for these serious young freedom fighters. By the late 1950s and early 1960s, increasing numbers of black rhythm-and-blues singers were recording on mainstream record labels; many of them regularly performed in Atlanta for enthusiastic fans. For example, an Atlanta concert advertised as the "Biggest Show of Stars for 1961" featured Fats Domino, the Shirelles, Chubby Checker, the Drifters, and Ben E. King.[89]

Even when student movement activists were unable to attend such events in the community, they still found ways to socialize. Quite often, movement people got together and danced the bop and the cha-cha. Ben Brown remembers that Ruby really enjoyed these parties. She was fond of dancing and quite good at it. "Ruby Doris was a social creature. Behind all of the dedication and stuff, she knew how to relax and have fun. She could tell some wild stories like all of us would do back in that day." Furthermore, these young activists enjoyed dressing in the popular styles of their era. Everyone wanted to look their best because there was always a lot of flirting and posturing at these gatherings. Most savored the relief they felt at being able to get together without the threat of violence that constantly plagued them during demonstrations; this, plus the music of their favorite rhythm-and-blues artists, made dancing irresistible. It felt so good to be a "normal" teenager—just for a little while. Even at parties, however, Ruby could never relax completely. Brown clearly recalls that thoughts about the movement were always with her: ". . . if the music started, [Ruby] Doris was going to have fun. But she might be standing there dancing with you, but she['s] going to be talking about what she got to do."[90]

Thus, Ruby and her Atlanta Student Movement colleagues tried to juggle a number of concerns. Sitting in at lunch counters and marching on picket lines for hours on end was time consuming enough. But movement people also sat through long meetings, plotting strategy and learning nonviolent techniques. All of this left little time for study, social life or anything else. Because of the many pressures to be balanced, the constant threat of danger, the uncertainty of their academic and financial futures, and the steady demand for a high level of physical energy, many young freedom fighters began to suffer some of the same symptoms as combat veterans. The movement had taken over their lives. They suffered flashbacks, anxiety, and insomnia.

Consequently, some of them only worked in the movement for a year or two before they left to go on with the rest of their lives. They just wanted to get back to "normal"—whatever that was for them now. The student routine of attending classes, studying, and socializing may have seemed dull before, but now, it looked appealing, even comforting. Its sameness ensured security and helped them remember that they had come to college in search of a better life for themselves. For Ben Brown, the decision to return to normal occurred when he graduated from Clark College in the spring of 1961: "I turned the page. Time I left here, I turned the page." Brown went to New York to work for a while, then enrolled in Howard University's law school. The movement had left him so "burned out" that he did not even want to participate in student politics while he was in law school. Mary Ann had also grown quite weary by the spring of 1961.

> I was totally washed out, burned out, everything when spring came. . . . That's why I went to California. I didn't want to stay

anywhere near [here], and it wasn't to get away from the South or that, but I just felt that I had become so entrenched and involved that I'd lost myself, really, in the cause.[91]

That same spring Norma June Davis graduated from Spelman, and she, too, put her protest activities behind her. Like her movement colleagues, Davis was exhausted, but there was also another reason why she stopped protesting. Shortly after her graduation Davis got married: "I had promised Leo [her husband] I wouldn't go to jail anymore when I married him."[92]

Whatever their reasons, some went on with their lives after working in the movement for a limited time. Yet there were others who saw things differently. The early skirmishes during the sit-ins had redefined reality for them. As far as they were concerned, the continued existence of racism and discrimination meant that pursuing the civil rights struggle was the only "normal" course of action they could possibly follow. Casey Hayden for example, characterized the early sit-ins as a life-altering experience: "A new kind of self was created. . . . A lot of the old self-definitions fell away. . . . What you were doing was being a participant with other people in the creation of . . . a movement."[93] Ruby clearly agreed. Increasingly, those closest to her began to recognize that the longer she worked, the stronger her commitment became: "she [Ruby] went off on a rocket . . . in terms of total commitment."[94] It seemed that just a few short months of movement work—from the Atlanta Student Movement's beginning in March 1960 through the end of the 1960–61 school year—had redefined reality for nineteen year-old Ruby Doris Smith. Because of the continued existence of injustice, she would be a freedom fighter for the rest of her life.

CHAPTER FOUR

Ruby Enters SNCC

⚡

THROUGHOUT THE 1960–61 SCHOOL YEAR, THE TEMPORARY STUDENT Nonviolent Coordinating Committee that sit-in leaders had established in April 1960 continued to meet and define its goals. Even as participants' heightened expectations propelled them past the limited goals that had originally drawn them to segregated lunch counters, they never lost sight of their founding statement.

> We affirm the philosophical or religious ideal of nonviolence as the foundation of our purpose, the presupposition of our faith, and the manner of our action. Nonviolence as it grows from Judaic-Christian traditions seeks a social order of justice permeated by love. Integration of human endeavor represents the crucial first step towards such a society.[1]

During the early months of their activism, these black middle-class students remained firmly anchored in the Judeo-Christian tradition of their culture. But this did not serve to limit their vision. On the contrary, they looked far beyond their hometowns, their region, or even their own country. They were moved by a feeling of connection to their ancestral homeland, Africa. Consequently, during that first summer, SNCC's Findings and Recommendations Committee suggested

> That we identify ourselves with the African struggle as a concern of all mankind. We understand there is a possibility that President Eisenhower will make a visit to Africa this fall, and agree that this is a desirable step-up. We feel that before going to Africa, the president should lend the prestige of his office to the

solution of the racial problem in this country, and thus he shall be even better prepared for his visit to Africa.[2]

But practical concerns quickly intruded on the heady excitement of this new international vision. One consideration was staffing. At SNCC's first official meeting in Atlanta during the spring of 1960, student delegates voted to hire a temporary office worker who would manage organizational affairs over that first crucial summer. After making the decision, however, the students realized they had a problem: they did not yet have an office. At this point, Ella Baker stepped in and offered them office space in the SCLC headquarters. SNCC gratefully accepted.[3]

Sit-in activity waned during the summer months of 1960. Most of the young freedom fighters returned to their homes and found summer jobs just as they always had. On the surface, their lives seemed to return to normal. It was good to be home again, to sleep in their own beds, and to eat home-cooked meals. They eagerly sought out old friends so they could compare notes about the latest fashions, the most popular dances, and the juiciest gossip. But somehow this summer was different. Suddenly the things they had always cared about seemed to matter less. Before they left school, they had been making plans to change the world. They could not simply go back to business as usual during the summer. Friends and relatives noticed a change in these returning warriors. In many ways they were still typical college students, but they seemed to square their shoulders and stand a bit straighter, and there was a righteous fire burning in their eyes.

Although the new temporary Student Nonviolent Coordinating Committee may have appeared to lie dormant over the summer, the young protesters' minds were working overtime, pondering issues of strategy, goals, and their movement's future. These budding activists quickly recognized the need for another SNCC conference. Held 14–16 October, this conference was designed to be "action oriented." Conferees attended workshops on a variety of topics that included "desegregation of public facilities, black political activity, discrimination in employment, and racial problems in education."[4] The workshop rooms hummed with the boundless energy and infectious enthusiasm that was so characteristic of early SNCC.

Amid the endless debates on tactics, goals, and vision, one major concern surfaced over and over again: the "jail-versus-bail" question. All over the South, thousands of black student protesters had been arrested. In most cases, they posted bail and were released. Yet some began to argue that there were compelling reasons why protesters should serve their full jail sentences rather than post bail. Proponents of this strategy reasoned that if demonstrators clogged the jails, they would put additional pressure on segregation by straining local resources. Moreover, providing bail funds for students was placing a terrible financial burden on local black communities. Finally, the presence of protesters in jail would provide powerful moral reinforcement of their position. Civil rights activist Bayard Rustin expressed the sentiments of many:

> There are not enough jails to accommodate the movement. . . . If one or two of us are arrested, the rest must nonviolently seek arrest. If, upon arrest, you pay your bail or fine, you provide room for a friend. Only so many can fit into a cell; if you remain there, there can be no more arrests. . . . Imprisonment is an expense to the state; it must feed and take care of you. Bails and fines are an expense to the movement, which it can ill afford.[5]

In fact, a few select members of some local movements had already begun to serve their full sentences when they were arrested. But delegates did not resolve the question at the October conference.

Although SNCC's decision on the jail-versus-bail issue would soon figure prominently in the beginning of Ruby's national activist career, she kept her distance while these deliberations continued. The glamour and the danger of protest activities proved to be much more attractive to Ruby than the early strategy sessions of the fledgling organization. Thus, as SNCC conferees debated and discussed, Atlanta students kept on demonstrating, and Ruby marched right along with them. On 19 October, only three days after the end of the SNCC conference, Ruby and other members of the Atlanta Committee on Appeal for Human Rights protested lunch counter segregation in selected downtown stores. Because the students wanted to make a dramatic statement with their fall demonstrations, they had persuaded Dr. Martin Luther King, Jr., to join them. He was arrested at Rich's Department Store.[6]

At this point Atlanta's city administration began discussions with student leaders. Mayor Hartsfield finally agreed to release student protesters from jail if they would stop demonstrating while he discussed desegregation with downtown merchants. Even though the students were reluctant to accept the mayor's proposal, because they wanted immediate desegregation, they decided to give him a chance. The merchants refused to compromise; they wanted to delay desegregation for a full year. They should not have to desegregate their facilities, the merchants argued, until Atlanta desegregated its public schools in the fall of 1961.[7] Despite the mayor's best efforts, neither side was willing to compromise. In late November, students resumed their demonstrations.

At the same time, SNCC held another meeting in Atlanta at the Butler Street YMCA. Mary Ann attended, but Ruby Doris did not.[8] Just a little over two months later, on 3–5 February 1961, SNCC held yet another Atlanta meeting. This marked the first time that Ruby attended a SNCC meeting. She went as a substitute for Atlanta student leader Lonnie King, a SNCC member-at-large.

As in previous meetings, those in attendance discussed the jail-versus-bail question.[9] But by this time, the context of the discussion had changed dramatically. On 1 February 1961, nine students from Friendship College in Rock Hill, South Carolina, had been convicted of trespass after demonstrating in downtown variety and drug stores. The nine had refused to post bail and had publicly expressed a determination to serve out their full sentences. All of the participants in that February SNCC meeting were quite moved by this stand:

> There are nine students serving thirty days on the York County Chain Gang for sitting at Lunch Counters and requesting service. Their sitting-in shows their belief in the immorality of racial segregation and their choice to serve the sentence shows their unwillingness to participate in any part of a system that perpetuates injustice. Since we too share their beliefs and since many times during the past year we too have sat-in at lunch counters, we feel that in good conscience we have no alternative other than to join them.[10]

Ruby's conscience was particularly stirred by this discussion because the action of the Friendship College students had moved the debate from the theoretical into the realm of the possible. Here was something that Ruby could really sink her teeth into.

Everyone at the February meeting enthusiastically agreed that a SNCC delegation should go to Rock Hill as soon as possible. But whom should they send? Listening to the discussion going on all around her, Ruby felt a little thrill of anticipation that raised the hair on the back of her neck. This was going to be a turning point for SNCC—she just knew it. After much debate, the group decided that they needed experienced protesters, so they selected Charles Jones, Charles Sherrod, Diane Nash, and Mary Ann Smith. Ruby was terribly disappointed that she was not chosen, but she was not about to let anyone know. She stirred uneasily in her chair as she struggled to hide the feeling of being let down. The excitement and momentum generated in the meeting made it that much harder for Ruby, but at the same time Mary Ann felt honored to have been chosen.

However, later when Mary Ann was alone and the excitement waned, a sobering uncertainty assaulted her. The prospect of arrest did not frighten Mary Ann because she had already been arrested more than once during her protest activities with the Atlanta Committee on Appeal for Human Rights. However, she had never served any real jail time—only a few hours. When she thought about serving weeks or months in a jail that was far from home, her apprehension and uncertainty grew. By the time Mary Ann went home to pack, she was having serious misgivings:

> There were four, the people that were going to go from that meeting. And I was one of them. And what happened is I went home, you know. [I was] supposed to pack my bags. . . . And Ruby Doris was getting all excited 'cause she wanted to go. And actually I started having second thoughts. Well, first I said, "now both of us can't go up there. SNCC has already decided which four people are going to go. . . ." And then as [Ruby] got more excited, I got more weak in the knees. And then I started thinking about all the little things I had in the making for the next year, you know. Academically—fellowships and what have you. And what's going to happen if I [get] up there and spend all this time in jail? So what happened eventually is Ruby Doris talked it up, and I just bowed out and let her go.[11]

Ruby's excitement knew no bounds. Here was her chance to help implement a policy that could have a profound effect on the southern freedom struggle. The Rock Hill action would soon prove to be a critical turning point in SNCC's development, as well as in Ruby Doris's activist career. In the case of SNCC, this was the first time that the group had stepped outside its role as a coordinating body and attempted to formulate and implement a national policy. For Ruby Doris, her decision to go to Rock Hill was an important departure from her past movement experience in at least two respects. First, she had never before shown any inclination to take the initiative or provide leadership. Yet here she was volunteering for a hazardous SNCC mission. Second, the targets of Ruby's activism up to this point had all been establishments whose policies directly affected her, since they were in her hometown. But her involvement in Rock Hill pushed Ruby out of her own community and into the national arena. Thus, on the eve of the Rock

Hill action, Ruby Doris Smith, full-time college student and part-time protester, was about to become Ruby Doris Smith, full-time freedom fighter. Nobody doubted that her initiation into full-time movement work would be difficult.

Serving a jail sentence in the rural South was a difficult proposition for any black person, let alone a college coed who was being groomed for the middle class. This was especially true in the case of Rock Hill, "a very tough and scary place."[12] Charles Jones, one of those chosen to go to Rock Hill, explains his apprehension: "I remember us being really concerned . . . about being in a different, new place with[out] any real contacts that we [knew]."[13]

Ruby's mother was very concerned about her daughter's determination to participate in this SNCC action. Ruby recalled, "I went home that night to explain to my mother. She couldn't understand why I had go to away—why I had to go to Rock Hill."[14] Diane Nash did not want her mother to worry, and so she simply did not tell her. Diane's mother discovered what her daughter had been doing only after she had been arrested. "I remember my mother once told me that she had been watching television once, just watching the news and, uh, all of a sudden I came on. The police were putting me into a [paddy] wagon. I was being arrested . . . and she said, 'what a shock.' "[15]

After they arrived in Rock Hill, Charles Jones, Charles Sherrod, Diane Nash, and Ruby Doris Smith assembled at the house of a local supporter and said a brief prayer. The occasion was heavy with anticipation, and nobody knew quite what to expect. The sober expressions on the protesters' faces reflected their feelings of apprehension. Time seemed to crawl by as they waited to go downtown. In the midst of this solemnity, Ruby Doris did something totally unexpected.

> We got up real, real early that morning. . . . Everybody was ready to go. And Ruby Doris said, "Well, everybody can just sort of sit down and do whatever because my hair is not right. And I'm rolling it, and I'm not leaving until it's curled. . . ." And everybody there just said, "Oh, okay."[16]

Perhaps Ruby was trying to maintain some sense of normalcy in the face of grave danger. Perhaps she was simply worried about her hair. Whatever the reason, her actions lightened the atmosphere briefly, but soon the demonstrators were on their way downtown to sit in at Good's Drug Store on Main Street.

Because the SNCC delegation had made no secret of their intentions, local police were ready. They hardly got a chance to demonstrate at all before they were arrested. It was all very orderly, it happened very quickly, and they were sentenced to thirty days in jail.[17] The men were forced to serve on the chain gang, but Ruby and Diane escaped this punishment since there was no chain gang for women. Instead, they were assigned to share a relatively large, but very uncomfortable, cell with five other inmates. Ruby had a difficult first night trying to sleep on an iron-slatted bed without a mattress.[18]

After that first night the two coed activists settled into a routine. Ruby usually woke up around a quarter of seven, just in time for a breakfast of syrup and grits or biscuits with fatback. Then she and Diane would clean the cell. They were particularly concerned about their bed linens because the jail provided clean sheets only once every two weeks and there was no provision for laundering blankets. Appalled, Ruby and Diane complained to the prison officials. By half past eleven, the women were served a lunch consisting of two vegetables along with biscuits. In the afternoon, Ruby read, worked on her diary, answered letters, and exercised. Finally, dinner (cornbread and buttermilk) was served at half past six every evening.[19]

Members of Rock Hill's black community were distressed by the poor quality of the food served in jail. Consequently, they sent the students a steady supply of home-baked delicacies. Reverend C. A. Ivory, a local black minister and activist, visited Diane and Ruby every day, and he never came without a desert—cake, pie, or cookies—baked by a member of his congregation. Ruby's family also sent baked goods. Even though she was glad to receive all of these treats, Ruby soon began to worry about gaining too much weight. She alluded to this in a letter to her sister: "I received the cookies along with your letter. Yum! Yum! Don't worry, I'll try to control my diet (smile)."[20]

Ruby Doris Smith and Diane Nash spent long afternoons discussing the movement. "We analyzed extensively the situation of segregation, and how to get out of it."[21] Ruby was convinced that regardless of how confining and uncomfortable her jail cell was, she had to serve her sentence because it would help in the fight against segregation:

> I feel, however, that because of my convictions this is the only thing that I could do. I know that this sacrifice is small when compared with the cause which motivated me to do it. I also realize that this is the only way that one can truly express the philosophy of non-violence—the willingness to suffer and accept the punishment of society rather than obey the evil of a system like segregation.[22]

Both women read a great deal and "compared notes on what they were reading."[23] The books Ruby read included *The Ugly American*, *The Life of*

Mahatma Gandhi, Exodus, The Wall Between, Elmer Gantry, and the Bible.[24] Diane also read the Bible, among other books. She came to believe that there were compelling parallels between the persecution of the early Christians and the treatment of the civil rights workers.[25]

From her cell in the York County Jail, Ruby tried to keep up with developments in the Atlanta Student Movement. She wrote to Mary Ann: "I was happy to receive your letter. . . . If you have time, keep me abreast of negotiations [between downtown merchants, city officials, and students]. They *don't* censor our mail." Ruby was also quite interested in the Rock Hill movement. She was particularly frustrated by the degree of local white intransigence: "The officials here are getting 'stiff' on picketing. The tension is *high* downtown. Whenever [the picketers] go down, a crowd of hoodlums gather around and eventually they begin to 'fight' (or beat up someone). The police come to [the] rescue after the incident gets out of hand—only to arrest the picketers."[26]

Ruby treasured communication with friends and family on the outside, and was very pleased that the *Atlanta Inquirer* had encouraged its readers to write to her:

> Persons who desire to write to RUBY DORIS SMITH should address all correspondence to Box 202, Atlanta University, or York County Jail, Women's Division, York, South Carolina.[27]

Members of the *Atlanta Inquirer*'s staff strongly supported Ruby's activities because most of them were Atlanta University Center students who had been involved in the local movement with Ruby. Before the *Inquirer*'s birth, the *Atlanta Daily World,* Atlanta's only black newspaper at the time, had been openly hostile to student protesters. The paper's position had angered many members of Atlanta's black business community, and they had canceled their advertisements in the *World.* When businessmen, particularly those in real estate, began to lose revenue because they had discontinued their ads, they decided to establish a rival black newspaper that would present a more balanced view of protest activities. The result was the birth of the *Atlanta Inquirer* on 31 July 1961. Atlanta student protesters made up a large proportion of the new paper's staff. In fact, Julian Bond, one of Ruby's close colleagues, was heavily involved with the *Inquirer,* serving as managing editor, reporter, and columnist.[28]

Ruby and Diane got an education in jail that neither expected. For the first time in their lives, these young coeds had the chance to talk with "bad women" and to realize that they were "just folks."[29] Ruby and Diane's interaction with these women gave them a new perspective on what it meant to be poor, black, and female in American society. It also allowed them to understand behavioral patterns that had previously seemed strange.

> For the first few days the heat was intense in the cell. Breathing was difficult. Everyone was perspiring profusely. We couldn't understand why women in the cell hesitated to ask that a window be opened or the heat be turned down. It turned out that it was because they were so often cold in their homes, and had come to value heat so highly, that they were willing to suffer from it if they could just have it.[30]

As Ruby and Diane read, reflected, discussed, and observed, their vision of the civil rights struggle that had brought them to this jail cell in Rock Hill, South Carolina, broadened dramatically.

But serious issues were not the only things on Ruby's mind. She still had many of the same concerns as the college coeds who slept in dormitories instead of jail cells. Although Ruby had been dating someone before she went to Rock Hill, her long absence caused problems in the relationship. Ruby complained to her sister: "Do you know that ole scroungy John hasn't written me? I guess you know, it's all over for us." Even as Ruby fretted about her boyfriend's inattentiveness, she was amused by the attentions of another man: "Do you know Rev. Ellison? He's been writing me letters like *mad*. Says he has a Cadillac and all that 'crab.' I wrote him back after the first letter, but when he started talking about being in love—Huh! I guess you know—I put him *down!*" In addition to her concern about relationships, Ruby also worried about her appearance. At one point she exclaimed, "My hair is awful."[31]

Upon completion of her thirty-day sentence, when Ruby returned to Atlanta on 18 March 1961, a group of seventy students from the Atlanta University Center schools met her at the airport. Descending the steps of the plane into the Atlanta sunshine, Ruby Doris was overcome with emotion. The waiting students surged forward to embrace her as she stepped onto the tarmac, and her spirit was renewed by their commitment. Then they all joined hands and sang, "We Shall Overcome."[32] As she closed her eyes to sing this civil rights movement anthem, Ruby felt a lump in her throat. The Ruby Doris Smith the group welcomed home was not the same young woman who had left just a few weeks earlier. This new Ruby Doris had a much broader and deeper understanding of the civil rights movement and her role in it.

A few weeks after Ruby's release from jail, the movement shifted its focus to a new target: interstate buses. This shift, and the resulting freedom rides, would generate national publicity. Segregated transportation had long been one of the most hated symbols of Jim Crow. Consequently, as early as the 1950s, African Americans in a number of southern communities, like Montgomery, Alabama, had attacked bus segregation. These had all been local efforts, however. By the spring of 1961, some activists thought that the time was right to attack bus segregation on the national level.

The confrontations faced by these freedom riders were dramatic, but they were not the first. One of the earliest "freedom rides" on record, that of Reverdy [sic] Cassius Ransom, occurred in 1906. Ransom, an elder and later a bishop in the African Methodist Episcopal Church, had a reputation as an outstanding speaker. Because of Ransom's oratorical abilities, William H. Council, president of the all-black Alabama State Agricultural and Mechanical College in Huntsville, invited him to deliver the address for the 29 May 1906 commencement. After he accepted the invitation, Ransom decided to travel from his home in Boston to Alabama by train. He asked the clerk at the railway station if he could purchase a ticket for a sleeping car, and the clerk assured Ransom that he would be allowed to occupy a sleeping car because he was an interstate passenger. But despite the clerk's assurances, Ransom was in for a rough ride when his train reached the South. White passengers, outraged that his sleeping car was not in the Jim Crow section, forcibly ejected him. Ransom described his ordeal:

> At this time the train was running at a high rate of speed. After that I was in a dazed state. All I know is they cuffed me, kicked me and dragged me again through those coaches, threw me up into the seat, and took my leather bag and slammed it at me.[33]

Even though he had paid for a sleeping car, Ransom was forced to ride in a Jim Crow car all the way to his destination.

A more organized group assault on segregated interstate buses occurred right after World War II when the Fellowship of Reconciliation of the Congress of Racial Equality sponsored their Journey of Reconciliation. In 1947, both CORE and FOR decided that their journey was necessary to test the South's compliance with the recent Supreme Court ruling in the Irene Morgan case, which outlawed segregated seating on interstate carriers. Although the sixteen interracial participants in the Journey of Reconciliation encountered a number of white passengers who were sympathetic to their cause, they also faced threats and violence. Jim Peck, one of the white participants, was arrested in Asheville, North Carolina. His subsequent experience with southern justice only served to emphasize the absurdity of segregation. During his trial, Peck was amazed that there were even Jim Crow Bibles in the courtroom:

> Along the page edges of one Bible had been printed in large letters the word "white." Along the page edges of the other Bible was the word "colored." When a white person swore in he simply raised his right hand while the clerk held the white Bible. When a Negro swore in, he had to raise his right hand while holding the colored Bible in his left hand. The white clerk could not touch the colored Bible.[34]

Fourteen years later, in 1961, Jim Peck would again join in an effort to challenge segregation in interstate travel. By this time, the Supreme Court had expanded its ruling in the *Morgan* case to include desegregation of terminal facilities.[35] Once again, CORE took the lead in organizing a group of freedom riders to test compliance, but this freedom ride would differ from the earlier one in two important ways. First of all, the later riders would travel all the way into the Deep South; their predecessors had never ventured out of the Upper South. Second, the 1961 freedom rides would follow in the wake of both a Supreme Court decision outlawing school segregation, and massive demonstrations to desegregate local facilities. This meant that many white southerners had already grown quite angry and resentful about attacks on their way of life even before the freedom riders appeared on the scene. Southern anger had been further inflamed by the very real prospect that the rides would attract national media attention. Thus, when CORE announced plans to sponsor a freedom ride in the spring of 1961, many, including the participants, believed that violence was inevitable.

James Farmer, the head of CORE, wrote to the president, the vice president, the attorney general, the Justice Department, the Interstate Commerce Commission, the FBI, and Greyhound and Trailways. He informed all of them about CORE's plans to test southern compliance with the Supreme Court's desegregation rulings. Farmer remembers, "We were hoping that, even though we'd received no letters, the FBI was going to protect us. . . . [However,] that was a vain hope. We learned later that the FBI had gotten our itinerary, since we'd sent everything to them, all the letters, and they had passed on our itinerary to local police whom they knew to be active in the KKK."[36]

The lack of assurances from anyone in the federal government did not dissuade Farmer and CORE. In March 1961, CORE issued a call for volunteers. In response, on 1 May, an interracial group of thirteen volunteers assembled in Washington, D.C. Ruby did not meet the others in Washington; she would join them much later when they reached the Deep South and SNCC became involved. After a short briefing session on nonviolence, they split into two contingents, one of which boarded a Greyhound bus; the other, a Trailways. Both were scheduled to travel from Washington, D.C. all the way through the Deep South to New Orleans. All of the participants were acutely aware of the danger they faced. As Farmer puts it, "I felt that these people were ready for anything, including death. And they knew that death was a possibility."[37] The first part of the ride, through the Upper South, proceeded without incident. But trouble started when they reached Rock Hill, South Carolina, the place where Ruby Doris and her three SNCC colleagues had just served a thirty-day jail sentence. As two of the riders headed for the white waiting room in the terminal, they were attacked by a gathering of local white people.[38] Things quieted down after this, and the riders passed through the rest of South Carolina and entered the state of Georgia.

After spending the night in Atlanta, the riders headed into Alabama on 14 May. As the buses went further into Alabama territory, the tension mounted. Just outside of Anniston, Alabama, a white mob slashed the Greyhound bus's tires and set it on fire with the freedom riders still on board. The mob "surrounded [the bus] and held its doors shut. They broke one of the windows and hurled a firebomb into the vehicle. It filled with smoke and burst into flames." Amid the panic and horror, one of the freedom riders, Albert Bigelow, took charge, opened the emergency door, and supervised the evacuation of the passengers. Once everyone was out, a local policeman dispersed the crowd. The bus was completely consumed by the fire. As a result of their ordeal, a number of the freedom riders had to be treated for severe smoke inhalation.[39]

The Trailways bus, which was an hour behind the ill-fated Greyhound, encountered its own share of problems. When it arrived in Anniston eight local white men boarded the bus and beat some of the freedom riders. The bus then proceeded to Birmingham, where a mob attacked a number of the riders as they left the bus. The attack left Jim Peck unconscious and lying in a pool of blood. Still another rider, Charles Person, was beaten so badly that his whole face was swollen, and he had a nasty gash in the back of his head. The next afternoon, all the freedom riders assembled in the Birmingham bus station while a hostile white mob gathered outside. The riders tried in vain to locate a driver who would take them on to Montgomery. When they realized that this was not possible, they opted to fly to New Orleans and assemble there. This was the end of the first freedom ride.[40]

At this point, Ruby Doris and SNCC became involved. It all started when Diane Nash contacted James Farmer after the freedom ride was interrupted. She told Farmer, "Your group of freedom riders are so badly chewed up that they cannot go on now." Diane then asked whether Farmer would object if Nashville members of SNCC continued the ride. Farmer reminded her that the riders would be facing serious violence, but Diane was undaunted. She felt that they could not afford to let violence stop them. "If we do," she insisted, "the movement is dead."[41] Thus armed with fresh SNCC recruits, the rides continued.

Diane Nash's recruits left Nashville in the early morning hours of 17 May aboard a bus bound for Birmingham. The trip was uneventful until the riders reached the outskirts of Birmingham. There, local police intercepted their bus and apprehended them. Police insisted that they were only placing the riders in protective custody. The group spent one very scary night in jail. Nobody slept much that night. They talked quietly into the wee hours of the morning. It was somehow comforting to talk about their goals, their dreams, their plans for the future. It made them feel almost normal again.

Then the long night was over. The knot of fear returned to their stomachs when they heard the footsteps of their captors and the jingle of keys in the corridor. Suddenly, the cell door swung open and Birmingham's notorious Commissioner of Public Safety, Eugene "Bull" Connor, materialized in the dim light outside their cell. Before the riders even had a chance to react, Connor and his officers roughly pulled them out of the cell and pushed them into waiting police cars, which took off at top speed with a screech of their tires. They drove straight to the state line. As soon as they crossed over into Tennessee, Connor put the students out on the side of the road, next to the railroad tracks.[42]

It was a beautiful spring day, but the freedom riders scarcely noticed the puffy white clouds in the deep blue sky or the sweet smell of the wildflowers dotting the roadside. Instead, they were already planning their next move. The commissioner's action only strengthened their resolve. The group walked to a nearby black home. From there, they were able to summon Nashville supporters, who immediately sent a car to pick them up and take them back to Birmingham. Within hours, the riders were in the Birmingham bus terminal once again attempting to continue their journey to Montgomery.[43]

While the Nashville group was trying to push past Birmingham, Ruby Doris Smith was busy raising the money for her transportation so that she could join them. By the time the Nashville recruits reached Birmingham for the second time, Ruby had enough money. She flew from Atlanta to Birmingham and went straight to the bus station. This is her description of the scene that met her when she arrived:

> I was alone. . . . When I got to Birmingham I went to the bus terminal and joined the seventeen from Nashville. We waited all night trying to get a bus to Montgomery. Every time we got on a bus the driver said no, he wouldn't risk his life. The terminal kept crowding up with passengers who were stranded because the buses wouldn't go on. The Justice Department then promised Diane that the driver of the 4:00 a.m. bus would go on to Montogomery. But when he arrived he came off the bus and said to us: "I have only one life to give, and I'm not going to give it to the NAACP or CORE!"[44]

Throughout the night, tension ran high in the Birmingham terminal. Ruby and the others were acutely aware of the violence that had plagued the CORE-sponsored ride that had preceded their effort. They were also aware that they could not expect any aid or protection from the federal government. In fact, Ruby had been in the SNCC office when Diane Nash had contacted Washington about the expected violence:

> I remember Diane Nash called the Department of Justice from Nashville, and Lonnie King—you know he was head of the Atlanta student movement—also called the Department. Both of them asked the federal government to give protection to the Freedom Riders on the rest of their journey. And in both cases the Justice Department said no, they couldn't protect anyone, but if something happened, they would investigate. You know how they do.[45]

The Justice Department's willingness to investigate was small consolation to the freedom riders in Birmingham trying to find a bus that would take them on to Montgomery. While the riders waited, they occupied themselves by singing freedom songs. As Ruby and the others clapped and sang, the words provided comfort and solace. Their voices swelled and reinforced each other. "Stand up and rejoice, a great day is here. We're fighting Jim Crow and the vict'ry is near," they sang. Then they followed with the chorus, "Hallelujah, I'm a traveling. Hallelujah, ain't it fine? Hallelujah, I'm a traveling down freedom's main line." They sang verse after verse, sometimes improvising on the spot. "I'm paying my fare on the Greyhound bus line. I'm riding the front seat to Montgomery this time."[46]

The few white passengers who remained in the bus station periodically cast puzzled, and sometimes hostile glances at these disruptive black students who sang into the early hours of the morning. Finally, the driver who had unequivocally insisted that he would not give his life for the NAACP or CORE returned to collect the group's tickets in preparation for the trip. The freedom riders boarded the bus, and it departed for Montgomery. By this time, they were exhausted after their long vigil in the bus station. The first part of the journey was uneventful, and many of them slept a little, but as they approached Montgomery, the atmosphere changed. The drowsy riders were jolted back to full awareness when, suddenly, policemen and highway patrol officers seemed to appear out of nowhere. Later the riders discovered that state authorities had provided this show of force because of federal pressure.[47]

A few miles further, just inside the Montgomery city limits, the helicopters and police cars disappeared as suddenly as they had appeared. An eerie quiet enveloped the bus. Nobody talked. The only sound was the rush of the wind past their windows and the hum of the tires on the pavement as the bus moved inexorably toward an uncertain fate. At the terminal a mob numbering approximately three hundred people was waiting for the unescorted bus. The riders were horrified to see all those hostile white faces, and to hear the racial epithets and death threats. The moment seemed frozen in time as the bus slowly pulled into its parking space in front of the terminal. The riders were close enough to the mob now to distinguish the features on the faces of individuals in the crowd. They even noticed inconsequential details like hair color and clothing styles. Many of the young men in the crowd wore short sleeved white T-shirts, and sported crew cuts. The women's hair color ranged from black to light blond, and some wore it teased and piled high on their heads in very elaborate styles. Smoke drifted lazily above their heads as a majority of the mob puffed nervously on cigarettes. But all of these individuals had one thing in common: their mouths were twisted into hideous and hateful snarls, and their eyes radiated pure and unadulterated hatred. In the face of this frightening spectacle, the riders' commitment never wavered. They were filled with a grim determination as they marched down the steps of the bus.

The first freedom rider to leave the bus was Jim Zwerg, a young northern white man. He was attacked immediately. Some of the white women in the mob shouted, "Kill the nigger-loving son of a bitch." As other freedom riders got off the bus behind Zwerg, the mob quickly turned its attention to them. In Ruby's words:

> The mob turned from Zwerg to us. Someone yelled: "They're about to get away!" Then they started beating everyone. I saw John Lewis beaten, blood coming out of his mouth. People were running from all over. Every one of the fellows was hit. Some of them tried to take refuge in the post office, but they were turned out. . . . We saw some of the fellows on the ground, John Lewis lying there, blood streaming from his head.[48]

By the time the police arrived, the mob had grown much larger and more unruly. The officers were forced to use tear gas to disperse them. Eventually, the wounded freedom riders made their way to Montgomery's black community, where they were housed for the night. The next day, Sunday, 21 May, Ruby and the others attended a mass meeting at Reverend Ralph Abernathy's First Baptist Church. While the meeting was going on inside the church, a white mob began to form outside. Local police again used tear gas, but things were so chaotic and dangerous that everyone had to remain in the church until four o'clock the next morning. "The tear gas was so bad," Ruby would later recount, "We had to close the windows. We could hear the mob in the street."[49] Despite this harrowing ordeal, the freedom riders were ready to continue their bus ride through Mississippi and on to New Orleans.

Alabama had been tough, but everyone expected Mississippi to be tougher. James Farmer sums it up: "If Alabama had been purgatory, Mississippi would be hell." Early the next morning, after a brief prayer service, the freedom riders boarded buses bound for Jackson, Mississippi. At the Mississippi state line, many began to feel a sense of impending doom. The riders' commitment did not wane, but their anxiety level certainly increased. Farmer noticed the change: "Some of the kids were writing something. Diaries? No. We don't write; we talk. I looked, and it was names and addresses of next of kin. The young men stuffed those grim messages in their pockets; the women in their bras."[50] Dave Dennis, CORE's field director for Mississippi, was also aware of the fatalistic atmosphere that permeated this part of the ride:

> When the group left Montgomery, the first bus load to go into Jackson, Mississippi, everyone on that bus was prepared to die. . . . One girl in particular just started pulling hands full of hair out. She just started screaming. Nothing happened, and there was

the cold shock. I mean, people just were doing strange things. One guy was beating his head up against the wall. We didn't. . . . It was just that right then and there everyone wanted to die. They had been willing to give up their lives.[51]

Each of the freedom riders coped with the rising tension in different ways. Amid all the anxiety, Ruby Doris had, according to John Lewis, "this sense of wanting to know about the different participants. How were people doing, uh, were you all right or not. She had this sense of caring about the different individuals. . . . She wanted everybody to be all right."[52] With each mile, their apprehension grew. By the time the buses reached the outskirts of Jackson, the riders had steeled themselves for the worst.

But the tension was broken, at least for a while, when an incident of mistaken identity occurred. As Jim Farmer laughingly recounts,

> We drove up to the Greyhound bus terminal. A crowd of people [was] there. I said, "Well, this is it. This is where we get it." The door opened and I led the group off the bus. It turned out that the crowd of people were not hoodlums. They were plainclothesmen and reporters. They were the crowd.[53]

These policemen and reporters were so sure that the freedom riders would try to use the facilities in the white waiting room that "they parted and made a path for [Farmer] leading right to the white waiting room, and [Farmer] thought maybe [he] could have pled entrapment when they got to court, because [they] couldn't go anyplace else."[54]

After they passed the reporters, and tried to use the white facilities, the freedom riders were quickly arrested. Ruby was not on the bus with Farmer; she was on the one right behind it. As this second wave of riders entered the Jackson terminal they too were arrested. The Jackson police hoped that their quick action would put a stop to the freedom rides, but they were sadly mistaken. After the arrest of these first freedom riders, other volunteers rushed in to take their places, and by the end of the summer, over three hundred freedom riders had been arrested by Mississippi authorities.[55] Many of these volunteers did not serve a full sentence. Rather, they posted bail at the last moment that they could without forfeiting their right to appeal. As the rides continued, Ruby and the others from the first group began serving two-month jail terms. Regardless of any fear and anxiety she may have felt, Ruby tried hard to reassure her family back in Atlanta. In a letter to her mother from Jackson's Hinds County Jail, Ruby insisted: "I'm doing fine.

There are seven of us in the cell now, although 3 are sleeping on mattresses on the floor (smile). We don't mind it."[56] The number of prisoners in Ruby's cell soon grew from seven to thirteen, and then to seventeen. Before Ruby and the other freedom riders were finally transferred to another facility, exasperated prison officials would stuff twenty-three women into the four-bunk cell with Ruby. Ruby still did not complain:

> It was a nice set-up. When the windows were open we could talk to the fellows. We sang. We wrote Freedom Songs. A Negro minister from Chicago sang: "Woke Up This Morning With My Mind Set On Freedom" so everyone began singing it. It started there. . . . Other songs were composed—"I Know We'll Meet Again" was written by a fellow I know from Nashville and Rock Hill. We would do ballet lessons in the morning to keep ourselves fit. There were different people from different areas. Somebody was giving Spanish lessons.[57]

The concern for others that John Lewis had noticed in Ruby during the freedom ride continued even after she was incarcerated. At one point, she asked her mother to bake some cookies for fellow freedom rider William Mitchell. Ruby felt worried about him. But she also showed consideration for her mother: "Now I know you're busy and don't have time to be waiting on me, but if you possibly could find time, please send him some [cookies]." In addition to the cookies, Ruby asked her mother to send her new plaid skirt and her Bible.[58]

While the Hinds County Jail was crowded, at least the treatment Ruby Doris and the others received was relatively humane. Things would soon take a dramatic turn for the worse, however. After the riders had spent only two weeks in the Hinds County Jail, state officials decided to transfer them to Parchman Penitentiary, which had a well-deserved reputation for being tough—especially on black inmates. Ruby never forgot that ride through the dark Mississippi countryside: "We were awakened at 4:00 a.m. to find out that we were all going to Parchman State Penitentiary. . . . It was a long ride in the night."[59] The atmosphere inside the big trucks transporting the students was hot and stifling, and many of the young protesters found it hard to breathe. This only increased the anxiety they felt. They realized their vulnerability; it would be easy for their racist prison guards to execute them here in rural Mississippi and bury their bodies where nobody would ever find them. This was Mississippi, after all. Cordell Reagon, one of the freedom riders on that nightmarish ride, remembers: "This was Jackson, Mississippi, in 1961. Well—I knew I was going to die. All I saw was these people taking us out in a field and shooting us. I prayed and gave up my life in my mind. . . . We all knew that we were going to get killed. They could kill every black man and black woman among us and it wouldn't even make the papers."[60]

When they arrived at Parchman, the freedom riders were forced to undress completely, and they were subjected to thorough body searches. They were not allowed to keep any of their clothing, not even their shoes. Ruby and the other women were issued skirts with stripes. Then the guards locked up the women in the maximum security section of the penitentiary. Despite all her previous prison experience, Ruby Doris was dismayed. Her cell was filthy and full of bugs.[61] All of the riders were profoundly affected by the treatment and conditions they faced at Parchman. One reported: "I lost my fear. It happened to all of us in that jail! We realized we could say to them, 'Kill me—I'm going to love you anyhow. But I am not going to cooperate with you.' We all realized that we were much more powerful than them. That's when we all became noncooperative."[62] The guards insisted that the prisoners make as little noise as possible, but some of the women defiantly talked and sang anyway. When they continued to ignore the guards' orders that they be quiet, their mattresses, towels, sheets, and toothbrushes were all confiscated. The men were forced to perform hard manual labor outside the prison under the watchful eyes of prison guards brandishing guns and nightsticks. Brutal beatings were common for even the smallest infractions.

During the next few weeks the inmate population kept growing due to continued arrests of freedom riders. Exasperated prison officials transferred Ruby and some of the other women to the prison infirmary in an effort to relieve overcrowding in the cell block. Though these accommodations were more comfortable, Ruby Doris found the view outside the infirmary window distressing: "There were fifty, sixty Negro men in striped uniforms, guarded by a white man on a white horse. It reminded you of slavery."[63] While Ruby was in Prachman, she spent a good deal of her time reflecting on her experiences in the black freedom struggle and on the dimensions of that struggle. Her interaction with the other freedom riders in Parchman changed her. In fact, they all changed each other. As one puts it, "There were [a] lot of little movements going into Parchman, but one big one coming out."[64]

When Ruby finally completed her sentence, a student leadership seminar happened to be starting in Nashville, Tennessee. It was a perfect setting for Ruby to continue to explore and discuss the dimensions of the African-American freedom struggle. Timothy Jenkins of the National Student Association, who originally conceived of the seminar idea, aimed "to pull the best people out of the movement . . . and give them a solid academic approach to understanding the movement." The central theme of the three-week seminar, which began on 30 July was "Understanding the Nature of Social Change." Among the scholars and consultants who participated were John Doar of the Justice Department, E. Franklin Frazier, and C. Eric Lincoln.[65] Student conferees included Ruby Doris, Dion Diamond, Chuck McDew, and Stokely Carmichael. During the workshop, participants engaged in long and sophisticated discussions on a variety of important matters, including nonviolence. They were no longer the idealistic, inexperienced college students they had been at the beginning of the lunch counter sit-ins. They were now experienced freedom fighters whose idealism had been tempered by experience.

During the discussions on nonviolence, Ruby Doris expressed her feelings in no uncertain terms. Stokely Carmichael recalls how vigorously she defended her position. According to Carmichael, Ruby argued:

> We have to understand this thing seriously; that we represent our community sure enough, but we only represent a small segment of our community when we come to talk about nonviolence, you know. The over-whelming majority of our people are not believing in nonviolence and we know that. So if we are going to make this a mass movement like we say, we have to understand that.[66]

Ruby Doris went on to insist that those who were committed to the movement had a responsibility to make allowances for the views of local people; they did not have the right to tell people how to struggle. At one point, she asked the key question "Who's to say that violence will not help in the struggle?"[67] Ruby also raised the related issue of self-defense. One of her coworkers, Constancia Romilly, remembers, "[Ruby] was also a very firm believer in self-defense; I know she was." Above all, Ruby Doris was realistic. She recognized that black people in the South carried guns. She had no intention of attempting to change their minds. Rather, according to Romilly, "her thing was, how could [civil rights workers] protect [themselves], but without bringing the wrath of the sheriff down on [them]."[68]

Another issue that Ruby raised at the conference involved the movement's targets. She was convinced that there were dangerous and formidable enemies within the black community that had escaped the movement's notice. As a fellow conferee, Chuck McDew, puts it: "That's one of the things I remember most about her. Ruby Doris was the one who started talking about the need to deal with black institutions. Well, she was very specific . . . and it had to do with . . . fraternities and sororities." Ruby was particularly concerned about the divisive effect of class and color issues on the movement. Black membership in Greek-letter organizations exacerbated those divisions, she reasoned, because influential members of these organizations effectively barred outsiders from privileged positions in the black community. In explaining this assessment, Ruby used the example of admission to medical school and law school. She pointed out that a preponderance of the graduates from the two institutions that produced the majority of black doctors and lawyers (Howard University and Meharry Medical College) were light-skinned men with fraternity connections. This occurred, she argued, because their fraternity brothers held powerful positions on admissions committees. McDew was amazed: "To me it was such a . . . brilliant sort of analysis—and simple at the same time."[69]

Through all the debates over strategies, philosophy, and tactics, a fundamental disagreement surfaced, one that concerned the critical issue of the group's goals. On the one hand, supporters of direct action thought that the organization should continue to attack the de jure segregation that severely circumscribed black lives all over the South. Proponents of voter registration, on the other hand, argued that real change would come only when significant numbers of disfranchised black southerners became registered voters. At the beginning of the Nashville seminar, Ruby Doris favored direct action, but she switched sides when she realized voter registration's potential for organizing and empowering local people.[70]

The voter registration/direct action disagreement soon threatened to tear the organization apart. Debate became especially heated at the SNCC meeting on 11 August 1961, at the Highlander Folk School in east Tennessee. As the discussion began, the emotions of the seasoned young freedom fighters quickly rose to the surface. Some of them, like Ruby, had just finished serving prison terms for participation in the freedom rides. Others were fresh from battles against intransigent city authorities in various communities throughout the South. Their nerves were rubbed raw, and their frustration level was at the breaking point. Hence, emotion quickly replaced reason, and the discussion reached an impasse. At the point when the organization appeared to be on the verge of splitting, Ella Baker suggested a compromise: SNCC should have two wings—a voter registration wing, and a direct action wing.[71] Once the compromise suggestion effectively neutralized much of the dissension, the organization decided to inaugurate its new policy by sending workers to support a voter registration drive in McComb, Mississippi. Because many of SNCC's most experienced workers could be found in the ranks of the freedom riders, the Highlander meeting voted to send some of these veterans to McComb.

The McComb Project had begun in July 1961. At that time, C. C. Bryant, head of the local NAACP chapter, convinced New York activist Bob Moses to come and organize a voter registration project. Once Moses arrived in McComb, he officially joined the SNCC staff and began recruiting personnel to come into the area. The group opened a voter registration school to prepare McComb's prospective black voters for Mississippi's tough literacy test. Along with their voter registration efforts, some SNCC personnel worked with local residents to initiate direct action protests against segregated facilities.[72] SNCC workers also started an alternative school for young McComb residents, which they christened Nonviolent High.

Ruby Doris was one of those asked to go to McComb. Even though she had just finished serving her sentence at Parchman, she agreed to return to Mississippi, but she stayed only a few weeks. While there, Ruby went door to door in the scorching Mississippi sun canvassing for voter registration. It was hot, tedious, and frustrating work. As Ruby talked to one McComb resident after another, she sensed their fear and felt their resignation. She realized that registering to vote could be dangerous for these people. She was asking them to put their livelihoods and even their lives on the line. Nevertheless, she knew that these people would have to have political power in order for change to occur. Trudging from house to house, Ruby remembered the boldness of the racist mobs that had attacked her and the other freedom riders. Those white racists had known that many in state and local government condoned and even applauded their attacks. Ruby also remembered the disgusting conditions she had faced in Parchman Penitentiary, and she knew that Mississippi officials had condoned and applauded that treatment too. These memories helped put the energy back in Ruby's stride as she approached the next house. She had to convince these black Mississippians to register and vote. They had to have power if they were ever going to banish those hostile white mobs from their state.

Ruby also taught at Nonviolent High.[73] Everywhere she went, her reputation preceded her. By this time, Ruby had become known as a savvy veteran of the civil rights struggle who was incredibly brave, as well as politically sophisticated. Regardless of her reputation, however, Ruby still looked and dressed very much like a college coed. C. C. Bryant, who met Ruby when she first arrived in McComb, remembers her as a "clean-cut youngster."[74]

By the time she returned home in the fall of 1961, Atlanta students had achieved a major victory. After months of negotiations, downtown merchants had finally agreed to desegregate their lunch counters by 17 September 1961.[75] In the meantime, Ruby Doris decided she wanted to re-enroll in college. She had dropped out during the second semester of her junior year when she decided to go to Rock Hill in the spring of 1961. Before she could resume her studies, Spelman College required her to reapply for admission. The personal statement Ruby submitted with her application was revealing:

> At the beginning of the second semester of the 1960–61 school year, I was torn between my desire to work wholeheartedly with the "student" movement and my desire to complete my formal education. I knew, on the basis of my academic record for the first semester, that I had to make a choice if I was going to really be successful in any one area. In an effort to think the situation over, I delayed registration for the second semester for a few days.[76]

Ruby went on to describe her movement experiences in modest terms as "eventful and somewhat exciting." She assured the admissions committee that her movement commitment would not interfere with her studies: "I feel at this point, the only really wise decision is to do everything within my power to complete my formal education at Spelman College. I intend, if I am admitted, to work as hard to achieve academically as I have worked in the past to achieve socially." Along with her application, Ruby submitted a number of recommendations—including one from Dr. Martin Luther King, Jr. Apparently, the admissions committee was favorably impressed because they permitted her to enroll in classes for the fall semester of 1961. Ruby Doris kept her promise to work hard, and she was rewarded by financial aid from SNCC, the National Council of Negro Women, and the American Baptist Home Mission Society.[77]

As Ruby readjusted to college life, she resumed demonstrating with the Atlanta Committee on Appeal for Human Rights. Even though downtown lunch counters were integrated by this time, many symbols of segregation remained. One of the most visible of those symbols was Grady Hospital, a public facility that admitted both black and white patients but had segregated entrances and segregated areas within the hospital. Throughout late 1961 and into early 1962, Ruby Doris, along with other Atlanta students, staged a series of protests at the hospital. Julian Bond recalls one demonstration when black students went in the hospital's white entrance. As soon as they stepped inside, the looks of surprise on the faces of white patrons quickly gave way to icy stares. A startled white receptionist immediately told them they could not use that entrance. "And besides," she added in a hostile voice dripping with sarcasm, "you're not sick anyway." The woman's challenge stopped the students in their tracks like a cold slap in the face. As they milled around in confusion, Ruby Doris separated herself from the group and boldly walked up to the receptionist's desk. She looked the woman in the eye, bent over, and vomited on the desk. Then she straightened up and demanded to know, "Is that sick enough for you?"[78] The receptionist's hostility quickly turned to speechless confusion. As the Grady protests continued, authorities began to make arrests. In February 1962, Ruby was among those arrested, but she did not serve time.[79]

Meanwhile, Ruby Doris continued her work with the Student Nonviolent Coordinating Committee. By this time, SNCC had begun to shift part of its focus from the McComb campaign to a fledgling movement in Albany, Georgia. The local black community there, assisted by some SNCC members, had begun direct action protests against selected segregated targets in the fall of 1961. Ruby Doris participated. For example, she was part of a SNCC group that traveled by train from Atlanta to Albany to test compliance with the Supreme Court's desegregation ruling that covered terminal facilities.[80] A few months later, during the summer of 1962, an integrated group of protesters was convicted of loitering at the Albany Holiday Inn. The group, which included Penelope Patch, Ruby Doris Smith, John Zellner, Reverend Samuel Wells, and Reverend Robert Kinlock, was sentenced to pay a two-hundred-dollar fine or serve sixty days in jail. They decided to appeal.[81] Their appeal was unsuccessful.

This period saw a profound change in SNCC's administrative structure that resulted in the addition of James Forman to the staff as the organization's first executive secretary. Forman had joined the group in August 1961. Previously, he had been active in local movements for racial justice in Fayette County in west Tennessee and in Monroe, North Carolina. By the fall of 1961, Forman was back home in Chicago, just beginning the school year as a teacher in a local elementary school. Out of the blue, he received a phone call from Paul Brooks, a freedom rider whom Forman had met some months before. Diane Nash had asked Brooks to persuade Forman to become part of SNCC's direct action wing because she thought his skills as a veteran organizer would be invaluable. Forman was more than a little reluctant. He told Brooks, "Man just wait a minute now. This requires a slight degree of thought. You don't just say am I willing to leave my job."[82] After much soul-searching, Forman decided to join the young student activists. He left Chicago and traveled to Atlanta where he found an organization that seemed to be in chaos.

When he arrived at the SNCC office, there was nobody around. The office was locked. After he had waited a long while, Forman finally forced the lock open. The sight that greeted him was more than a little disconcerting.

"There it was—the national offices of the Student Nonviolent Coordinating Committee. . . . Greasy walls. A faint light from a dusty, plastic skylight overhead. The mustiness, the smell, the mail scattered all over the floor."[83] Two days later, when SNCC workers began coming back from McComb, some of them gradually began to drift into the office. Forman's introduction to his new colleagues was quite discouraging; he realized that the disorganization in the office mirrored a lack of organization in the group. Forman's worst fears were confirmed at his first staff meeting, which happened to be the exhausting and emotional Highlander meeting on the direct action—voter registration split. A horrified Forman watched the organization argue its way to the brink of disintegration. A short time later, he was one of those who breathed a sigh of relief when the crisis was past. It was in that amiable postcrisis atmosphere that SNCC decided to elect a direct action coordinator, a voter registration coordinator, and an executive secretary to stay in the office. Many wanted Ella Baker to serve as executive secretary, but she declined. There were others who urged Forman to consider the job. Although this suggestion surprised Forman, who had never even considered administration, he wanted to do whatever he could to help the young organization. But he had reservations: "I was in a quandary, for I didn't want to work as an administrator. I knew that I had some administrative qualities, more perhaps than any of those assembled, but I felt that my best skills lay in other areas— agitating, field organizing, and writing."[84]

Despite his reservations, Forman accepted the position. He soon realized, though, how hard it would be to define the limis of this brand new administrative post in an atmosphere that was hostile to traditional notions of administration. Many in the group seemed to display "a lack of concern with internal organization" and "a generalized disdain for leadership: All of us sitting in the room were leaders, people said."[85] But Forman was undaunted, he was determined to bring order to the rapidly growing organization. Because of the sheer volume of the office work confronting him during the early days of his administration, Jim Forman welcomed Ruby Doris's assistance when she began to spend many of her afternoons after school in the SNCC office, assisting wherever she could.

Some of Ruby's colleagues in the Atlanta Committee on Appeal for Human Rights also worked with SNCC during this period. Other Atlanta committee members objected to sharing their personnel. They expressed those objections in no uncertain terms when James Forman tried to recruit the committee's Julian Bond to serve as SNCC's press secretary. Forman also remembers that Ruby thought the Atlanta committee was obliged to help SNCC any way it could. She "spoke up about the need to help the Student

Nonviolent Coordinating Committee."[86] It seemed that Ruby's broad movement exposure afforded her a vision that transcended local interests.

In this chaotic but exciting atmosphere, Ruby Doris began to assume increasing responsibility. Whereas most of the staff members had no desire for office work because they were much more interested in the glamorous and dangerous work out in the field, Ruby's dedication prompted her to step into this administrative void. She recognized that the organization would cease to function without proper administrative guidance. As she increasingly performed office duties, colleagues became aware of Ruby's growing power. Reginald Robinson recalls that by early 1962, "you got your money from Ruby; you got your orders from Ruby."[87]

By this time, SNCC's young activists had forged a powerful bond between them. Referring to one of the major SNCC conferences held during this time, Jim Forman describes that connection: "The meeting was permeated by an intense comradeship, born out of sacrifice and suffering and a commitment to the future, and out of the knowledge that we were indeed challenging the political structure of the country, and out of a feeling that our basic strength rested in the energy, love, and warmth of the group. The band of sisters and brothers in a circle of trust, felt complete at last."[88]

The existence of this bond did not eliminate problems in the office, however. Many in the group continued to resist any efforts to strengthen the administration. But despite this sentiment, Jim Forman and Ruby Doris Smith worked tirelessly throughout 1962 to create a more structured administration. The longer they worked together, the more Forman recognized the compatibility between his and Ruby's administrative views. He also recognized her growing influence, so Forman was quite pleased in the spring of 1963 when Ruby Doris formally joined the SNCC staff and became his administrative assistant: "I felt . . . very secure with her in that particular function handling the day-to-day administration of the organization, which, you know, permitted me more time to do other things."[89]

Even with a permanent and dedicated administration in place, however, some of the group's organizational problems continued. Chairman John Lewis discussed them during a 1963 meeting:

> We have had an open policy—"whosoever will come" philosophy—and a high degree of autonomy. As a result people have been abusing it, leaving projects and going to New York or other projects at will. . . . Staff discipline at the moment is at a low ebb. We have begun to get a decent subsistence, at least a regular one;

and we have lost some of our concept of sacrifice and identification.[90]

As Forman's administrative assistant, Ruby Doris was obliged to deal with
these difficulties. It took all of her considerable talents, along with a variety
of administrative techniques, to impose some order on such a chaotic, independent organization.

Recollections of Ruby's administrative style are quite varied. That suggests
that her style was multifaceted, flexible, and not easily characterized. A flexible and creative approach was necessary because of the broad assortment of
situations, problems, and individuals that regularly confronted Ruby Doris.
At times, she could be an uncompromising taskmaster. She was especially
tough when it appeared that staff people were trying to take unfair advantage
of the organization's resources. Stanley Wise, who would eventually succeed
Ruby Doris as executive secretary, admired her attitude:

> She absolutely did not tolerate any nonsense. I remember some
> people came in there [the Atlanta Central Office] once from Mis-
> sissippi. They had driven their car over there, and they said they
> needed new tires. And she pulled out [a card] from her little file.
> She said, "Listen, I've given you sixteen tires in the last four
> months. . . . I've sent you four batteries; you had two motors in
> the car. You're not getting another thing. Now take that car out
> of here and go on back to Mississippi." That's what she told
> them.[91]

Wise was amazed at the extent of Ruby's knowledge about the history of this
one car, given the size of the SNCC fleet.

SNCC freedom singer Matthew Jones, Jr., recalls that his brother, another
member of the freedom singers, was also a target of Ruby's wrath. When the
group performed on the West Coast, Ruby arranged round trip transportation
for them by automobile because she determined it to be the most economi-
cal. The group had an uneventful trip out to the West Coast, and gave a
successful concert, but when they assembled for the return trip, Jones's
brother arrived too late. The cars had already left. He immediately called
Ruby to explain that he was stranded in Los Angeles, but she refused to send
him the money for a plane, train, or bus ticket. Since Jones should have been
responsible enough to meet the prearranged transportation at the appointed
time, she reasoned, the organization should not have to pay for his mistake.
Ruby's parting advice to Jones as she hung up the phone? "Well, walk

back."[92] Ruby could also be uncompromising about procedure. "When she became in charge of the payroll," notes Reginald Robinson, "and you had reports to do—you had expense accounts to turn [in]. Well, if you didn't do what you were supposed to do, Big Mama [Ruby] would cut your money." Charles Jones sums up Ruby Doris's no-nonsense approach: "You didn't run any games on her."[93] Jack Minnis, a member of SNCC's research staff, offers an even more blunt appraisal: "She had a 100-percent-effective shit detector."[94]

All of Ruby Doris's SNCC colleagues agree that her primary administrative goal was the effective functioning of the Student Nonviolent Coordinating Committee. She had very definite ideas about how SNCC should be administered, and she never failed to stand up for her beliefs, whether others agreed with her or not. As SNCC colleague Worth Long put it, "She's set in her ways, and she's mostly right. . . . She would take a principle[d] stand. . . . She'd argue, and she'd huff and puff too." During the free wheeling discussions in SNCC about organizational policy, Long remembers Ruby as "a formidable opponent. I wouldn't want to play poker with her."[95] Coworker Curtis Hayes was struck by Ruby's intensity: "I guarantee if you ever see a picture of Ruby in a meeting, . . . she'll be on the end of the chair. You'll never see her sitting back like this. . . . Whoever's talking, she'll be leaning into them. And her eyes will be right into them. . . . And when you get to that point she don't agree with? She was all over you."[96]

Most in SNCC agree that although Ruby never backed down from a confrontation, her administrative style was not always confrontational. Rather, she could be quite creative and diplomatic in her efforts to persuade people to support her positions. As Jack Minnis puts it, "Ruby Doris was very good, I thought, at imposing order very surreptitiously. She was capable of getting people to do what she wanted them to do by convincing them that it was what they wanted to do."[97] Ruby's strength, bluntness, and mental acuity were only part of her office demeanor. She also displayed softness and sensitivity when the occasion demanded it. Worth Long recalls an illustrative incident. "We didn't have no money and no hopes of no money, [and] we need[ed] to pay the staff. People were in bad shape. And we took the thing personally, you know. . . . And that moved her to tears. She felt like it was her responsibility almost."[98]

Ruby's attempts to formulate and refine her administrative technique were complicated by the reality of her gender. Even though many of the young SNCC activists saw themselves as equals regardless of gender, most still had definite expectations regarding male ways of acting and female reactions. Men within the organization would often assume a macho persona. There were variations of this persona, but essentially men flirted, flattered, and swaggered. In return, they expected women to be compliant and agreeable.[99] Charles Jones labels this kind of male behavior "sexual power games." He bluntly declares, "There were certain times when sex—the use of it or the potential use of it—became a means to manipulate people to get what we needed." Apparently, then, macho behavior was sometimes calculated and deliberate. At other times, however, male-female encounters were characterized simply by lighthearted banter and good-natured flattery. Some of Ruby's SNCC colleagues remember that attempts to use flattery to persuade Ruby were usually ineffective; flattery sometimes annoyed her to the point where "she would read you out in a meeting."[100] Michael Simmons unequivocally agrees: "You could not speculate on sexism with Ruby in order to get what you wanted. . . . You could not play them [sic] kind of games with Ruby."[101]

While Ruby Davis refused to be manipulated by the flattery of others, she was not above using these tactics herself. Dion Diamond is sure that Ruby's security about her femininity, combined with her keen understanding of human nature, sometimes convinced her to attempt to charm her adversaries: "Ruby used her femininity. . . . she [realized that she] . . . could manipulate [male] chauvinism."[102] It seemed, then, that Ruby did not mind engaging in a little lighthearted bantering and mild flirtation of her own. Nevertheless, all agreed that Ruby drew a line: she did not simper; she was not coquettish or coy.

Even though Ruby was one of the few female administrators in SNCC, most did not consider her ability to exercise power to be the least bit extraordinary. So many of these student activists had grown up in families with strong black women who worked outside the home and exercised authority inside the home, that a black female authority figure in the central office seemed quite normal. In fact, Michael Simmons thought Ruby's administrative position was actually a traditionally female job.[103] Curtis Hayes concurs: "[Ruby] was a normal figure for me."[104]

Regardless of the judgment of others, Ruby Doris was tough, committed, and uncompromising in her devotion to the Student Nonviolent Coordinating Committee. Above all, she continued to be a team player, just as she had been during her Atlanta Student Movement days. As far as Ruby was concerned, SNCC would be able to function efficiently only if individuals placed the greater good of the group before their own personal opinions and ambitions. Consequently, movement colleague Bob Zellner points out, the group could always rely on Ruby Doris to enforce its decisions.[105] In the view of Curtis Hayes:

She wasn't deceitful, . . . and . . . she tried to be evenhanded with stuff. But she was hard on somebody who didn't respect what the plan was whatever SNCC had decided to do. I mean she was hard on enforcing the collective decision. And if somebody walked outside of that, she would cut you off. She would make it hard for you.[106]

Ruby Doris's ability to implement decisions was crucial, declares Worth Long: "The office would not have run except for her; and then the field would not have survived."[107]

Ruby Doris's attepts to balance her movement duties and her college commitments during the 1962–63 school year took a serious toll on her health. By the summer of 1963, health problems forced her to enter the hospital. For some time, Ruby had been plagued by digestive problems, and the jail sentences she served only exacerbated her condition. In addition to her digestive problems, Ruby Doris began to suffer from hemorrhoids by early 1963. It was at that time that her doctor recommended surgery. Ruby was thoroughly exasperated by this turn of events. Not only did she have to suffer with an uncomfortable condition, but she also had to cope with the frustration of having her work interrupted.

Yet during this trying period Ruby still found time to worry about others. She was especially concerned about SNCC's Danville, Virginia, project director, Avon Rollins. Rollins, a close friend of Ruby's, was also experiencing some health problems. While she was in the hospital, Ruby Doris wrote to Avon:

> You know, I really wish that you would find time to go back to New York if the M.D. thinks you should. I know how you must feel about the Danville Project. You couldn't want to be there more than I want to go to Miss. But, Avon I know that the struggle will be around for a long time and we make a terrible mistake if we neglect our bodies (physically) in our rigor to obtain Freedom for our people.[108]

Ruby Doris went on to advise Rollins that he had a responsibility to take care of himself because of "the cause that [he had] dedicated [his] life to." She wrote that she had faced the same realities and had concluded that she must take care of herself so that she could continue the struggle. Ruby Doris's concern about her health also prompted her to be conscious of her weight. She proudly reported to Rollins, "I've lost a few pounds since you last saw me—a part of my physical fitness program."[109] This accomplishment required a great deal of effort from Ruby, since, coworkers recall, "she liked to eat."[110] Ruby acknowledged her weakness for food and even joked about it just before she was taken to surgery: "They'll be coming for me in a couple of hours now. The anxiety is not so bad but they won't let me eat (smile) and that I can't take so easily."[111]

Given the frantic pace of SNCC activities during this period, no time would have been convenient for Ruby to take an extended leave, but this proved to be a particularly inconvenient time. As she was recuperating from surgery, the March on Washington happened. While Ruby fretted in the hospital, her SNCC colleagues were stewing about the direction the march was taking. Most in SNCC believed that the older civil rights groups were trying to compromise their position. SNCC chairman John Lewis had been invited to share the podium with the leaders of the other groups, but when those leaders discovered how critical Lewis's speech was, they insisted that he change it.

In the original text of his speech, Lewis declared: "In good conscience, we cannot support the Administration's civil rights bill, for it is too little, and too late. There's not one thing in the bill that will protect our people from police brutality." Lewis then went further and suggested that a revolution was in order: "All of us must get in the revolution—get in and stay in the street of every city, village and hamlet of this nation, until true freedom comes, until the revolution is complete."[112] The leaders of the Southern Christian Leadership Conference and the National Association for the Advancement of Colored People were aghast at Lewis's call for a revolution. Convinced that they were making progress by working within the system, they thought that Lewis's militant tone could spawn a dangerous backlash. They demanded that he change the speech. Eventually, Lewis and SNCC capitulated, but they were not happy about it. From her hospital room, Ruby Doris expressed her disillusionment: "I sure hope to be up and out by the 28th. Although I'm disgusted with the 'water[ed] down' outcome of the March on Washington, I'd like to be on hand to observe the feat."[113]

The controversy over Lewis's speech further exacerbated tensions between SNCC and the other groups. For some time previous to the March on Washington, disagreements had been brewing between SNCC and the NAACP, and between SNCC and SCLC. One of the major sources of disagreement involved the issue of leadership. From its earliest existence, SNCC had embraced a much more flexible concept of leadership than had any other civil rights group. Most SNCC members felt that everyone had the potential to become a leader. So, when they went into a community to help people organize, SNCC staff members tried to teach local people how to empower themselves and develop their own leadership capabilities. Conversely, the NAACP and SCLC thought of themselves as advocates for the people. They felt that they should provide the leaders for local movements whenever they were called in to help. Because of this profound philosophical difference, collision was inevitable whenever SNCC and the other groups were working in the same area.

The tension between SNCC and the other groups that was evident at the March on Washington in August 1963 would only get worse by early 1964. By that time, serious changes in SNCC would provoke a philosophical re-evaluation by many of the group's members that would push them even further away from the others. Likewise, 1964 would prove to be a turning point for Ruby Doris. During that year, she experienced a series of critical events that would have profound consequences for her as a freedom fighter and as a woman.

→ CHAPTER FIVE ←

Freedom Summer and Sexual Politics

DURING RUBY'S EARLY YEARS WITH THE MOVEMENT, SHE WAS TRANS-formed from a middle-class college coed to a committed professional activist and a savvy and tough administrator. This transformation accompanied her passage into young adulthood, since she was only seventeen years old when she started movement work. During these tumultuous years when SNCC was seeking to define itself, Ruby Doris was exploring and testing the limits of her own womanhood. Like other normal young women her age, she wanted and needed a social life.

Despite her sometimes blunt, sometimes intimidating office persona, Ruby Doris Smith socialized. She went to parties, she enjoyed dancing, she liked playing bid whist, she dated, and she eventually got married. Charles Jones recalls: "Ruby had her men, man, whatever. Ruby wasn't a wallflower." Regi-nald Robinson remembers how Ruby interacted with the men she dated: "If she was your lover, . . . she was devoted to her men too. I mean . . . these guys [the men she dated] idolized her and worshipped her. . . . Ruby had a kind of authoritative kind of way, but she was as soft as cotton. She was as sweet as she could be. But she was as matter of fact as any, anybody else that's got to give orders."[1]

However, the power that Ruby exercised in the Student Nonviolent Coor-dinating Committee had a profound impact on her social relationships. While fellow activists were the most accessible partners available to her, Ruby's office demeanor made it difficult for some men to approach her. Dot-tie Zellner observes, "Inside SNCC here were these men who would take on ten sheriffs, and if they had to take on Ruby they were terrified. . . ."[2] Accord-ing to others in SNCC, Ruby Doris's exceptional personality and position meant that only a certain kind of man would have been able to have a relationship with her. Reginald Robinson is of the opinion that a prospective mate of Ruby's would have needed a personality opposite to hers. Since she was strong, blunt, opinionated, and committed, he argues, she needed a mate who did not feel the need to challenge her: "You couldn't compete with Ruby on that level. I mean it would have been a destructive relationship."[3]

Other strong African-American women in SNCC also wrestled with the problem of balancing their social lives with their movement commitments. Those with leadership responsibilities often felt the need to cultivate a tough, assertive image. Some were convinced that dating a SNCC man could compromise that image and ultimately diminish their effectiveness. As one puts it: "Probably if you looked at all our personal lives, we've probably had a very difficult personal life in terms of relations with men. Many of us made decisions not to go with SNCC men, because in some kind of way we didn't need to be fucked . . . it was very confusing." This woman was talking about much more than sex. According to movement scholar Sara Evans, "The slang usage of 'to be fucked' meant to be abused or taken advantage of." Evans concludes, "Women found it difficult to be tough and vulnerable at the same time."[4]

When Ruby Doris began to date, she too faced this dilemma. To understand her dating relationships, it is necessary to juxtapose Ruby's social experiences against the kind of relationships that existed generally within SNCC. Most in the organization were just at the age where they were testing and trying out their budding sexuality. As SNCC staffer Jean Wheeler Smith acknowledges: "There was a lot of sex in SNCC . . . we were twenty years old . . . what do you expect?"[5] This experimentation and maturation occurred against a backdrop of extreme danger and unswerving commitment. Those circumstances played an important role in shaping the relationships these young freedom fighters had with each other. Charles Jones says that relationships born in that atmosphere were often short lived: "Sex, enjoying each other's affection—both touching and sexual involvement—was a way of reassuring each other that we were going to be okay. . . . It wasn't a question of a long-term commitment. It was a question of a mutual need that members of the movement themselves shared with each other."[6] In the words of Bobbi Yancy, "Relationships may have happened as much out of stress as anything else." Many of those relationships did not last once the couple left SNCC. When the stress of the movement was no longer present, people were unable to "relate to each other in a normal way."[7]

Regardless of the difficulties, Ruby dated SNCC men. She also socialized with a select circle of friends in the organization. Her friends remember that she was outgoing and gregarious. She liked to tell jokes. Ruby and her SNCC friends danced. At times, SNCC personnel had parties at each others' houses, and at other times they went to local nightclubs. Freddie Greene Biddle and Ruby used to frequent a little cafe close to SNCC's Nelson Street office. The women enjoyed relaxing over a beer while they listened to the cafe's jukebox. Even on these occasions, though, SNCC business was never very far from their minds. "Even when you were out socializing, there was always something about SNCC that [came up]."[8]

During the late summer of 1963, Ruby's days of casual dating ended. She had just been released from the hospital after her hemorrhoid surgery and had gone to recuperate at her sister Catherine's house. At that time Catherine was married to Casper Robinson. One day Casper's brother, Clifford, stopped by for a visit. Clifford had no idea they had a houseguest, but when he and Ruby saw each other for the first time, sparks flew. In a lot of respects, Ruby Doris and Clifford seemed to be opposites. She was outgoing; he was reserved. She was committed to the movement; he was not involved. Yet the chemistry between them was so irresistible that by the end of 1963 they were married in a civil ceremony before a justice of the peace. It happened very quickly, and Ruby and Clifford did not tell any of their friends or family about their marriage plans.[9]

Ruby's SNCC colleagues saw so little of Clifford while the couple dated that they did not realize how serious the relationship was. Stanley Wise had no inkling of it: "I mean I never saw them stand together, I never saw them hold hands, I mean I didn't even know they were married until I went to their house and saw that's who Cliff was." Wise is sure that Ruby Doris and Clifford kept their romance secret because they were intensely private people.[10] But Bobbi Yancy points out that secret romances often occurred in SNCC for a variety of reasons. She thinks that Ruby Doris may have been concerned about how marriage might affect her colleagues' perceptions of her. Yancy reasons, "[Ruby] may have felt that it was going against her image to have this person on the side."[11]

Whatever their reasons, Ruby Doris and Clifford did not tell anyone of their marriage plans, and even after they were married, the newlyweds never made a formal announcement. Family and friends just gradually discovered it. Some were surprised that Ruby Doris was married at all, and even more were surprised that her new husband was not involved in the civil rights movement. Clifford did not remain an outsider very long, however. In 1964 he became a mechanic on the SNCC staff, working on the cars in the Sojourner Motor Fleet, which his wife administered. Bob Zellner thought that Ruby and Clifford made a good team, since Clifford took care of the SNCC cars, and Ruby Doris cared for SNCC members' souls.[12]

Many SNCC colleagues agree that the only reason Clifford joined SNCC was that he loved Ruby Doris and she was committed to the organization. Essentially, when Clifford Robinson married Ruby Doris Smith, he also married the Student Nonviolent Coordinating Committee because such a large part of Ruby Doris's identity was inextricably bound up in SNCC by this time. Reginald Robinson voices the view that many of Ruby's movement colleagues had of her husband: "He was not involved—he was Ruby's husband."[13] According to Stanley Wise, "He loved Ruby and that's [SNCC] what Ruby did, and that's what he would be doing."[14] Clifford himself freely admits that if he and Ruby had not been married, he never would have joined SNCC. As Willie Ricks sums up the newlyweds' relationship to SNCC, "Cliff was the husband, but Ruby Doris was the boss [in the organization]."[15] Regardless of the extent of his involvement, Clifford Robinson had to cope with an uncommon situation. He was married to one of the most powerful women in a major civil rights organization, and that meant that he and his new wife faced a number of difficult issues.

Prior to her marriage, Ruby had been working full-time at breakneck speed in SNCC. It was not going to be easy to fit a husband into her already full life, but she tried. The effort was often exhausting. It made her even more critical of coworkers who, in her view, were not working up to their capacity. Freddie Greene Biddle recalls Ruby's impatience:

> I think one of the things that really used to get to her is disorganized and just lazy folks[s]. 'Cause she used to always maintain that she did so much . . . and then other people would just sit around on their butts doing nothing. . . . She's always running, and she's always in a rush because of her own personal situation.[16]

According to Biddle, Ruby Doris regularly and bluntly expressed her displeasure to coworkers. "[She would] say, 'What are you all [doing] dragging in here? We all have the same thing to do.' "[17]

Yet regardless of the difficulties, Ruby enjoyed the rewarding aspects of marriage. Joyce Ladner noticed that Ruby's new relationship brought out a side of her that differed dramatically from her SNCC persona: "I remember that side of her, the softness, and her ability to relate as a woman to a man." Ladner also saw that Clifford "absolutely adored Ruby. He would just sit and look at her. He loved her."[18]

Despite their closeness, the newlyweds faced a problematic atmosphere in SNCC because of Ruby's powerful position. Many in the organization had trouble reconciling their vision of Ruby the SNCC administrator with Ruby the young wife. They were particularly puzzled by her decision to marry someone who was not as committed to the movement as she was. As Dorie Ladner puts it:

> I was a little surprised that she got married as early as she did. I always [pictured] her staying single much longer and, uh, being more or less the woman who was in charge and . . . see the other side of it was that she wanted a family, but her husband was also very supportive of her. And I saw him as being weaker than she. . . . And he looked up to her. . . . When I met Cliff and saw his bearing, I knew that she was in control.[19]

Ladner concludes, "He seemed to have been in awe of her, and under her spell."[20]

Was Ruby Doris the dominant partner in her marriage as Dorie Ladner's account suggests? Although memories differ, a number of SNCC colleagues agree with Ladner's assessment. But others who were also close to Ruby, like Freddie Biddle, saw another side. Biddle thinks that Ruby "had this husband who wanted to really dominate her." She continues: "[Ruby] was definitely sensitive to what he liked and what he didn't like. But yet she tried as much as possible not to, not to be dominated by that whole process."[21] In all likelihood, both Ladner's and Biddle's descriptions are accurate, since they were observing these newlyweds during the most fluid point in their relationship when Ruby and Clifford were testing limits and trying to establish a balance of power.

Regardless of how hard the couple worked on their relationship, however, some disagreements were inevitable amid the volatile atmosphere of the civil rights movement. Among the movement colleagues who sometimes caught a glimpse of this was Emma Bell Moses: "I think the root cause of those problems was [that] she was spending a great deal . . . of time away from her husband and he wasn't that involved in the movement."[22] Another who saw evidence of strains was Gwen Robinson:

> I can just remember, you know, you run in the office and he's [Clifford's] standing there waiting on her to go. And, you know, everybody's saying, "Ruby Doris, so and so and so." And he's saying, "Look, we got to go." And she's saying, "Cliff, wait a minute," I mean, "I got to take care of this." And him stalking off mad. And she saying, "Oh, God . . . later for him, then." I imagine she caught hell when she got home.[23]

It seemed that there were times when Ruby's commitment to the movement and her commitment to her husband pulled her in different directions.

Clifford freely acknowledges how consumed Ruby was by her work in SNCC. She never had any free time because [SNCC work] "was going on all the time around the house." Whenever he felt that Ruby was doing too much movement work after office hours, Clifford insists, he "was there to stop it."[24] Because she was sensitive to Clifford's feelings, Ruby Doris sometimes made extraordinary efforts to plan activities he would enjoy. For example, Freddie Greene Biddle recalls Ruby would invite some of her office coworkers to their house to play cards because she knew Clifford enjoyed this and he would participate.[25]

Ruby and Clifford soon faced a development that complicated and enriched their relationship at the same time: Ruby Doris became pregnant. In typical Ruby Doris fashion, she refused to let the pregnancy interfere with the pace of her movement work. During the early months, she kept her condition secret from friends and coworkers. But those closest to her guessed the truth because, even though she never missed a day at work, she spent a lot of time in the bathroom with morning sickness. The pregnancy affected Ruby's sense of smell. She was particularly sensitive to the smell of perspiration, and there were certain kinds of cologne that nauseated her. Nevertheless, Ruby Doris continued to work long days in the SNCC office right up to the end of her pregnancy. In fact, she was on her way home from the office when she went into labor.[26]

Ruby Doris and Clifford were overjoyed by the birth of their son, Kenneth Toure Robinson. Ruby chose her child's middle name to honor the president of the West African nation of Guinea, Sekou Toure. Immediately after Toure's birth, Ruby made it clear that she would return to work as soon as possible. Her determination to end her confinement prompted her to begin doing physical exercises just a few hours after the birth. Catherine was shocked when she visited Ruby in the hospital and found her on the floor in her hospital room exercising. Whether her exercise program paid off or her stubbornness prevailed, Ruby Doris went back to work in just two weeks.

Previously, Ruby had had to work only at balancing movement work and marriage. Now she had to add motherhood to the equation, and it was not easy. The first problem her new status created was the issue of day care for the baby. Again Ruby took Catherine by surprise.

> We had not really made a commitment about me keeping her baby while she . . . [went] back to SNCC. The baby was two weeks old, and I wasn't working. And [Ruby] came and knocked

Ruby Doris on her father's knee, her older sister Mary Ann standing beside her.

Ruby Doris (left) and Mary Ann in about 1943.

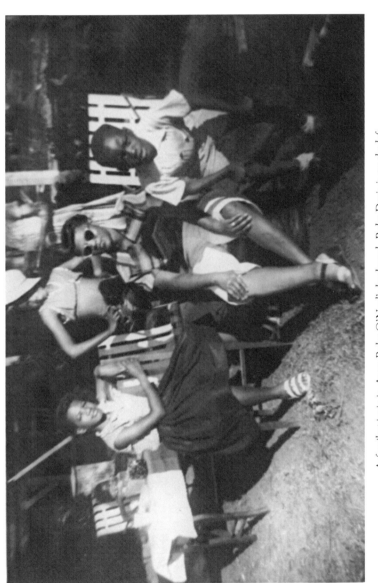

A family picnic in Aunt Ruby O'Neal's backyard. Ruby Doris is on the left.

Ruby Doris (left) and Ruby O'Neal during a rare Atlanta snowfall.

Ruby Doris's high school graduation photo.

Luther Judson Price High School, Atlanta.

The demonstration for slain postal worker William Moore in Norfolk, Virginia, in 1963. Ruby Doris is third from the right. Avon Rollins is on the extreme right.

The Moore demonstration. Ruby Doris is third from the right. Avon Rollins is on the extreme right.

Julian Bond at the Moore demonstration.

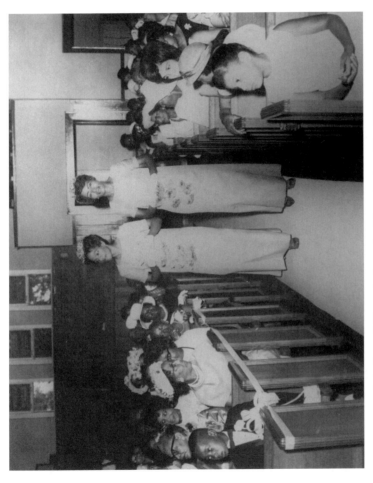

Ruby Doris (left) as a bridesmaid in Mary Ann's wedding (1965).

The Smith sisters: Mary Ann, Ruby Doris, and Catherine, about 1966.

Ruby Doris and her son Kenneth Toure Robinson.

Ruby Banks O'Neal and Alice Banks Smith (Ruby Doris's mother).

*Members of the Smith family (1993) in front of the family home on Fraser Street.
From the left: Catherine, Shelvis, Willie, Terria, Alice Banks Smith, Mary Ann,
Kenneth Toure, and Bobby.*

Funeral Services
for

MRS. RUBY DORIS SMITH ROBINSON

Saturday, October 14, 1967
1:00 P. M.
West Mitchell C. M. E. Church
Rev. E. H. Hicks, Pastor

OBITUARY

Mrs. Ruby Doris Smith Robinson was one of seven children born to Rev. and Mrs. J. T. Smith. Born April 25, 1942, the Atlantan received her elementary and secondary education in the Atlanta Public School System. Upon completing her undergraduate study at Spelman College, she received the degree of Bachelor of Science in Physical Education in 1965.

At an early age Mrs. Robinson became affiliated with the West Mitchell CME Church where she served as member of the Youth and Collegiate Choirs and the Christian Youth Fellowship. In 1956, Ruby Doris was delegate-elect to the National Youth Conference of the CME Church which convened in Memphis, Tennessee.

The principles which governed the life of the deceased can be observed in her past labors in the Civil Rights movement. Ruby was a charter member of the Student Non-Violent Coordinating Committee of which she later became the Executive Secretary.

Survivors include her husband, Mr. Clifford Robinson, Jr; a son, Kenneth Toure; her mother and father, Rev. and Mrs. J. T. Smith; two sisters; four brothers; seven aunts; eight uncles; a mother and father-in-law.

The church bulletin for Ruby Doris's funeral services.

FLOWER LADIES

Mrs. Carolyn Banks
Mrs. Wilma Blanding
Miss Nadine Cook
Mrs. Wilhemina Glover
Mrs. Valarie Lipsey
Mrs. Dessie Robinson
Mrs. Maudette Twyman
Miss Veronica Vaughn

ACTIVE PALL BEARERS

Julian Bond
Charles Black
Benjamin Brown
Ralph Featherstone
William Hansen
Frank Holloway
Donald Stone
Alfred Wyatt

HONORARY PALL BEARERS

Dr. Ralph Abernathy
Addis Davenport
James Forman
Carl Holman
Lonnie King, Jr.
Dr. Martin Luther King, Jr.
John Lewis
Robert Mance
Dr. James D. Palmer
William Porter
Frank Smith
Stanley Wise

ORDER OF SERVICE

Prelude .... Mr. Claude Dunson

Hymn .... Come Ye Disconsolate

Scripture .... Rev. O. M. Sims

Prayer .... Rev. B. B. Carter

Remarks (Three minutes)
Mrs. Vivian Sherrard
Rev. O. C. Woods
Mr. John Lewis (SNCC)

Solo .... Mr. Earlie Hicks, Jr.

Eulogy .... Rev. E. H. Hicks

Acknowledgement .... Mrs. C. P. Eagleson

Postlude

- - - - - - - - - - - - - - - - - -

Interment: Southview Cemetery

- - - - - - - - - - - - - - - - - -

The members of the bereaved family express
their sincere gratitude for cards flowers, telegrams
and the many kindnesses shown during the illness and
death of their loved one.

Ruby Doris Smith Robinson's grave in the Southview Cemetery.

up on my door with the baby and a bag. . . . And I said, " I don't know how to tend to this baby. I never had [any children]. . . ." She said, "Well you'll find out." She said . . . "The bottle is in the bag," and she just left that baby with me.[27]

This child care solution was only a temporary one.

Ruby explored a number of other options. She sometimes took Toure to work with her, where she would set up a little playpen for him. Stanley Wise explains, "[Ruby] brought the baby constantly by the office and [would] whip out that breast and pull him right up to it and just go right on meeting."[28] Ruby was not the only SNCC mother who brought her child to work. While it did not happen regularly, there were others, and there was a little nursery in the back to accommodate them. The sounds of crying babies added to the frenetic atmosphere that already permeated the SNCC office. The phones rang constantly. Sometimes it was the press asking for information, other times it was field workers who needed help. People were dashing to and fro answering calls and attending to all the details necessary to keep the organization in operation. But over all the din, Ruby seemed to be able to hear the least little noise Toure made even though he was in the nursery all the way in the back.

Ruby enjoyed having Toure with her in the office, but this arrangement could sometimes be quite frustrating. While she always tried to give 100 percent of her energy and concentration to her movement work, she wanted to give her all to her son too. Because she could not do both simultaneously, Ruby had to find another solution. At this point, her family gladly stepped in to offer their help. Many mornings, Ruby would dress Toure, gather up all his things, and dash to her parents' house. On the drive over, Ruby's mind was spinning with all the details of the work that awaited her. But as soon as she took the baby in her parents' house, her mind would focus completely on her son once again. Even though the comforting warmth of the house where she had grown up made Ruby feel a bit better about leaving Toure, she still felt guilty, and she missed him. He missed her too. Toure cried every time she left him. The sounds of his distress bothered her so much that Ruby would often ask her brother Bobby to play with her baby and distract him so that she could slip out without Toure knowing it.[29]

Eventually, the baby became used to spending many of his days at his grandparents' house, and he settled into a comfortable routine.

But [Toure] stayed there so much until he became adopted. Toure learned to count to ten before he was eighteen months old. Greg

[Ruby's youngest brother] taught him. He would do this because Greg would pretend to box with him and then pretend to be knocked out. And Toure would count him out.[30]

While her awareness of the closeness between Toure and her family undoubtedly relieved some of Ruby's anxiety, separation from her baby was still difficult.

Freddie Greene Biddle witnessed at least one time when the frantic pace of Ruby's life threatened to overwhelm her:

I remember once Ruby came out [of her house] with all these bags and her pocketbook and all this stuff, and we're going to the office, and she's going to drop, uh, Toure . . . off. . . . Well she's backing out of the . . . driveway and I'm in the car. . . . She had all these bags and stuff, and so then all of a sudden she said, "Oh shit." [I] said, "What's wrong?" She'd forgotten the baby.[31]

There never seemed to be enough hours in Ruby's day to get everything done. And even though she was surrounded by supportive family members and friends, the major responsibility of caring for Toure rested squarely on Ruby's shoulders. Clifford rarely offered to help because he had very traditional views of husband–wife roles. He felt that Toure was "definitely her responsibility."[32] As Mildred Page Forman recalls, it was a responsibility Ruby eagerly embraced despite her hectic existence:

That was, I think, one of the best moments of her life. She was ecstatic over the baby and the husband, and she was a good mother; and she was always mothering that baby. . . . I think that was, in fact I think that was the best thing that could have happened to her. Because she just, she just beamed and glowed with the baby.[33]

Many of Ruby's colleagues realized how hard she worked to balance movement commitments and personal responsibilities, and they were sure that both areas of her life were equally important. As one puts it, "It is clear that she wanted to stay married to Cliff . . . but she also wanted to be very active in SNCC."[34] Many mornings after Ruby left Toure at her parents' house, she would be the first person to arrive at the SNCC office. As she unlocked the office door, Ruby's guilt about leaving Toure weighed on her mind and on her soul. But once inside, her focus began to shift to the work that awaited her. Ruby sat down heavily in her chair because she was often so tired. With all her responsibilities, both personal and professional, she never had time to get enough rest. Yet she did not feel sleepy during those solitary early morning hours. Rather, Ruby was often seized by a terrible physical weariness. It almost felt as if she had weights attached to each one of her limbs.

Nevertheless, Ruby's commitment to SNCC and the African-American freedom struggle always allowed her to push her weariness aside and attack the mountain of work piled high on her desk. By the time coworkers began arriving, Ruby was answering phones and issuing orders at the frantic pace that was so characteristic of her. Some are convinced that Ruby's attempts to be wife, mother, and SNCC administrator eventually proved to be too much. One theorizes:

> She died of exhaustion. . . . I don't think it was necessary to assassinate her. What killed Ruby Doris was the constant outpouring of work, work, work, work with being married, having a child, the constant conflicts, the constant struggles that she was subjected to because she was a woman. . . . She was destroyed by the movement.[35]

While Ruby juggled motherhood, marriage, and the movement, SNCC faced a major decision. From late 1963 into early 1964, the organization debated the wisdom of becoming involved in a joint effort with other civil rights groups that would soon be labeled Freedom Summer. Bob Moses, who had been working in Mississippi since 1961, and Allard Lowenstein, a white activist and veteran of demonstrations in Jackson, Mississippi, conceived of the Freedom Summer idea in the fall of 1963. Earlier that year, both had been involved in a SNCC freedom vote campaign, an alternative election that had given the disfranchised black citizens of Greenwood, Mississippi, a chance to vote for their own slate of candidates. Lowenstein and Moses reasoned that a high incidence of participation in the freedom vote campaign would disprove segregationists' claims that black Mississippians were incapable of, and uninterested in voting. Lowenstein had recruited one hundred northern white students to work in the campaign, and voter turn out was high. Because this strategy had been successful, Moses and Lowenstein thought of recruiting even more northern white students to come to Mississippi the following summer. The inclusion of so many white outsiders in a SNCC project could have a profound impact on the character of what was then a mostly southern and black group. But both Moses and Lowenstein were convinced that the project's potential to effect change was much more important than any possible impact on organizational character. They were sure that if SNCC could send large numbers of white outsiders into the state, they could register large numbers of black voters, and educate them about the obligations and privileges of citizenship. This would lead to a shift in the state's political power, they reasoned, that would mark the beginning of the end of segregation in the state.[36]

Lowenstein and Moses initially presented their idea to the Council of Federated Organizations, and it provoked heated disagreement. Although COFO was a federation of the major civil rights groups, the majority of COFO staff were also SNCC members. Consequently, when SNCC's Executive Committee met on 30 December 1963 to consider the Moses–Lowenstein proposal, that discussion was a continuation of the COFO debate. A number of SNCC people expressed grave misgivings about the plan to flood the state with "thousands" of outsiders. Native Mississippian and SNCC staff member Hollis Watkins was unalterably opposed to such a plan. Watkins asserts that his opposition was regional rather than racial; he was opposed to the volunteers because they were from outside the South, not because most of them were white:

> The basic reason I didn't want people from the North to come to Mississippi was because we had begun to get the local people from Mississippi to come together to take initiative themselves and take responsibility for making their own decisions and acting on them and being prepared to suffer the consequences of their actions, take their losses, take their wins. And I felt that having people from the North, especially with the attitude that I perceived the people from the North of having—of being superior to the southerners, knowing it all, coming as a savior—would squash that leadership ability.[37]

As the meeting dragged on, many stood up and expressed their frustration in no uncertain terms. So many of them had been working in SNCC since the earliest days. They had faced extreme danger, and even death. Through these experiences, they had grown; they had gained confidence in their ability to end segregation. The Student Nonviolent Coordinating Committee had helped them each realize their own potential. It had freed their minds and empowered them. Furthermore, these native black southerners trusted each other, and they trusted each other's commitment. Many of these young movement veterans felt that the Freedom Summer proposal constituted a challenge to their authority over their own movement. Listening to the anguished voices and the emotional arguments, Ruby was moved by the look of betrayal she saw on the faces of many of her coworkers. She had recruited some of these people into movement work, and she felt their pain.

There is no record of how Ruby voted on this proposal. Constancia Romilly, however, remembers that Ruby opposed it.[38] While it is not clear whether Ruby objected to the race of the volunteers, some of her coworkers, including Worth Long, recall that she agreed with Hollis Watkins's concerns about outsiders in the movement: "Ruby didn't trust outsiders."[39] Accordingly, throughout this period, Ruby Doris continued her strong advocacy of southern college recruitment. At a February 1964 staff meeting, she agreed with her colleagues who suggested that the organization increase the number of SNCC recruiters on southern black college campuses. Ruby urged, "We should flood the *southern* campuses with material and field workers for one month" [emphasis added]. She went on to advise that: "Part of the problem with college contacts is that we've been sending out people who couldn't recruit from the campuses. Campus recruiters should be brought in for a month to reorganize their tactics."[40]

Ruby recognized that the addition of more southern black students to SNCC's membership would present certain unique challenges. She observed: "We can't redevelop student groups on the pattern of 1961. Now they have a different role." Clearly, the organization was changing, and new recruits who refused to embrace that change would have little in common with veteran activists. As Ruby put it, "The students are still sitting in at lunch counters and we are working on more complex and developed areas."[41] Thus, even the recruitment of southern black students presented serious challenges for black movement veterans. Logically, then, the addition of a large number of recruits from outside the region and outside the race would present a set of even more complex challenges to the organization.

Regardless of her personal feelings, once the decision was made to bring in northern white volunteers, Ruby Doris provided her full support: "She threw herself into it, and . . . again she tried to build a fervor and build a spirit so that we could be ready for whatever came."[42] Ruby spoke out about the positive role these white outsiders could play—even in the face of violence: "The dead become a symbol [and should] be replaced by thousands [of] others. . . . We recruited these summer people for a purpose."[43]

Even as Ruby publicly supported Freedom Summer, however, she privately wrestled with nagging questions that would not go away. During a June staff meeting, she identified one of those questions:

> We know that the summer project was conceived with the idea that there would be bloodshed, but what does it mean to say that

violence will be brought to the door step of the White House. No one in Birmingham rose after the shootings and bombings. There was no program. If we must operate off the land like guerrillas we must function that way.[44]

Ruby's concern about the question of bloodshed was part of a larger question in SNCC about the wisdom of self-defense in certain circumstances. Ever since its founding, SNCC had been committed, at least tactically, to nonviolence. But many had always been uneasy with that commitment. It was the reality of their black southern upbringing that spawned this uneasiness. In fact, the right to bear, and the ability to use, firearms effectively had been a cherished part of white southern notions of honor, chivalry, and manhood stretching all the way back into the nineteenth century. In the case of black southerners, this tradition combined with the oppression that confronted them to create an even more urgent need. "All of our parents had guns in the house," points out Joyce Ladner, "and they were not only for hunting rabbits and squirrels, but out of self-defense."[45]

As members of SNCC contemplated the very real prospect of racist violence during Freedom Summer, some began to rethink their commitment even to tactical nonviolence. In a letter to Howard Zinn, Staughton Lynd, a white professor at Spelman College and director of the SNCC Freedom School program, reported on an extensive discussion of violence versus nonviolence at a SNCC staff meeting he had recently attended. After a great deal of debate, the group had concluded that "no SNCC worker or summer volunteer should carry a weapon, and there should not be weapons in SNCC offices or Freedom Houses."[46] The group was unable to decide, however, what the proper course of action would be for a SNCC staff member or volunteer who was placed with a local family that kept guns in the house. The observations of SNCC staffer Don Harris were typical of the testimony offered by many. Harris told of a mass meeting that had been held in Albany, Georgia, after a young boy was shot by a policeman. Twelve hundred people had come, and "they were mad." Harris was convinced that SNCC could have organized the crowd into an effective demonstration, "but [SNCC members had] talked nonviolence and it [had] cut the meeting immediately. Some people had put [SNCC] down because of it." Harris's weariness and frustration showed in the tone of his voice when he demanded to know "what right [SNCC had] to stop these people from doing what they want[ed] to do."[47]

Ruby Doris attended this 1964 meeting, and she, too, expressed frustration about SNCC's continued support of nonviolence. She reminded the others that "in 1961 people had arms, but nothing was made of it." Since then, she observed, things had changed drastically: "We are asking people to expose themselves to more and more." It seemed to Ruby that in the current, more dangerous atmosphere, SNCC's continued insistence on nonviolence was becoming counterproductive. She used the example of the movement in Cambridge, Maryland, where SNCC took "people into the streets, stirred them up, and then turned them back with talk of nonviolence."[48] Finally, Ruby and the others who attended that staff meeting agreed to continue to support SNCC's policy of tactical nonviolence. But many, including Ruby, were uneasy with this decision.

Another issue that confronted SNCC staffers as they prepared for Freedom Summer was the question of SNCC's image. The early student demonstrators who had made up the founding nucleus of SNCC had always made a point of dressing in their best clothes when they demonstrated. The men had generally been clean shaven with close-cropped hair, while the women had taken care to make sure their hair was neatly straightened. In short, they projected a safe, middle-class image that played well before the news cameras. During these early optimistic days when the sit-ins were just beginning, these young activists were precisely what they seemed to be—patriotic, middle-class college students who fervently believed in a moral and just American system.

In a short time, though, their experiences altered them in fundamental ways. As Casey Hayden explains, "A new kind of self was created. . . . A lot of the old self-definitions fell away."[49] As they felt differently and saw themselves differently, some began to dress differently. Particularly after SNCC staffers moved into Mississippi in 1961, some took to wearing denim overalls and work shirts. One Mississippi veteran noted, "[The] reason we originally [wore] overalls and denim was to identify with people we were working with."[50] Increasingly, this tendency spread throughout the organization. By late 1963, some began to worry about the significance of this "SNCC uniform." John Lewis queried: "We have adopted a uniform which we wear everywhere in a self-righteous way. Do we really wear it to identify with the working class, or is it now a status symbol?"[51]

This discussion continued on into early 1964. By this time, people were raising questions about the way their image affected their ability to communicate with the people they were attempting to organize. All too often, some insisted, SNCC organizers ignored local views and sensibilities. The question of SNCC's image would take on added significance during Freedom Summer, when the organization's ability to recruit and inspire local people under very dangerous circumstances would be directly affected by peoples' perceptions. C. C. Bryant, longtime resident of Pike County, Mississippi, and head of its chapter of the NAACP, worried that some of the organization's workers looked sloppy and unkempt. He charged, "This, you know, tended to turn people off."[52] While Ruby Doris was quite concerned about this issue, she had her own ideas about how to address it. As others debated the wisdom of wearing jeans, Ruby argued, "It isn't so much what you wear but the condition of the clothes worn."[53] In fact, Ruby's personal wardrobe choices did not follow the SNCC trend. Throughout this period, she generally continued to wear skirts and blouses.

Many of these young activists were assailed by doubts about whether Freedom Summer would make any real difference. Despite the doubts, they tried desperately to cling to their belief in the power of the vote to change black lives. They were convinced that substantive change would not occur unless black Mississippians became active participants in their state's political affairs. Guided by this belief, at its monthly state convention in Jackson, COFO announced its intention to form a new Mississippi Democratic party that would "challenge the state Democratic party's delegation at the national convention in Atlantic City in August."[54] Shortly after this, the Mississippi Freedom Democratic Party was officially founded on 26 April 1964 at a rally in Jackson. In addition to the slate of delegates they chose to represent them at the Democratic National Convention, party members nominated their own candidates for the Democratic congressional primary. This challenge to Mississippi's entrenched white political establishment was brash and unprecedented. Black attorney and activist Len Holt declared, "These few dare to dream of challenging the traditional Mississippi Democrats. . . . It was ridiculous by any standard other than that of SNCC."[55]

As the summer approached, SNCC members worked tirelessly organizing freedom schools and workshops designed to educate prospective black voters and summer volunteers. But their hard work would not banish their doubts. Ruby Doris and her SNCC colleagues had become quite suspicious of a federal power structure in Washington that they judged to be unjust and entrenched. Although they knew they had the law on their side, many doubted that the federal government had the will to challenge Mississippi's recalcitrant racist officials. This doubt and budding disillusionment prompted Ruby to ask probing questions about the significance of Freedom Summer in general and the Mississippi Freedom Democratic Party in particular. She knew that the "Freedom Democratic Party and Freedom Vote campaign [were] radical programs." But, she went on to ask, "what would the seating of the delegation mean besides having Negroes in the National Democratic Party?"[56]

Motivated at least in part by her distrust of America's political system,

Ruby had concluded by now that economic reform was the only effective way to combat oppression. It was frivolous to worry about equal access to lunch counters, or even voting rights, when so many African Americans were worried about having "the basic necessities of life." In order to address the issue of economic reform, Ruby believed that SNCC should explore "new and creative tactics."[57] For example: "Agitation [that] demonstrates and exposes this country internationally. . . . We could employ radical action such as asking for political asylum."[58]

Ruby went on to argue that such complex solutions would require restructuring and tightening of SNCC's administrative apparatus. This restructuring could also help to solve internal problems that had begun to cause strains in organizational unity. One of the most serious of those problems, according to Ruby, was the lack of staff discipline that John Lewis had complained about in late 1963. Staff discipline, she said, was an issue that the SNCC administration desperately needed to address: "People are irresponsible because we've allowed them to be so and left them in the projects." Ruby charged that discipline problems were not only severe but widespread as well: "We have personnel and staff problems in all projects." In an effort to address problems of unity and discipline, Ruby urged the group to overhaul its administrative structure. She suggested that the coordinating committee that determined policy should be larger and more inclusive. Student workers should be appointed along with staff to this restructured committee, and they should quickly set a very clear list of priorities for the coming months. At the top of that list should be SNCC's educational program because its policies, which included leadership institutes and student recruitment, were designed to empower local people.[59] While many agreed with Ruby's ideas, the group took no action on them.

In the months preceding Freedom Summer, the group's administrative structure was severely tested as the central office's workload increased rapidly. Even after the summer was underway, administrative duties continued to increase. SNCC's Mississippi activities were coordinated through both the SNCC office in Greenwood and the COFO office in Jackson. But Atlanta remained SNCC's nerve center, and Ruby Doris Robinson was left in charge of the Atlanta office. Although she did visit Mississippi, and go to the orientation sessions in Oxford, Ohio, Ruby spent almost all of Freedom Summer in the Atlanta office out of the spotlight. The work of organizing such a huge effort and coordinating the activities of so many groups and communities produced unparalleled administrative headaches. It was a thankless, tiresome, and glamourless job that took its toll. Just before the summer started, Ruby Doris had predicted, "[I] feel [the] summer's going to teach us lesson [s] & force us to face up to many things we're now avoiding."[60] Her words proved to be prophetic.

One of those things that SNCC members were forced to face was the profound consequence of their own expansion. The rapid growth of the SNCC membership in late 1963 and early 1964 had brought in people whose vision was at odds with that of the founding members. In the stressful atmosphere of Freedom Summer, deep differences, and the simmering resentments they produced, were more noticeable than ever. Both activists and scholars of the movement agree that the relationship between black and white women in SNCC was one of the most important and visible areas affected by these differences. During that long and difficult summer, tempers flared. Some black women, including Ruby Doris, began to articulate their pent-up anger and frustration about a variety of issues. When black women lashed out, some white women quickly became defensive and assumed that they were the special targets of this black female anger. A number of movement scholars who have accepted this white female assessment have concluded that the problem is firmly rooted in a general and pervasive black female resentment of white women. But such an assessment ignores the historically problematic intersection of race and sex in America. Only an exploration of this broader historical perspective will yield a complete understanding of the complex female relationships in SNCC and their impact on Ruby and her impact on them.

The issue of black–white female relationships in SNCC was a painfully sensitive one during the turmoil of Freedom Summer, and it remains exceedingly emotional now. Mary Aicken Rothschild is one of those movement scholars who have attempted to tackle this volatile issue. In her book, *A Case of Black and White*, she concludes that the friction between black and white women in SNCC was provoked by black male/white female sexual encounters. Once white women became involved with black men, she reasons, black women became bitter because they did not want the competition:

> While a few black and white women staff members identified themselves as a group with interests occasionally in conflict with black men, young black women in the movement did not generally join with northern white women in any effort to overcome sexist practices. When there were sexual problems on a project, for the most part young black women remained bitterly divided from white women, whom they saw as stealing their men.[61]

Rothschild goes on to charge that not only did white women who were involved in interracial liaisons become "the focal point for a great deal of bitterness" from black women but their work was criticized too. She continues, "In most cases [the white woman] was written off as an ineffective worker."[62]

Like Rothschild, historian Sara Evans attributes black–white female friction to black women's frustration over stealing their men. Furthermore, in her work *Personal Politics*, Evans expands this line of reasoning to say that black women were also frustrated because white women got differential treatment in movement work: "A black woman pointed out that white women would perform the domestic and mundane tasks in a feminine kind of way while [black women] . . . were out in the streets battling with the cops. So it did something to what [our] femininity was about. We became amazons, less than and more than women at the same time.' "[63] But Evans's and Rothschild's conclusions are only part of the picture. They ignore a very important fact: black women were not the only ones who were frustrated.

On the contrary, white women in SNCC lived with their own share of anger and frustration when they saw black women doing the kind of work that they were not allowed to do. Cynthia Washington, a black SNCC staff member who worked in Mississippi, reports:

> During the fall of 1964, I had a conversation with Casey Hayden about the role of women in SNCC. She complained that all the women got to do was type, that their role was limited to office work no matter where they were. What she said didn't make any particular sense to me because, at the time, I had my own project in Bolivar County, Mississippi. A number of other black women also directed their own projects. What Casey and other white women seemed to want was an opportunity to prove they could do something other than office work. I assumed that if they could do something else, they'd probably be doing that.[64]

Washington recognized how hard the work of a project director was; besides that, it "wasn't much fun." Because of her insider's view, she was at a loss to understand why white women were complaining about not being appointed as project directors. In fact, their discontent with their situation only convinced Washington "how crazy [white women] were."[65]

Cynthia Washington's view was undoubtedly shaped by her position as a project director in SNCC; she was a woman who had at least a measure of authority in the organization. Similarly, Ruby Doris Robinson's view of white women was filtered through the prism of her experience as a powerful woman in SNCC. Yet white women, both scholars and activists, who have sought to evaluate Ruby's feelings about them have rarely taken this important perspective into consideration. For this reason, some scholars have dismissed Ruby Doris as one who simply hated white women. For example, Sara Evans declares, "Robinson herself hated white women for a period of years." Ruby's supposed hatred of white women, Evans reasons, was bound up in negative views of herself: "[Ruby] realized that [white women] represented a cultural ideal of beauty and 'femininity' which by inference defined black women as ugly and unwomanly."[66] Such reasoning suggests that Ruby and other African-American women reacted to society's assessment of them by hating the ideal (white women) rather than by affirming themselves. In the midst of their jealousy toward white women and their insecurities about themselves, this argument continues, black women felt anti-white-female anger—especially when competition for black men was involved.

Such a simplistic explanation of Ruby's behavior and beliefs seriously underestimates the complex of historical and cultural factors that have always shaped the existence of African-American women in this country. Being an oppressed *black* woman has always been quite different from being an oppressed woman in American society. For over three centuries, African-American women have been judged as morally inferior and physically undesirable. Black women have reacted to society's negative perceptions in a variety of ways. It is this important reality that provides the context necessary for understanding the tensions between African-American women and their white sisters in the movement.

Many of Ruby's black colleagues recall how their perceptions of proper morality were carefully and deliberately shaped during their childhood to blunt the impact of society's negative assessment. The upbringing of SNCC project director Gwen Robinson is illustrative. Although her family was not middle-class, they had middle-class aspirations. Hence, they taught their daughter that nice girls carefully guarded their virtue and their virginity. By contrast, in a shotgun house across the street from Gwen's family lived a poor woman who had a number of children but no permanent man. This prompted Gwen to associate sex outside of marriage with poverty and female exploitation. Above all, Gwen knew that being thought of as a "nice girl" was crucial.[67] According to Reginald Robinson, such views were widespread among the black women in SNCC: "What else was working on the sisters was the whole tradition of how sisters was told about sex and what role it played. . . . You don't raise your legs for nobody but who you're going to marry."[68]

Widespread black middle-class acceptance of such notions was reinforced by the extraordinary efforts made by black colleges to supervise the moral and social development of their female students. Consequently, regardless of society's assessment, black families, black communities, and black institutions all worked together to create black "ladies." The pressure black women felt from their own communities to uphold such high standards was enormous and unremitting. But at the same time, the scorn of an American society that viewed them as morally defective could be painful and destructive.[69] Such unrelenting scrutiny and criticism followed black women from slavery into freedom, into the twentieth century, and into the civil rights movement. It was a terrible burden to carry around.

Added to the weight of this burden was the issue of physical appearance. From their earliest days in this country, African women had been judged by a European standard of beauty. No matter what they did or how hard they tried, black women had only to look in the mirror to see that they could never measure up physically. Gwen Robinson's awareness of the standard idealized by so many was born of her experience on the Spelman campus. Spelman was famous for the beauty of its student body. Translation? A large proportion of the students had light skin, keen features, and straight or nearly straight hair. Here is Robinson's analysis of the prevailing view at Spelman in the early sixties:

> First of all, the best of all possible worlds is that you are light as you can be, you have green eyes, or light brown, and you have long straight hair. [Morehouse students] would be lined up outside your door, trying to get a date. Then you could be paper-bag brown or above and have long hair that you have to straighten, you know, that's still real cool, right? 'Cause we were all straightening—tough—in those days. Then, of course, you could be darker and have straight hair, long straight hair. . . . Then the last of the last category was that you were dark skinned and you had short hair or medium-length hair, you know?[70]

Having physical features that did not measure up to the white standard of beauty could often be painful for black women. Because she was dark skinned, Robinson learned that the pain was caused less by white reaction than by black rejection: "Some of the Morehouse guys were so nasty to a person who looked like myself. Overt. I mean, straight up."[71]

Clearly, black women's features marked them for life. But even if they could not change the standard, there were some subtle changes they could make in themselves. As many scholars of the black female experience have discovered: "Cosmetic preparations for lightening skin and straightening hair represent a multimillion dollar market among Negroes not favored with Caucasoid features. Among the less affluent and more credulous, urine rinses for the face and 'mammy-leg' presses for the hair contribute to the unending search for some approximation of the white ideal."[72] There were times when the use of those methods could result in at least a little discomfort. But the physical discomfort was not nearly as intense as the mental distress that many suffered when they recognized that such methods were incomplete and temporary. One black woman cried out in frustration:

> My hairdresser straightens my hair with a hot comb, but it never really looks naturally smooth. It looks straightened and . . . the more humid the air, the more it reverts. Especially in a steaming bath. Sometimes I use a hot comb on myself . . . because a press doesn't last very long. But unless you're very skilled, you can burn yourself. I've often burned the edges of my face.[73]

Young black girls learned early never to get caught in the rain without an umbrella or something to keep their hair dry. They learned to worry about their hair "going back" (reverting) at parties if they danced too vigorously and worked up a sweat. Of course, it was very difficult to enjoy swimming, since they constantly worried about just how wet their hair would get. In short, hair was a major preoccupation and a constant struggle. Everything in their environment reminded black women that they could not keep it straight—but somehow it always seemed important enough to keep on trying.

Ruby Doris Smith Robinson had to carry her share of this black woman's burden. She was not particularly light skinned. She had broad features and short kinky hair. All around her in American society in general, and on Spelman's campus in particular, Ruby faced daily reminders of the negative implications of her looks. Her colleagues say, however, that Ruby was not bound by society's judgment and neither were they. Because many in the organization were questioning standards and values in a variety of areas, they did not blindly and completely accept American standards of beauty. This allowed them to view Ruby in a different way. "Even though [Ruby] didn't fit the 'American model' of attractiveness, she was nevertheless a striking-looking woman, imposing really," declares Dottie Zellner. "From my perspective, Ruby did not fit any of the female stereotypes."[74]

A number of Ruby Doris's male colleagues also showed a willingness to look beyond contemporary white American standards of beauty. Curtis Hayes describes his first impression of Ruby:

Ruby Doris was the first woman I saw with an Afro hairdo. . . . It blew my mind. . . . [When] I met Ruby, she had on a . . . croaker-sack skirt . . . burlap, and a blouse similar to a T-shirt, and kinky hair, and some sandals. And everything about her would have been considered ugly, *and she was fine.* [Emphasis added][75]

Stokely Carmichael agrees: "I found Ruby Doris to be a real pretty sister with a pleasant smile. . . . If she wasn't my sister, you know, I'd say she had a fine body."[76] Even though Michael Simmons did not think Ruby was attractive when he first met her, he soon changed his mind: "I mean it was very clear to me that at another time and place that, like, I definitely would have tried to hit on her."[77] Thus, Ruby Doris Smith Robinson received mixed messages about her looks. She lived in a society that bombarded her with negative assessments of her kinky hair, broad features, and skin color, but she was surrounded by people who questioned society's judgment.

However, regardless of what anyone thought, Ruby Doris maintained a positive self-image. That self-image, coupled with Ruby's unshakable belief in the righteousness of the cause she had embraced, left her little time to worry about others' judgments. Charles Jones explains: "Ruby Doris . . . was a very practical black—in color, and in hair, and in attitude—woman. . . . She didn't have any illusions."[78] As Stokely Carmichael read her: "She had no complexes at all. She was convinced that there was nothing that she could not do. Her self-confidence, you know, when you consider the batter-ing that especially African women have to take on the question of self-con-fidence in this country, she was a tower of strength."[79] Ruby made a similar impression on Dion Diamond: "For a woman who knew she was less than the European attractive model, I mean Ruby was very comfortable with her-self. . . . *I mean she was still a woman* [emphasis added]."[80] Michael Simmons adds, "She saw her . . . womanness . . . in a way that did not set any limits on what she could do."[81] Clearly, the nurturing atmosphere in the Student Nonviolent Coordinating Committee helped Ruby recognize the best in her-self, just as it helped her colleagues. According to Casey Hayden, "You really kind of stopped thinking in terms of the limitations of . . . sex or class or race."[82]

Because she had such a positive sense of herself, Ruby Doris went to the trouble to look nice. The care she took in selecting her clothes, which her sisters had noted during her high school years, did not end once she entered the movement. While by this time she was less inclined and less able to indulge her expensive tastes in clothes, Ruby still took pains with her appear-ance, sometimes under very difficult circumstances. Some of Ruby's movement colleagues had trouble reconciling the strength of her commitment with her fastidious personal grooming. But their failure to understand reveals more about them than about Ruby. Even though they may have believed the stereotypical notion that women who were assertive, strong, and committed were almost never attractive, Ruby refused to let this notion circumscribe her existence.

Ruby confronted negative perceptions of her actions as well as of her looks. Her position and stature in SNCC challenged popular notions of proper female behavior. According to 1960s middle-class American values, women were not supposed to exercise power over men. But Ruby did. Even though her coworkers accepted her ability to exercise power as an integral part of her persona, some of them reacted in ways that forced her to confront the issue of her own femininity within the context of her activist leadership role: there were times when some treated her like "one of the boys."

Ruby was not the only black female freedom fighter to face this issue. On the contrary, others have routinely had their femininity called into question, not only because of their actions, but also, and more importantly, because of their color. Consequently, any attempt to analyze the impact of this issue on black women activists must explore the peculiar status of black women in American society, a status firmly anchored in the nineteenth century and slavery.

> The slave system defined Black people as chattel. Since women, no less than men, were viewed as profitable labor-units, they might as well have been genderless as far as the slaveholders were concerned. . . . Judged by the evolving nineteenth century ideology of femininity, which emphasized women's roles as nurturing mothers and gentle companions and housekeepers for their husbands, Black women were practically anomalies.[83]

Those negative notions have affected the consciousness of a broad segment of the American population for a very long time. Even after the institution of slavery was outlawed, questions about black women's femininity persisted. An examination of the most enduring black female stereotype, the black mammy, illustrates pervasive negative views of black femininity. As one scholar explains, this mammy image has endured because it is an important part of southern culture as well as the counterpoint to white women's identity:

> A [white] lady was expected to be a wife, a mother, and a manager; yet she was supposed to be delicate, ornamental, virginal,

and timid. . . . If the image of the delicate alabaster lady were to retain some semblance of truth, it would be necessary to create the image of another female who was tougher, less sensitive, and who could perform with efficiency and grace the duties of motherhood for her mistress and of course for herself. The image of the southern lady, based as it was on a patriarchal plantation myth, demanded another female image, that of the mammy.[84]

The typical mammy that many white Americans found so comforting was fat, very dark skinned, and always kerchiefed. She sang a lot too, since she was so happy taking care of her white folks. There was absolutely nothing about her that made her desirable and attractive. Rather, she was a figure of black womanhood that was essentially desexed. Some white southerners cherished this view so much that in 1911 they started a movement to establish memorials to the "old black mammies of the South." A school was even established in Athens, Georgia, that was christened the Black Mammy Memorial Institute.[85]

This symbol of desexed black womanhood lived on into the twentieth century and was widely popularized with the advent of the motion picture industry. Film historian Donald Bogle describes the mammy of the screen as a character who was invariably "big, fat, and cantankerous" and always headstrong and independent. Portrayals of her date back as early as the era of silent films. In 1914, Hollywood released a comedy called *Coon Town Suffragettes* which was a blackface version of *Lysistrata* featuring a group of bossy mammy washerwomen who orchestrated a campaign to keep their "good for nothing" husbands at home. A short time later, Hollywood introduced a character that was a variation on the theme, and she proved to be mammy's very close cousin. This mammy mutant, Aunt Jemima, was every bit as big, fat, and dark as mammy, but her personality was quite different. She was generally "sweet, jolly, and good-tempered," but above all, she was still desexed.[86]

The mammy/Aunt Jemima image was later joined by a complementary stereotype: the tragic mulatto. At first glance, the tragic mulatto appears to offer an alternative view of the black female persona. Upon closer examination, however, it becomes clear that this image actually serves to reinforce the notions of sexlessness and unattractiveness that are integral to the mammy image. Early-twentieth-century filmmakers most often presented the tragic mulatto as an attractive, sexually desirable woman whose only real flaw was her possession of just enough "Negro" blood to taint her. Thus, the not-so-subtle message was that in order to be alluring and feminine, one must look like a white woman. If the tragic mulatto were a "real" black woman like mammy, sexual attractiveness and femininity would be completely beyond her reach.[87] Such screen images of black women and the messages they conveyed were quite widespread and incredibly compelling during the first half of the twentieth century.

The weight of so much negative tradition undoubtedly pressed heavily on many black female activists over the years. The harsh judgments engendered by this tradition moved the legendary Sojourner Truth to complain: "Dat man ober dar say dat women needs to be helped into carriages and lifted ober ditches, and to hab de best place everwhar. Nobody ever helps me into carriages, or ober mud puddles, or gibs me any best place!" Truth concluded by crying out in frustration, "And ain't I a woman?"[88] The cry of Sojourner Truth from the nineteenth century resonated with the young Ruby Doris Smith Robinson and many of her activist sisters in the civil rights movement of the twentieth century. As Ruby wrestled with the same negative views of black femininity that had confronted so many before her, her reactions were shaped by her own self-image, by the strength of her commitment, and by the fluid nature of the Student Nonviolent Coordinating Committee.

An assessment of her colleagues' judgment of her unique reactions provides important insights into Ruby's struggle to resolve this supreme contradiction of her existence. Within SNCC Ruby was widely perceived as a woman who did not conform to contemporary notions of femininity. The following comments are typical: People in SNCC "didn't view her as a man or a woman; they viewed her as a strength."[89] "I think that everybody accepted her as one of the boys."[90] "Guys would argue with Ruby, but the guys respected her. She was like one of them in a way."[91] "Her personality was so strong you didn't see a lot of . . . didn't nothing else matter."[92]

Constancia Romilly was among those who were particularly impressed by Ruby's commanding, and not necessarily "feminine," voice: "Ruby . . . was tough as the men, and as courageous, and her voice was as strong as any man's voice. . . . Yes, she had a, she had a carrying voice, and a very well-defined [voice]. When she spoke, you could definitely hear what she had to say."[93] Curtis Hayes describes Ruby's voice as authoritative, masculine, but not too heavy: "She didn't have a whiny female thing. Wasn't none of that."[94]

While Ruby's appearance and voice set her apart, her courage and assertiveness distinguished her as well. During Ruby's early movement days, she gained a reputation for bravery. Dottie Zellner recalls that by the time she became involved with SNCC in late 1961 and early 1962, "the men held [Ruby] in incredible respect. . . . [there was] a mystique about her bravery."[95]

Most could recount at least one Ruby Doris story that added to the mystique. For example, Willie Ricks remembers that the Atlanta police would often issue parking tickets to cars in front of the SNCC office—whether they were illegally parked or not. This thinly disguised attempt at harassment offended Ruby's sense of justice and moved her to action. One day she ran downstairs just as a white policeman was placing a ticket on a car. She snatched it off and tore it into small pieces in front of the officer. When she turned to walk back into the office, the policeman just looked at her. He did not attempt to stop her. By this time, she was married and she was eight months pregnant.[96]

James Bond, who worked in the SNCC print shop, witnessed another Ruby Doris incident when a group of SNCC staff went to the airport to meet some of the organization's celebrity supporters:

> So we went out there and met the first plane which was coming from California, which had Marlon Brando and Tony Franciosa on it. And then we had to go meet a second plane, which had Paul Newman on it. So we took them down to the other gate. . . . Ruby Doris was with us. And as we stood out at the gate waiting, . . . the first person to come off the plane was Governor [George] Wallace. And Ruby Doris went up to him and said "How are you, Governor," and introduced herself and said, "I've spent some time in your jails." And he said "Well, I hope they treated you well, and if you're ever back, look me up."[97]

She never did.

While Ruby's brashness and courage were not considered normal character traits for American women in the 1960s, they were typical of many African-American women in the civil rights movement. Consider the example of Annelle Ponder. After Ponder, an SCLC voter education teacher, was arrested in Winona, Mississippi, her white prison guard demanded that she use a title of respect when addressing him. She refused. Fannie Lou Hamer, who was arrested with her, remembers hearing the guard snarl, "Cain't you say yessir, nigger? Cain't you say yessir, bitch?" Ponder answered, "Yes, I can say yessir." The guard then demanded that she say it. Ponder's reply? "I don't know you well enough." The guard was so incensed that he beat her. Hamer remembers, "She kept screamin' and they kept beatin' her . . . and finally she started prayin' for 'em, and she asked God to have mercy on 'em because they didn't know what they was doin.' "[98]

Then there was the case of Annie Pearl Avery. During the course of a demonstration in Montgomery, Alabama, Avery came face to face with a white policeman who had a billy club aimed straight at her head. He had already beaten several others. Avery "reached up, grabbed the club and said, 'Now what you going to do, motherfucker?' " The policeman was awed. Avery slipped back into the crowd of demonstrators.[99]

Betty Cotton, a young high school student and native Mississippian, provides still another example of black female brashness and courage. Cotton impulsively decided one day that she would not allow white people to push her around anymore. She acted on this impulse after SNCC had dispatched her, along with Chuck McDew, to Liberty, Mississippi, to investigate the burning of a black church. While Betty and McDew were walking down the street, some white women approached from the opposite direction. As custom dictated, McDew stepped off the sidewalk to let the women pass, but Betty had other ideas. McDew explains: "And the women went to pass and tried to push Betty aside. . . . Betty hit this one woman with her shoulder and knocked her down . . . in the street." McDew's reaction? "Oh shit!" He knew that because of what Betty had done, their lives were in danger. Predictably enough, the white women notified the sheriff, and a posse was dispatched immediately. In the meantime, McDew and Cotton made their way to a root cellar, where they hid until the danger was past.[100]

These actions that seemed so normal within the black community, particularly in the context of the civil rights movement, were completely contrary to wider American notions of proper female behavior. American women of this era were regularly told that women's place was in the home. Some experts, like psychiatrist Marynia Farnham and sociologist Ferdinand Lundberg, insisted that "career and higher education were leading to the 'masculinization' of women." In his commencement address at Smith College, Diplomat Adlai Stevenson's comments complemented this view when he told the audience:

> The assignment to you, as wives and mothers, you can do in the living room with a baby in your lap or in the kitchen with a can opener in your hand. If you are clever, maybe you can even practice your saving arts on that unsuspecting man while he's watching television. I think there is much you can do about our crisis in the humble role of housewife.[101]

While it is doubtful that assertive black women like Ruby Doris would have taken such advice seriously, they were still subjected to society's pressure to conform. If they did not, their femininity was questioned not only by people

126

outside the movement but sometimes by those inside it. SNCC staff member Cynthia Washington offers an example of the latter:

> I remember discussions with various women about our treatment as one of the boys and its impact on us as women. We did the same work as men—organizing around voter registration and community issues in rural areas—usually with men. But when we finally got back to some town where we could relax and go out, the men went out with other women. Our skills and abilities were recognized and respected, but that seemed to place us in some category other than female.[102]

Thus, well before Freedom Summer, Ruby and the other black women in SNCC were struggling with their own issues of physical appearance, femininity, and self-image. They brought that struggle with them to Mississippi in 1964, where they encountered young, idealistic white female volunteers who were waging their own struggle to confront issues of identity and self-worth in a sexist society. In most instances, this was the first time that these young white women had ever had such close and intimate contact with African Americans and southern culture. Very quickly, African-American women concluded that these white women did not understand them or their culture.

Part of the reason for this lack of understanding was simply a matter of ignorance black women found annoying and insulting. When white SNCC staffer Dottie Zellner went south to join the movement, she knew so little about African-American culture that she, "didn't even know who Ray Charles was."[103] Gwen Robinson remembers: "It was an interesting experience dealing with white women. . . . we went through some interesting stuff, you know, everything. Hair—you know—I mean . . . the white folk constantly wanted to feel your hair and understand, well why does it do this when you put water on it. . . ."[104] Robinson felt insulted by this reaction sometimes, but tolerant of it at others. Because of her middle-class upbringing, however, she rarely communicated her resentment to white women. The painful truth remained a family secret. Such repressed resentment on the part of Robinson and other black women, undoubtedly offered a fertile breeding ground for real anger—later.

Ignorance was only one of the obstacles facing some of those eager white women who sought to understand African Americans. Another was the rampant racism in American society. These women had been exposed for years to subtle and not-so-subtle messages popularizing negative black stereotypes and supporting notions of black inferiority. Psychiatrist Alvin Poussaint examined the importance of this long-term exposure in his study of the adjustment of white women volunteers to the rigors of Freedom Summer. During their weeks in Mississippi, many of these women struggled to confront the racist stereotypes that their society had accepted for so long. In Poussaint's estimation, some of them lost that struggle, and their racist tendencies became obvious. He labels such behavior the "white African queen complex":

> At the center of this "complex" is probably a tabooed and repressed fantasy of the intelligent, brave, and beautiful white woman leading the poor, downtrodden, and oppressed black man to freedom and salvation. One white female worker told me she sometimes felt like "the master's child come to free the slaves." Another confided, "What an electrifying feeling it is to be worshipped by the Negroes."[105]

Black women bitterly resented this attitude and the condescending behavior it spawned.

A further complicating factor in this problematic relationship was the issue of class. Many of the white women who journeyed south that summer were truly middle-class or even upper middle-class. On the other hand, many of the African-American female veterans, including Ruby Doris, were from families with middle-class aspirations but only working class incomes. Some of these black women had faced very difficult economic circumstances during their lives. When middle-class white women doing office work in the movement began to complain about being oppressed, Ruby Doris and other black women like her lost their patience.

But it is important to recognize that long before the large influx of white female volunteers into SNCC during Freedom Summer, black and white female staff members had regularly interacted with each other. During those early years, SNCC staff remained quite small, mostly southern, and exceedingly close knit. These young activists made a conscious effort to ignore race—at least within their own organization. In this atmosphere, black and white women seemed to get along: "In the early days, it was very much . . . I mean what one did in one's personal relationships was as important as what one did publicly. So there was a lot of effort—people were willing to put a lot of effort into transcending race."[106] Ruby Doris was no exception. Connie Curry, a southern white woman who worked with early SNCC, remembers feeling quite close to Ruby. In fact, Curry recalls, "I used to try to sit by her [at staff meetings] because I liked her." And again: "I just always felt sort of at home and safe with her as another human being. I was older, but that means at eighteen [years old], she gave off emanations that would allow me as a white person to feel comfortable around her."[107]

But even before the unsettling experience of Freedom Summer, there were some black-white female conflicts. Almost everyone agrees that the white women who joined early SNCC were an eager, idealistic, and vocal presence in the organization. After the first few years of SNCC's existence, some among their black counterparts charged that white women were becoming too vocal and too eager; and were trying to exert too much influence. According to Bobbi Yancy, Ruby shared this perception, and she remarked on it openly and often; in fact, according to Yancy, Ruby bluntly advised the white women office workers to stay out of her way, let her do her job, and concentrate on their supportive work.[108] Dorie Ladner adds, "I think that [Ruby] felt that [white women] had a different agenda and that they had to be kept on the course as to what the agenda of the blacks was."[109]

At least one white female SNCC staffer, Constancia Romilly, understood why Ruby and the other black women were suspicious:

> If I were to put myself in Ruby Doris's head, what I would say is, you know, "here comes Dinky Romilly; here comes Mary King. Why are they here? They don't have any intrinsic interest in promoting the rights of black people. They're middle-class white women. . . ." And I can understand that . . . she would be very suspicious of that.[110]

Joyce Ladner, too, questioned white female intentions: "See, a lot of white women who came into SNCC, even though they felt they were 'discriminated against,' confined to the office setting, . . . they still tried to dominate the office. I mean it was a matter of [not] being content anywhere—if you put them in the field. They were white women: that's all that was necessary to know about them." Ladner describes the impact of this tense atmosphere on Ruby Doris:

> The impression Ruby conveyed was that . . . white women were always at kind of an uneasy peace around her. She didn't mistreat them, but they sure didn't pull that shit, I mean bullshit on her. She was the last person they would run to with some complaint about, "Oh we're poor, oppressed white women here. . . ." She'd been in jail and was from a poor background herself. So it was hard for her to have sympathy for a girl from Sarah Lawrence who felt put upon.[111]

Because of her authority, Ruby Doris had to cope with a variety of attitudes and reactions exhibited by white women staff and to balance these against the feelings and perceptions of black women staff. In the midst of this, she was still dragging around her share of the black woman's burden, still coping with the historical and recent negative assessments of black female morality, femininity, physical appearance, and capabilities. In the meantime, Ruby developed a sophisticated leadership style and political ideology. All of these factors influenced her interaction with white women in SNCC. Each interaction was different, depending on the woman and the circumstances.

Yet some claim that by 1964 Ruby Doris harbored a pronounced dislike for all white women. Ann Romaine, a southern white woman who worked with SNCC, met Ruby Doris in late 1964. She was quite aware of the gossip, that Ruby Doris hated white women. "That was kind of the word around. By the time I came on the scene in late '64, oh yeah, she had a lot of problems [with white women]." Romaine declares that Ruby's dislike was accompanied by an intense wrath: "The one thing you saw about her was how much anger she had. She had a tremendous, tremendous amount of anger."[112] Other white women also remember that anger, an anger that they assumed was directed at them. Casey Hayden observes: "She had a certain intensity or anger or turmoil, you know. She wasn't a peaceful person."[113] What had happened since SNCC's earliest days? Why did some in the organization begin to suspect that Ruby Doris hated all white women by 1964?

A large part of the answer lies in the dynamics of Freedom Summer. By that time, Ruby had become quite a powerful force in SNCC, and her duties were many and varied. Part of those duties included making personnel decisions that were particularly problematic, given the large influx of white volunteers into Mississippi in the summer of 1964. As Ruby worked to keep the organization running smoothly that summer, she was confronted by countless personnel conflicts and difficulties, many of which resulted from differences in background, perspective, and skill level. These fundamental differences provided a fertile breeding ground for serious conflict. For example, many of the northern students brought with them office and organizational skills that surpassed those of the local black staff. At the same time, some black staff members who had seen the organization through very tough times questioned the commitment of white northerners who had yet to expose themselves to physical danger in defense of black rights. The situation was further complicated by an air of superiority that characterized many of these northern white recruits, who were not even aware of the potentially disastrous effects of their attitude. The comments of one white, summer volunteer illustrate the complicated relations between white volunteers and black staff:

> [The black project director] and I absolutely drove each other crazy because I didn't understand him [and] he didn't understand me. I had all these skills and, you know, worked eighteen hours a day. _____ was real laid back and, of course, was being courted by the local women . . . and I was self-righteous as hell about all this. . . . So I was always after him about being immoral, irresponsible. . . . Hell, he was probably [overwhelmed] . . . by these college kids from the north. I mean, how the hell was he going to compete with that? . . . I just moved in and took over. I mean I wasn't trying to supplant him, I just did. I had absolutely no sensitivity to what that might have been doing.[114]

Another white volunteer experienced similar problems. She recognized that she possessed a number of characteristics, including her gender, that aroused the ire of some of her black coworkers. She exclaimed in frustration:

> Several times I've had to completely re-do press statements or letters written by one of them. It's one thing to tell people who have come willingly to Freedom School that they needn't feel ashamed of weakness in these areas, but it's quite another to even acknowledge such weaknesses in one's fellow workers. Furthermore, I'm a northerner; I'm white; I'm a woman; I'm a college graduate; I've not "proven" myself yet in jail or in physical danger. Every one of these things is a strike against me as far as they are concerned. I've refused to be ashamed of what I cannot change; I either overlook or purposely and pointedly misinterpret their occasional thrusts of antagonism.[115]

This white woman correctly observed that many black staff members already in Mississippi regarded the coming of white women volunteers with a special foreboding. Southern black staff had no illusions about the kind of reaction that white women's working close to black men would provoke in Mississippi in 1964, and many were alarmed. Chuck McDew recalls, "You'd have to force the field secretaries to be with them [white women] because it was just a troublesome sort of thing."[116] As a native Mississippian, Freddie Greene Biddle was also aware of the potential for danger:

It was . . . the question in terms of Southwest Mississippi, a fact of not feeling it was safe having them [white women] there. . . . It was not the question only of protection for them. I remember it was also the protection of the rest of us, because it would be extremely dangerous being in the car with a white girl and something happen[s]. I mean you can get hurt.[117]

Dorie Ladner echoes Biddle's fears: "You could have a picket line and the moment a white woman appeared on the line, [local] white men would become very angry and aggressive."[118]

It was difficult for these young white female summer volunteers to accept the notion that their mere presence might endanger the movement and the lives of their coworkers, especially when they observed black women out in the field doing the kinds of things they wanted to do. It seemed so unfair. Because they were involved in a movement about social justice, restrictions placed on their actions were particularly difficult for white women to accept—regardless of the reason. Many black staff members saw this white female frustration from a much different vantage point, however: "One of the problems was that . . . [white women] were so insensitive to . . . the danger they were bringing on the other people. . . . it was like a red flag."[119] Others thought that some of the white women completely misunderstood efforts to keep them out of potentially dangerous situations: "White women wanted to . . . do certain things. And not understanding the seriousness, you know, of the movement and the nature of a lot of things, . . . they mistook some of the things that men would do . . . as being . . . male chauvinistic . . . things."[120]

Was there any chauvinism associated with attempts before, during, and after Freedom Summer to restrict white female behavior? Perhaps. Was there any danger associated with a white female presence in SNCC projects in Mississippi and other areas in the rural South? Undoubtedly. But regardless of the safety issue, some white women remained determined to help when they could. Long before Freedom Summer, some black staff members had witnessed the serious consequences of such well-intentioned white female assistance. In fact, Chuck McDew was the recipient of some of that assistance on one occasion when he had been in jail for about two weeks on a charge of criminal anarchy. Even though he had not been allowed to contact anyone, McDew's guards seemed to be treating him reasonably well, but that all changed drastically and abruptly.

One day the guards came in and just started beating me, kicking me, socking me, knocking me around, and cursing me. [They said] "you black son of a bitch" and all of that. And I didn't know why. I mean . . . heretofore they hadn't abused me physically. And then finally, one of them . . . just came in later as I was just laying there thoroughly whipped, trying to recover, and kicked me in the side. [He said,] "Son of a bitch, that's what you get for marrying a white woman."[121]

Since he was unmarried, McDew was completely baffled. Only later did he discover that this was all part of a plan formulated by a white female SNCC supporter: "I'd been in prison about two weeks. . . . They wouldn't let anybody see me. I found out later that this woman had conjured up the great idea that, well, they can't deny him a visitor if it's his wife." So she had gone to the jail posing as McDew's wife and had demanded to see her husband. The result was not what she intended. McDew explains, "I bear the scars of that foolishness today." After McDew was released from jail, he confronted her and exclaimed, "Is you fool? If you don't get out of here, I will kill you."[122]

Many black SNCC staffers expressed similar outrage when it seemed that white women's actions, no matter how well intentioned, were placing them in jeopardy. That outrage was directed not only at the white women involved but also at black staff members who encouraged them. Freddie Greene Biddle cites an illustrative incident: "There was this crazy guy, Cliff Vaughs, I remember who came . . . across the country. And then everybody was mad because he rode through Mississippi on a motorcycle with this white girl on the back. . . . People were mad and hated things like that because you use your resources to protect something foolish. I mean, that was just clearly foolish."[123] Biddle and many of her coworkers were angry at the white woman for making the trip, but they were also angry at Vaughs for taking her. Such anger motivated some in SNCC to warn their black male coworkers, "If you get lost with your white woman, we [are] not looking for you."[124] Thus, when black staff members welcomed white women volunteers during Freedom Summer, many did so with a great deal of reluctance and a sense of foreboding.

Another problem that many associated with a white female presence during Freedom Summer was the prospect of interracial dating. In fact, black male/white female romantic encounters violated one of the Old South's most sacred taboos and created an emotional and dangerous atmosphere for civil rights work. Consequently, those contemplating such involvement often had to choose between their own desires and the health of the movement. One white woman who was thinking of volunteering for Freedom Summer was asked by the SNCC staffer interviewing her:

> how she'd deal with a Negro man who caught up to her on the street and asked to sleep with her. She said she might. [The interviewer] asked her what she'd do if [he] told her, as a staff member, that sexual activity would endanger everyone, and not to do it. She said she might go ahead and do it anyhow.[125]

In addition to being horrified about the dangerous atmosphere created by these interracial liaisons, many black project directors and field-workers were also alarmed about the impact of these relationships on the local black population. Both of these concerns prompted Holly Springs, Mississippi, project director Ivanhoe Donaldson to ban such relationships. He reasoned:

> Interracial relationships will provide local whites with the initiative they need to come in here and kill all of us. Even if the whites don't find out about them, the [black] people will, and we won't be able to do anything afterwards to convince them that our primary interest here is political. Our entire effort will be negated if we lose the support and respect of the people. I don't intend for that to happen. . . . We're here to work. The time for bullshitting is past.[126]

There are some in SNCC who charge that these relationships also had profoundly negative consequences for African-American women in the organization that transcended issues of effectiveness and safety in the movement. Michael Simmons charges that when black men drew criticism for their involvement with white women, many tried to justify their behavior by denigrating black women. They claimed that black female deficiencies had driven them to choose white partners. Simmons has no doubt that such arguments indicated black male acceptance of the well-established negative stereotypes about black women.[127] Such pronouncements must have been very difficult for black women to hear. On other occasions, according to some, black men simply lied and denied their involvement. SNCC staff member Fay Bellamy found such dishonesty particularly troublesome: "[Black women] didn't care what you did. They just cared that you lied about it. . . . if you weren't comfortable with what you're [doing], then something is wrong with what you're doing." Many black women termed this "talking black and sleeping white."[128]

134

The concerns about interracial sexual liaisons shared by Fay, Ruby, and other black SNCC women cannot be fully understood without an examination of the other side of this attraction. While it is true that some black men in SNCC found some of the white women staff members and summer volunteers to be attractive, some of these white women felt a powerful attraction to black men as well. As one expressed it: "My sexuality for myself was confirmed by black men for the first time ever in my life, see. In the white society I am too large. . . . So I had always had to work very hard to be attractive to white men. . . . Black men . . . assumed that I was a sexual person . . . and I needed that very badly." Another white woman volunteer had similar feelings: "In terms of black men, one of the things I discovered . . . [was] that physically I was attractive to black men whereas I never had been attractive to white men."[129]

Even before Freedom Summer the increasing frequency of white female attractions to black men had led some to suspect that such behavior was becoming a fad. Constancia Romilly, for one, thought so:

> I, by this time, had gotten the idea that there were a lot of white women running around, through whatever sociologic, psychological, pathological—whatever rationale [there] was. There were a lot of white young women college students, running around thinking that the greatest thing in the whole wide world was to have a black boyfriend and, you know, run off to the movement.[130]

But in 1964, because of the numbers of white women involved in Freedom Summer, even more attention than ever was focused on the potential for this kind of liaison.

Yet this is only part of the story of relationships in SNCC. Sexual attraction between SNCC workers went far beyond these two most publicized groups. The danger and stress that constantly confronted the volunteers and staff members bred an atmosphere conducive to a broad range of sexual attractions, especially since these young people were just at the age where they were experimenting with their sexuality. Dion Diamond discusses the sexual energy that seemed to permeate field activities:

> Civil rights workers were . . . somewhat analogous to a present-day jock, or a movie star, or a player of a big band. And there were groupies. I mean it was instant access to, at least for the men, sex. Unabated sex. And I think if there were one hundred

... black civil rights workers, I would dare say that 99 percent took advantage of it.[131]

Similarly, Ann Romaine recalls, "It [sexual tension] was very strong in the atmosphere."[132]

In Gwen Robinson's estimation, the field staff adopted a macho persona in order to survive the extreme rigors of the field. She termed it "macho to the max." Part of this persona was a kind of sexual assertiveness that was not directed exclusively at white women. Quite often black women had to deal with advances from coworkers. Because of the limits placed on her sexual views by her black middle-class upbringing, Robinson found such behavior patently offensive. Her response to it? "Go to hell."[133] Fay Bellamy recounts how another black woman tried to head it off during a SNCC conference at Gammon Theological Center: "Annie Pearl Avery said . . . put a little announcement out. She said, 'Anybody that comes to my door and tries to come in there without permission, I'm going to hurt you.' "[134] What is most important to recognize here is the existence of sexual attractions between black men and various women in SNCC—not just white women. According to Martha Prescod Norman, a northern black SNCC worker, it was absolutely untrue "that black men who were in the movement, you know, who were fighting for civil rights . . . had so little race consciousness that all they had to do was see a white woman and they lost their minds."[135]

But despite the existence of a broad range of sexual attractions and combinations, the focus of many has remained fixed on black male/white female liaisons, particularly during Freedom Summer. Such an exclusive focus has led to grossly distorted assumptions regarding black female attitudes. Many of these distorted assumptions originated with white workers in the movement but were later popularized by scholars of the movement. For example, Doug McAdam, in his work *Freedom Summer*, insists that black women were angry at white women and black men because of the "sex thing." He reasons that one of the most important explanations for that anger was that "sexual or romantic relationships granted the white women unique access to some of the most influential black men within SNCC. In turn, this access threatened to eclipse the political stature and influence that the black female staffers had struggled long and hard to achieve."[136] There are many who strongly disagree with this assertion.

For example, in her examination of the history of African-American women in the movement, Paula Giddings argues that just the opposite was true: "In fact, the influence of Black women was actually increasing. . . . it was White women who were being relegated to minor responsibilities, in part because of indiscriminate sexual behavior."[137] SNCC organizer Charles Jones also provides an alternative viewpoint:

> I think a lot of what white women were perceiving in terms of reactions of black women was somewhat limited, I think. They were limiting it to the sexual level. But what we're talking about is power games period that women were playing with women, some of whom happened to be black, some of whom happened to be white. And the jealousies or the envy were on a lot of different levels. . . . *White women couldn't come in and get over on their bodies alone.* [Emphasis added].[138]

Ruby Doris and her black female colleagues would have been appalled at the suggestion that any woman in SNCC could sleep her way to the top. They knew that white women's access to influential black men in the bedroom did not necessarily translate into power in the conference room. Ruby Doris Robinson, Gwen Robinson, Fay Bellamy, Cynthia Washington, Diane Nash—these are just some of the black women whose heroism and commitment guaranteed them a hearing in the conference room. The importance of their actions and positions was not diminished in the least by the sexual preferences of white female staff or volunteers.

Of all the distracting and destructive effects that interracial liaisons produced, African-American women in SNCC were particularly concerned with the effect on preexisting relationships. This concern undoubtedly influenced black female reaction to Jim Forman's choice of partners. Freddie Greene Biddle contends that the main reason why many were so upset when SNCC's black executive secretary, Jim Forman, became involved with new white staff member Constancia Romilly was that Forman was already married at the time. Many SNCC staff members knew and liked his wife, Mildred. When he began to develop an obvious romantic interest in Romilly, they became upset. Dorie Ladner, for example, felt sympathy for Mildred and anger at Romilly: "We were openly hostile to Dinky [Romilly]."[139] Ladner recalls that because Ruby Doris was friendly with Mildred, she was particularly upset with Forman and angry with Romilly.

Ruby made no attempt to hide her anger. Her friend and colleague, William Porter, recounts an informal conversation with her in the office one day:

> Just before the March on Washington happened, . . . Ruby and I were talking about it, and it got back to . . . Jim that Ruby and I

were talking about the March on Washington, mainly . . . who we were talking about that time, . . . Dinky. And Dinky had real long hair, and Ruby and I said one day—I'm sure it was just jokingly . . . we said, "okay, let's go to the March on Washington and let's march right behind Dinky and then we can step on her hair."[140]

Dorie Ladner expressed her anger too. When SNCC sent a delegation to Atlantic City, New Jersey, for the 1964 Democratic National Convention, Jim Forman attended, along with Romilly. His wife, Mildred, remained in Atlanta. One day while Forman and Romilly were strolling on the boardwalk a group of reporters accosted Jim and began to interview him. As soon as Ladner realized Forman was about to be interviewed with Romilly by his side, she reacted swiftly. "I remember trying to push Dinky out of the way."[141]

At the same time, Romilly was aware of how much black female hostility was directed toward her. She declares that she did not cause the dissolution of Forman's marriage but most people thought she did. Because they saw her as the instigator, Ruby Doris and the others were so hostile towards her that Romilly stopped going to the office. Despite her memory of all the antipathy, though, Romilly still insists, "No I don't think Ruby Doris hated white women."[142] Jim and Mildred later got a divorce, and he and Romilly were married. According to some, this was only one of many examples of white female destruction of stable black relationships. As Michael Simmons puts it, "[Black women in SNCC] did not hate white women . . . even though they were being ripped off . . . I mean because white women had no respect for relationships of black men and black women—which every black man knew."[143] Clearly, black female views of interracial relationships were far more complicated than simple sexual jealousy.

All around her, Ruby Doris saw the complications arising from sexual liaisons, and pressure for sexual liaisons, among SNCC staff and volunteers. She also witnessed the inordinate amount of attention that black male/white female liaisons received during the Mississippi summer project of 1964. This angered Ruby Doris because it shifted the focus away from the movement's main goal. As Connie Curry puts it, "[Ruby Doris] did hate the phenomenon that was caused by the supposed chaos that came out . . . black guys trying to go to bed with white women and all of that— . . . she may not have hated [white women] individually, but I bet you ten dollars she hated the chaos caused by that."[144] John Lewis remembers how Ruby chided those coworkers she suspected of becoming involved in such liaisons:

Ruby was very . . . she had a very, sort of facetious and sarcastic way of dealing with things. She would say things like "I saw you. I saw you talking to. . . ." There was a white woman named Sheila Kessel. "I saw you talking to Sheila—you watch it." But she had her own way of jumping on the black men. And she used to say, "Don't talk to me; don't speak to me." And I think some of the white women thought that she was . . . thought that Ruby was anti-white. Not necessarily anti-white, but anti-white-woman. But it's not that she didn't like it or couldn't stand it, but I think she saw that white women . . . were trying to use black men . . . to do their own thing. And she had . . . a way of trying to not necessarily put you down but to let you know in her own way, "I don't like what I saw. I don't appreciate it."[145]

Other black women in SNCC shared Ruby's concern about the potentially destructive impact of these relationships. Their concern, along with their belief that some white women put their own desires ahead of the movement's goals, only served to widen the rift between women, prompting Casey Hayden to note, "Little by little, there was a separation between black and white women."[146] Later, by the time Ann Romaine became associated with SNCC, the rift had become pronounced: "Black women just kept themselves apart . . . pretty much."[147]

Another factor contributing to the rift was the amount of attention that white women—especially the volunteers during Freedom Summer—received merely because they were white. One black female civil rights worker expressed her resentment about this to Dr. Alvin Poussaint in no uncertain terms: "We've been getting beaten up for years trying to integrate lunch counters, movies, and so on, and nobody has ever paid us no attention or wrote about us. But these white girls come down here for a few months and get all the publicity. Everybody talks about how brave and courageous *they* are. What about us?"[148]

Thus, although the gulf between black and white women was a formidable one, the issue of interracial sex was only part of the problem. Yet many white women in this emotionally charged atmosphere had trouble understanding the black female perspective. In many cases, their preoccupation with the black male/white female issue prompted them to make erroneous assumptions about motivations for black female behavior. The recollections of one white female volunteer are particularly revealing: "I just never was able to connect . . . with the two black women on our project. . . . They just seemed

139

to hate me. . . . It was probably the sex thing, *but I never got close enough to find out*" [emphasis added].[149]

Amid this sort of misunderstanding, the notion that Ruby Doris hated white women became quite widespread. Her demeanor undoubtedly helped strengthen this notion. She could be curt and blunt, sometimes to the point of rudeness. But white women were not the only ones who received this kind of treatment. On the contrary, many remember that she could be abrupt with everyone from time to time. As one SNCC staffer puts it, "There were a lot of people in the organization who didn't like [Ruby Doris]. Really didn't like her, I mean. . . . And she wasn't really concerned how you felt personally. I mean, you know, she had a business relationship with you—and if you did nothing, then you were ignored."[150] She simply had no patience for anyone or anything that had a disruptive effect on SNCC's operations.

During Freedom Summer, Ruby Doris was harried, harassed, and stretched to the limit by her administrative duties. In that context, the disruptive effect that a white female presence in SNCC could often cause was just another headache. Quite naturally, this perception influenced the way Ruby Doris reacted to white women. But her reaction was also filtered through the prism of her experience as a black woman in a society that embraced starkly negative views of her physical appearance, morality, and femininity. Although society's judgment had remarkably little effect on Ruby's self-image, or on her dealings with others, she was acutely aware that white America, and black America, too, had always measured her and other black women by a white female standard of beauty and morality. As she sought to refute the validity of that measurement she was confronted by a white female presence in SNCC that mushroomed during that critical summer of 1964. Sometimes she could be kind. Sometimes she was unkind. She liked some, and disliked others. The attitudes of some angered her, while the commitment of others cheered her. In the cauldron of conflicting emotions swirling around in the civil rights movement generally and Freedom Summer in particular, Ruby Doris's feelings about white women were varied and problematic. They were inextricably bound to her perceptions of white female attitudes, her feelings about African-American womanhood, and above all her commitment to the movement.

By the fall of 1964 when Freedom Summer drew to a close, Ruby Doris had experienced some profound changes in her life. With her marriage to Clifford, her personal life had changed drastically. At the same time, Ruby's views of the crusade for social justice had become increasingly radicalized. It had been a long, hard summer, and like so many of her SNCC colleagues, Ruby was both mentally and physically exhausted. At this point, Ruby Doris was presented with an exceptional opportunity: a chance to leave the country for the first time in her life. She was thrilled about the prospect, and she was even more thrilled about the destination. Ruby Doris was going to West Africa—the land of her ancestors, and the land of recent successful liberation struggles. This trip would soon push Ruby Doris Smith Robinson to the next stage of activism.

CHAPTER SIX

The Final Phase of Activism

᠅

SNCC's PREPARATIONS FOR THE AFRICAN TRIP WERE CARRIED OUT IN the midst of a good deal of organizational soul-searching that was prompted by the unique experience of Freedom Summer. SNCC veterans had been profoundly touched by the brutality, broken promises, and insensitivity that accompanied events of that summer. They knew they would never be the same again. And because the addition of large numbers of new staff people had caused a dramatic and irreversible change in the organization's structure, veterans knew that their beloved Student Nonviolent Coordinating Committee would never be the same again either. In the wake of the momentous, traumatic, and tragic events of that summer, many veterans mourned the loss of the camaraderie that had existed among members of early SNCC. They fondly recalled the common bond and vision they had shared during the early years because of the similarities in their backgrounds: most attended southern black colleges, most were from Christian backgrounds, and all shared middle-class values and aspirations. They were truly brothers and sisters united in the struggle.

However, many of the group's new recruits were northerners who did not share the background, perceptions, or even goals of the earlier veterans. Indeed, many of these newcomers brought with them a vision of the civil rights struggle that was at odds with that of many SNCC veterans. Ruby and her colleagues from early SNCC were clearly disconcerted by this alien vision. Consequently, in September 1964, just as Freedom Summer ended, Ruby suggested that the organization adopt a policy of forced southern recruitment. She also advised that SNCC should limit the number of northerners it accepted. Ruby challenged the organization to decide "what kind of a staff [it] wanted to have" and to establish clear-cut and binding criteria for hiring staff.[1] Previously, the organization had accepted just about anyone who wanted to do movement work.

This was only one of a number of issues that needed the staff's attention in the critical weeks following Freedom Summer. But everything would have to wait because in September 1964 a select group of SNCC staff accepted an invitation to visit the West African nation of Guinea. These SNCC veterans were drawn to the African continent by obvious and compelling kinship and ancestral ties. They also shared a spiritual kinship with African freedom fighters battling to rid their continent of European domination. By the time of the SNCC trip, Africans had won a number of victories that were enthusiastically reported in America's black press. For example, *Ebony* had excitedly proclaimed in December 1960, "Freedom comes to 83 million as African rule passes from whites to blacks."[2] Although the rest of the article reported the problems that faced many of the emerging African nations, it still contained words of hope and pride.

But of all the newly emerging nations, the Republic of Guinea struck a particularly responsive chord in African Americans. In 1958, the French, who controlled Guinea and the eleven other colonies included in French West African territory, had offered all their colonies a chance for immediate independence. The offer was conditional, though; only those that continued a "political association" with France would continue to receive badly needed French aid. Those that chose complete independence, on the other hand, were assured that all aid would be discontinued immediately. When the twelve French West African colonies held elections, only one—Guinea under the leadership of Sekou Toure—voted for immediate independence.[3]

The French responded by quickly withdrawing all of their assistance from the fledgling country. Before the separation was complete, however, French President Charles de Gaulle gave the recalcitrant colony one last chance. He flew to Guinea to try to persuade Toure to change his mind, but Toure, whose long reputation as an uncompromising man of principle had earned him the nickname "l'enfant terrible," sent de Gaulle packing. Within a month of Toure's rebuff, the French withdrew everything. All French colonial personnel were sent home, including teachers, judges, and desperately needed medical personnel. Material resources were removed as well; medical supplies, maps, even china plates from the governor's palace were all returned to France. Anything of value was confiscated. The last French personnel leaving the country even ripped the telephones off of the walls.[4]

France had left the new country in desperate straits, but Toure continued his defiance of French authority anyway. His courageous, but solitary, stand made him a potent symbol for African Americans. Therefore, when he visited the United States in 1960, many in America's black press praised his courage and proclaimed his importance. *Ebony* reported: "The pomp and circumstance which surrounded Sekou Toure on his state visit dramatically underscored the importance of Guinea and the rising new states of Africa. As the only French possession to reject de Gaulle's constitution and as the world's youngest republic, Oregon-sized Guinea stands as a symbol to the awakened masses of Africa and Asia."[5]

SNCC's young freedom fighters were eager to exchange ideas and forge alliances with Toure and with other African revolutionaries. They were convinced that the internationalization of their freedom struggle would have profound consequences for the movement's future. Because of the trip's importance, there was a good deal of disagreement and political posturing on the question of who should go. Many argued that SNCC's highest officers should go, while others insisted that those who had worked the hardest in the field should be chosen. Finally, a staff vote settled the question of the delegation's membership, or so everyone thought. But the controversy would not die. Some continued to complain because they had not been chosen. One staff member dismissed some of those individuals as "immature." He continued, "Most of the people complaining about those chosen are not doing the job anyway."[6] Others questioned the selection process itself.

Despite the complaints and the disagreements, members of the delegation departed on 11 September 1964. The group, which included Jim Forman, John Lewis, Bob and Dona Moses, Prathia Hall, Julian Bond, Bill Hansen, Donald Harris, Matthew Jones, Jr., Fannie Lou Hamer, and Ruby Doris Smith Robinson, represented a broad cross-section of the SNCC membership and leadership. After arriving in New York, they prepared to board a Pan American Airways flight bound for Dakar, Senegal. The scene in the airport was chaotic as passengers milled around and Pan American employees dashed to and fro checking on planes and counting passengers. This was the first time that most members of the SNCC delegation had ever traveled outside the United States, and they could barely contain their excitement. Regardless of how much education they had, most of them had learned virtually nothing about Africa, since almost nothing was taught about it in most American schools. Instead, these SNCC people had been exposed to a dizzying array of vicious myths and stereotypes perpetrated and publicized by Hollywood, the media, and the U.S. State Department. But, finally, they would get the chance to see for themselves.

As delegation members sat musing about their thrilling prospects, Pan American agents came to an unpleasant conclusion: they had overbooked the flight. An airline representative asked if the group would be willing to take a later flight. While disappointed delegation members deliberated, Ruby Doris purposefully strode over to the jetway where other passengers were about to board the flight. Before anyone could stop her, she sat down in the middle of the jetway. Ruby's one-woman sit-in worked; the SNCC delegation was given seats on that plane.[7]

The flight was long, but the group soon landed in Dakar, Senegal, on the west coast of Africa. The sights, sounds, and smells differed from anything that Ruby and her colleagues had ever encountered. They saw people of all ages and both sexes sporting garments made of bright African tie-dye. Gold and silver jewelry glinted against rich, dark African skin tones. Lush vegetation flourished everywhere the young civil rights veterans looked. Some of the plants were familiar to the SNCC veterans, only bigger than the ones at home. Others were totally foreign, with huge blossoms that looked quite exotic to these serious freedom fighters.

After a brief stopover in Senegal, the SNCC delegation took a short flight to Conakry, Guinea. All around them the group heard the lilting speech of Guinea's residents, defined by African accents but punctuated by French expressions—a part of the colonial legacy. As the delegation members absorbed Guinea's unique sights and sounds, their consciousness was profoundly altered by the chance to shed their minority status. In the land of their birth, they were constantly conscious of their blackness; it seemed that everyone in a position of authority was white. But in the land of their ancestors, people who looked like them were everywhere, and they were doing everything. Mrs. Hamer exclaimed, "I saw black men flying the airplanes, driving buses, sitting behind big desks in the bank and just doing everything that I was used to seeing white people do."[8] Ruby Doris was equally thrilled. According to Stanley Wise, Africa was a "revelation" to her. "She said the cities are as beautiful as they are here and they are as complete and blacks do everything. Everything."[9] But the delegation viewed these sights through the prism of their American attitudes. Julian Bond recalls that the problem inherent in their unique vision forced most to confront a very painful reality. Bond, like all the others, had received constant messages of black inferiority from American society all his life, and these messages had subtly altered his consciousness. Thus, when he saw a black pilot preparing to fly the group from Dakar, Senegal, to Conakry, Guinea, Bond half-jokingly remarked, "Does he know what he's doing?"[10]

As Ruby and the others confronted the realities of their backgrounds— both African and American—they felt exhilaration, but also pain. Part of that pain was rooted in African reactions to attempts by some members of the delegation to embrace their African heritage. Some in the group bought African garments and had their hair braided. "I can remember Ruby Doris getting herself all done up," says Matthew Jones, Jr. But the makeovers elicited an unexpected response from Sekou Toure's advisors; they thought such actions were naive—and they said so. Jones remarks, "This was confusing for us."[11] The experience showed Jones and other members of the group just how American they were.

Members of the SNCC delegation had frequent discussions with Sekou Toure and his ministers about the global nature of the freedom struggle and their place in it. They even stayed at President Toure's villa. One of the group's members describes a typical evening at the presidential residence:

> Wednesday evening the President dropped by the Villa. This is a habit of his. One does not know when he will arrive. After all, it is his private quarters. Apparently, he found Julie relaxing with her hair down [and] wearing a house coat. Harry was asleep. John, Julian, Don, and I, were in our quarters with Ruby [watch that connotation!] taking our physical exercise.[12]

Ruby Doris was thrilled by this personal contact with the president. She was particularly impressed by Toure's obvious concern for working-class people and by how he treated Mrs. Hamer, a working-class woman.[13] Mrs. Hamer's reaction to meeting Sekou Toure for the first time also moved Ruby Doris a great deal. During that meeting, Mrs. Hamer "started to cry and said that she didn't know quite what she would do with this experience." Such a meeting was particularly significant because "for so long, [Mrs. Hamer] and a lot of poor black folk had tried unsuccessfully to meet with the president of her own country . . . and she could never see him." But in the land of their ancestors, Mrs. Hamer was received by an African head of state, Sekou Toure, who offered "great words of encouragement and hope and a declaration that this Africa was their home and its people their family."[14]

Aside from meetings with government officials, the delegation was treated to a variety of sports and entertainment. Yet whatever they did, the civil rights struggle was never far from their minds. SNCC members eagerly discussed and debated issues of social justice with their African hosts, and both sides were inspired by these talks. As they explored perceptions of the struggle, the SNCC veterans were struck by how much misinformation had been spread about their movement and about the position of black people in American society. For example, the erroneous portrait of black life painted by official U.S. government sources distressed Julian Bond: "There were all these pictures of Negroes doing things, Negro judges, Negro policemen, and if you didn't know anything about America, like Africans would not, you would think these were really commonplace things. That's the worst kind of deceit."[15]

Most members of the delegation returned home on 4 October, after almost three weeks in Guinea. An excited and energized Ruby Doris stepped off the plane brimming with ideas and plans. She had been touched by the genuine affection displayed by the people she met. As Stokely Carmichael declares, "Mrs. Hamer and Ruby Doris just had a time in that country [Guinea]."[16] Beyond merely touching Ruby's emotions, however, the trip to Africa had dramatically altered her consciousness.[17] It had stimulated Ruby's interest in Pan-Africanism: "She talked about how Pan-Africanism could be important within the United States. Within the southern United States, she had a concept of the South as an ancestral home for Africans who came here."[18] The trip had also stimulated broad ideas for international plans.[19] Soon after her return, Ruby Doris suggested that SNCC should explore the possibility of establishing Friends of SNCC groups in Africa, the Caribbean, and Europe.

While the African trip proved personally and professionally fulfilling for Ruby Doris and the rest of the delegation, it raised eyebrows among some members of the American press. An article published in the *Washington Post* in late 1964 charged that the SNCC delegation had met with President Sekou Toure without notifying the State Department and observing proper diplomatic protocol. The article implied that at the very least, SNCC owed the State Department a report on the group's meetings with Sekou Toure. Furthermore, it speculated about whether or not "SNCC [would] put into practice the revolutionary techniques of these emerging [African] countries."[20]

In the meantime, all the serious problems that the delegation had left behind when they went to Africa were still plaguing their organization when they returned. In retrospect, Jim Forman thought those problems were so severe that the delegation should have postponed their trip:

> The trip to Guinea had been a serious mistake. It took away many people who should have helped to steer the organization in the period of transition from summer into fall. Instead of our small group going away, we should have had a long retreat for ourselves and others. People were tired. But we did not think three weeks would make such a difference.[21]

During that relatively short time, SNCC's problems had intensified. Courtland Cox had been left in charge. Much to Forman's dismay, Cox had scheduled a staff meeting on what to do with the large number of summer volunteers left over from Freedom Summer.[22] Just prior to the Africa trip, the organization had vigorously debated this question and had allowed some of the volunteers to become permanent staff members. Both Forman and Ruby had hoped this would end the matter. But now other volunteers were still clamoring to join. Many old-timers were reluctant to accept too many more newcomers, who would undoubtedly change their organization even more. At the staff meeting that Cox had scheduled for October, immediately in the wake of the Africa trip, Forman and Ruby led the fight to block the new hirings. Even before the meeting was called to order, a sense of dread and expectancy settled over the group. For a moment or two Ruby replayed pleasant African scenes in her mind. She could still hear the lilting laughter of Sekou Toure and his ministers when one of her SNCC colleagues told a joke during dinner one evening. She could almost feel the comforting warmth of the African sun on her back; just for a moment, it seemed to dispel some of the gloom in the meeting. But the sense of well-being, belonging, and order inspired by Ruby's African memories vanished when the meeting started. The noise level in the room soared as frustrated SNCC veterans began expressing some of the anger and helplessness they felt. Their organization was changing too fast, and they knew they could not stop that change. Because so many of them were worn out from the disillusionment of Freedom Summer and the betrayal of the Mississippi Freedom Democratic Party, they lacked the energy to fight this internal battle. Thus, in October 1964 many veterans, including Ruby and Forman, watched with a sense of foreboding as eighty-five new people became members of the SNCC staff.[23]

Along with their concern about staff size and composition, Ruby and Forman were worried about the organization's administrative direction. In earlier years when SNCC had been a much smaller organization with a close-knit staff, decisions had been made by consensus. In view of recent changes, however, Ruby Doris and James Forman regarded the consensus method as no longer practical, or even possible. Instead, Forman envisioned an overhauled administrative structure that would make SNCC "a strong, centralized organization expanding its power and moving toward becoming a mass organization."[24] Ruby Doris enthusiastically supported this position.

Although SNCC's October staff meeting had been difficult, the group faced even more tense times one month later during a staff retreat held at the Gulfside Methodist Church in Waveland, Mississippi. In advance of the retreat, a number of staff members prepared position papers on a variety of volatile issues. Charles Sherrod's paper analyzed the crucial changes that had occurred in the civil rights struggle since 1960. He argued that while the early demonstrators had been able to appeal to the "white man's guilt," by

1964 SNCC workers were confronted with "a 'backlash' of the white man's conscience." In this hostile atmosphere, Sherrod insisted, SNCC needed to "organize along more rigid lines" to ensure the movement's success.[25] Others at the retreat also raised issues pertaining to administration and organizational goals.

Listening to this discussion about administrative structure, Ruby Doris Robinson felt an overwhelming fear that threatened to engulf her. She was absolutely certain that in order to survive and prosper, SNCC needed a stronger and more centralized administration. But she was equally certain that only a few of her colleagues agreed with her. Ruby was very uncomfortable. The room was too hot, and she was restless; she was fretting about the future of her organization. Ruby also worried about SNCC's members—particularly, about the feelings of the new staff members. As she put it: "I am concerned that the band of brotherhood has not been expanded. We don't really make people feel a part of that band."[26]

Over the next few days, as participants debated the wisdom of changing the group's administrative structure, some even accused Forman of trying to seize power because of his support for more centralization. Forman was incredulous. His advocacy of stricter administration was because of his concern for the group. He wanted to scream at them in frustration. He wanted to make them understand. As he looks back on the vicious atmosphere, Forman comments:

> The atmosphere of this Waveland meeting reached a new low in bad vibrations and secretive maneuvers. People were cutting each other up in small ways, but never openly criticizing a person. Instead of speaking out, a number of people could be seen circulating around the room, whispering. At one point, Stokely Carmichael came up to me and said, "Forman, don't you understand what's going on here? Those people are just angry 'cause you got so much power. And that's all they're trying to do, undercut that power."[27]

Because Ruby was perceived as both a staunch supporter of Forman's administrative views and a powerful administrator in her own right, the negative attitudes that affected Forman were also directed at her. She, like Forman, was incredibly frustrated. She almost felt like jumping up in the midst of the gathering and shouting at her colleagues, "We all have to make sacrifices to keep SNCC going. We can't all be leaders!" But she did not. Instead, she was momentarily paralyzed by feelings of impotence and sadness as she realized how bitterly divided the SNCC staff really was.

While arguments over administrative structure occupied a great deal of time at the retreat, the group still managed to discuss other topics. One position paper in particular generated more controversy than the others. That paper, originally presented anonymously, addressed the issue of gender discrimination in SNCC. This was not the first time that charges of gender discrimination had created controversy in SNCC. Just a few months earlier, in the spring of 1964, a number of SNCC women had held a strike to protest unequal treatment. Although many members of the SNCC staff vividly recall the strike, most disagree on the details. Mary King insists that she organized the strike, along with coworkers Judy Richardson and Betty Garman. King recalls that a number of women, including Ruby Doris, sat-in both inside and outside of Jim Forman's office. She describes the demonstration as "a show of force" and also "a plea for recognition,"[28] rather than an attempt to address specific grievances. She claims that all those involved, including Forman, "had many laughs" about the women's strike.

Jim Forman's memory of the demonstration is quite different from Mary King's. In his version, he encouraged the women to become militant in their demands for better treatment, and he suggested that they engage in role-playing to make their point. According to Forman, he even invited the women to focus their mock demonstration on his office. But Mary King categorically denies his voluntary involvement: "It is not true . . . that Jim invited this demonstration. It was certainly not his idea."[29] Black female staff member Bobbi Yancy remembers the strike but does not recall whether or not it was Forman's idea. However, she is certain that he "was open to [the strike]."[30]

Stanley Wise's account of the strike differs markedly from both King's and Forman's. As he tells it, Ruby Doris called a meeting of the women office staff and suggested that they have a strike. And the strikers did make a specific demand:

> Women would do absolutely nothing until men recognized that first of all [they] couldn't grab your butts, couldn't grab your breasts. . . . All of the women, every woman did absolutely nothing. They didn't speak; they didn't type any letters; they didn't answer any phones; they slapped you if you touched them.[31]

Wise recalls the strike's dramatic effect: "The organization came to a screeching halt. . . . It was unbelievable. . . . [The women] issued a memorandum of agreements that these were the kinds of activities that women would no longer tolerate in the organization—from anybody."[32] Whether or not the strike was Ruby's idea, most agree that her presence in the office emboldened women demonstrators. As Bobbi Yancy puts it: "I would say that [Ruby's] influence has to be credited with playing a very important role because she was the figure [men] clearly backed off [from]. And that certainly gave other women courage."[33]

Yet despite Ruby's sympathy for some gender issues, some insist that she was extremely critical of the anonymous Waveland paper that charged the organization with gender discrimination. The paper's authors did not mince words: "Consider why it is in SNCC that women who are competent, qualified and experienced are automatically assigned to the 'female' kinds of jobs such as: typing, desk work, telephone work, filing, library work, cooking, and the assistant kind of administrative work but rarely the 'executive' kind." The authors went further and explained why they kept their identity secret: "This paper is anonymous. Think about the kinds of things the author, if made known, would have to suffer because of raising this kind of discussion. Nothing so final as being fired or outright exclusion, but the kinds of things which are killing to the insides—insinuations, ridicule, over exaggerated compensations."[34]

One of the authors of this paper, Mary King, characterizes the audience reaction as one of "crushing criticism." She asserts that when people discovered that she and fellow white office worker Casey Hayden had written the paper, they were both subjected to taunts. So many members of that Waveland audience were preoccupied by questions of administrative structure, disillusioned by events of Freedom Summer, and generally uncertain and even frightened about the future of their organization. In such an atmosphere, complaints about too much typing and not enough fieldwork seemed petty and silly. In fact, very few women in SNCC were interested in exploring gender issues at that time, and a number of black women went so far as to repudiate the paper. King specifically recalls, "Ruby Doris had little sympathy for the questions Casey and I raised."[35] At the same time, however, Casey Hayden does not remember Ruby Doris and the others at Waveland being so critical. Rather, she is convinced that Ruby was actually sympathetic to some of these views.

Regardless of her reaction to the Waveland paper, Ruby's abhorrence of unfairness in any form prompted her to continue to confront gender issues in the organization from time to time. One of those confrontations occurred shortly after Stokely Carmichael made his now infamous remark at Waveland about women's position in SNCC. In an informal atmosphere after the day's session had ended, Carmichael declared, "The position of women in SNCC is prone!" Carmichael has always maintained that he made the remark in jest and that his SNCC colleagues who were present that evening laughed about it. In fact, Mary King, in her memoir *Freedom Song*, supports this view. When the remark was repeated outside of that jovial, relaxed context, however, it did not seem as funny to some of those who heard it secondhand. After Waveland, the infamous comment made the rounds very quickly. One day when Stanley Wise and several others were standing in the SNCC office discussing it, Ruby overheard part of the discussion. Wise tells what happened next:

> Ruby heard [Carmichael's remark] from the hallway, right. And I was outside her office, too. I didn't say it, and I don't know whether Stokely said it or not. I don't remember who said it. But she came out of her office and went [he imitates a slapping sound] right across the side of my face. I said "Ruby, what . . . ?" I mean she just knocked me right across my face. And somebody told her, "Ruby, you know Stanley didn't say that."[36]

She later apologized.

Most of those at Waveland recognized that incidents indicating differential treatment based on gender did occur in SNCC from time to time, even though many did not want to discuss them. However, few thought such incidents meant that the Student Nonviolent Coordinating Committee was a sexist organization. In recent years, movement scholars have formulated various conclusions as they have sought to answer the question; was SNCC sexist? At the same time, former SNCC personnel reflecting on the question of sexism in their organization offer a variety of explanations and assessments. For example, when he was asked if SNCC was sexist, Michael Simmons answered, "Absolutely." As far as he was concerned there was a double standard in the Student Nonviolent Coordinating Committee—at least at times.[37]

Other staff members agree that women were treated differently. For example, Gwen Robinson remembers men and women interacting freely in the SNCC office. "But," she insists, "I also have an image . . . that the males were dominant." According to her recollection, men just naturally assumed the dominant role: "I then start[ed] seeing the women who were doing, you know, a lot of work. But the people who would say something to you first, or you know, tease you, or [talk] to you initially tended to be the guys." Was such female reticence a product of traditional notions of male dominance?

Perhaps. In any case, needs of vocal male staff members were sometimes noticed and addressed more quickly than those of women. Most in the organization agree that harried and harassed central office staff tried very hard to be fair, but some say that expectations of female reticence and male dominance sometimes got in the way. The results could be disastrous, as Gwen Robinson charges: "I was discriminated against as a woman to get resources. And I couldn't get the cars that we needed. I mean I couldn't get equipment."[38] Likewise, Fay Bellamy insists that some gender discrimination existed in SNCC: "Even though the women were in the meetings and things together, the men seemed to . . . have the final opinion."

Despite male expectations of a certain amount of female deference, Bellamy goes on to explain, "there were some sisters who felt that they should have [the final opinion]." In fact, Fay Bellamy was one of those African-American SNCC women who valued their own opinions and expressed them forcefully whenever the occasion demanded it. One of those occasions occurred when demonstrators in Selma, Alabama, were attempting to march across the Edmund Pettus Bridge. Bellamy, who had been working in Selma for some time, was prepared to take her place with the other marchers, but the men had other ideas:

> And I remember when the demonstration was headed up, Forman kept saying, "Get in the back, Fay. Get in the back." I said, "Why?" And he said, " 'Cause we don't want you to get hurt." I said, "Forman, will you shut . . . up? I mean, you got all these [white folks] up here—white preachers, white rabbis, white Catholics, white this and white that—and you gonna tell me to get in the back 'cause I'm female and you want to protect me? You must be insane."[39]

Fay Bellamy was the only woman who marched in the front ranks that day.

Forman's expression of concern for a woman's welfare in a potentially dangerous situation is echoed by some of the male SNCC staff members seeking to evaluate the question of chauvinism in their organization. For example, Hollis Watkins observes:

> If there was a task that had to be done, whoever was available went ahead and did it. And if there were two tasks that had to be done and there were a man and a women to do it, then out of the protective mode that we had there for our women in the movement, the men would generally suggest, "well, let me take on the

more dangerous one because I'd rather confront the plantation owner with the gun than to have you confront him."[40]

In view of the dangerous conditions that existed, Watkins sees such a gesture not as chauvinism but as realism.

Within SNCC, black male notions about the protection of women were influenced by historical realities. Both during slavery and after emancipation, attempts by black men to fulfill traditional male roles, including the role of protector, had been severely circumscribed. For generations, because of their own powerlessness, black men had been unable to effectively defend their wives and daughters against the abusive treatment of a racist society. Finally, when the civil rights movement began to empower black people to assert themselves, many men saw this as an opportunity to fulfill traditional male roles. Their performance of these male roles, particularly the role of protector, allowed black men to affirm their manhood while they worked for social change.

This affirmation, although it soon collided with a budding consciousness of gender discrimination among some white women, was understood by most black women for they shared a history of oppression with their men. Consequently, there were many instances when black women in SNCC did not see black male efforts to protect them as chauvinist. Martha Prescod Norman's attitude and experiences illustrate this line of reasoning. Right after Norman arrived in the South, and had her SNCC orientation, she "went out canvassing with George Greene and Stokely Carmichael, . . . and [she] really decided that was a little too dangerous for [her] tastes." After that first experience, she "tried real hard not to get in a car with them too often." Norman did not feel that SNCC men who expressed concern for her were trying to limit her activities. On the contrary, she adamantly states that it was her decision to let them protect her: "I placed limits on myself." Furthermore, protection notwithstanding, Norman did not feel restricted: "I think there was no way I could have had an image of being limited as a woman."[41]

Martha Norman was not the only black SNCC woman who felt that gender did not determine her role in the organization. Dorie Ladner's experience corroborates Norman's:

I did not feel that there was a role that someone could carve out for me and describe for me to fall into. So when I started out, I started out as an equal partner with my fellow comrades, and that's where I remained.[42]

And, of course, there was the example of Ruby Doris, as Michael Sayer points out:

> Because you couldn't have known Ruby Doris, you couldn't have worked alongside or behind Ruby Doris and then asked the question, "How come women don't play a leadership role in the movement?"[43]

Jean Wheeler Smith, campus traveler and SNCC staff member, concedes that the organization may have appeared sexist to outside observers because "admittedly the structure, the administrative structure on paper was men." But, she argues, "the women had access to whatever resources and decision making that they needed to have or wanted to have and I don't remember being impeded in this." Joyce Ladner agrees, and goes on to argue that part of the organization's response was shaped by the actions and mind-set of the women—particularly the black women—who joined the group:

> None of these women I began to meet knew they were oppressed because of their gender. No one had ever told them that. . . . They had grown up in a culture where they had had the opportunity to use all of their skills and all of their talents to fight racial and class oppression—more racially than anything else. They took their sexuality for granted for it was not as problematic to them as their race and their poverty.[44]

Both Jean Wheeler Smith and Joyce Ladner are convinced that some of the scholars who have examined the question of gender discrimination in SNCC have reached erroneous conclusions. In some cases, the problem is the result of an inappropriate application of current feminist theory to 1960s reality. As Smith puts it, "As time has gone by the history just sort of gets rewritten and revised . . . to the convenience of the people who are rewriting it."[45] Thus, regardless of outsiders' judgments, Ruby, along with many of her movement sisters, refused to be dominated and would not be intimidated. On the contrary, there were times when men were more than a little uncomfortable in Ruby's presence. Fay Bellamy remembers, "A lot of guys would come out of [Ruby's office], like, whipped, you know, having dealt with her."[46]

It would seem, therefore, that in the fluid atmosphere of the Student Nonviolent Coordinating Committee, some stereotypical notions of gender roles existed, but they existed alongside the shared assumption that people had the right to challenge them. Indeed, one movement scholar concludes that in comparison to the larger society around it, SNCC was relatively egalitarian:

> Rarely did women expect or receive any special protection in demonstrations or jails. Frequently direct action teams were divided equally between women and men, sometimes on the theory that the presence of women might lessen the violent reaction.[47]

According to Dottie Zellner: "SNCC had all of the sexism that the society had . . . there's no way that it wouldn't. . . . But . . . the ethic—see there was a very strong ethic inside SNCC—that ethic did break down some of the sexism without us really realizing it."[48] Consequently, Ruby's Student Nonviolent Coordinating Committee was affected by sexism but not dominated by it. In such an atmosphere, Ruby's leadership challenged notions held by some and affirmed hopes cherished by others.

Nonetheless, at that fateful Waveland retreat, SNCC's fluidity exploded into divisiveness amid the rancorous debate over administrative structure and gender discrimination. Yet despite all the tension, the hurt feelings, the grumbling, and the resentment, conferees found the time and the means to relax and enjoy themselves. Michael Sayer remembers, somewhat painfully, the form that the recreation took one evening after the day's session had ended:

> There came some point during that [Waveland meeting] when it was just recreation time. . . . So someone suggested we have a football game. And we played tackle football with no equipment. Ruby was quarterback. We played eleven on a side. Here's Ruby, I mean tough Ruby was quarterback, and I was playing the line and she ran over me. And, first of all, I was just hurt. This was not a cute thing that we were doing.[49]

It seems that the intensity generated in the earlier business meeting followed these young activists onto the football field.

At the close of the Waveland meeting, much was left unresolved and unclear. What was clear, however, was that the Student Nonviolent Coordinating Committee of November 1964 was far different from the organization established by idealistic black college students in April 1960. What was equally clear was that the Ruby Doris Smith Robinson of November 1964 was in many ways a much different person from that young college coed who participated in her first demonstration in March 1960. In some respects, the evolution of SNCC paralleled that of Ruby Doris's thinking. By this time, both had broadened their vision of the movement's constituency and its goals.

During this critical period, late 1964 and early 1965, Ruby Doris continued to take courses at Spelman College; in the spring of 1965, she received her bachelor of arts degree. Also in the spring of 1965, Ruby became a member of SNCC's powerful and important Personnel Committee. That committee had the difficult task of attempting to solve the organization's worsening personnel problems. Serving with Ruby on the committee were Cleveland Sellers, Jessie Harris, Amanda Purdue, and Wilson Brown. In addition to her committee responsibilities, Ruby Doris continued to perform a number of other critical administrative functions. She was the one who received SNCC's incoming donations, she made car assignments, and she had the authority to make staff assignments. In fact, she had sole responsibility in so many areas that Cleveland Sellers referred to her as "a bureaucratic hang-up in the office."[50] As Ruby Doris received more power to govern, however, SNCC became progressively less governable. Often, and increasingly, people in the field would ignore the dictates of the central office staff in Atlanta—no matter who issued the orders.

Gwen Robinson recalls the impact of this open defiance on her attempt to secure a car when she was a project director in Laurel, Mississippi. Gwen requested a car from the SNCC fleet in Atlanta, but the central office decided that she should claim a SNCC car that had been confiscated from Cleveland Sellers by the sheriff in Holly Springs. The central office sent written authorization to a very grateful Gwen Robinson, who immediately made the trip to Holly Springs. After much discussion she was able to claim the car. Finally, Gwen had the transportation she needed. It made her duties as the Laurel project director so much easier, and she quickly settled into a comfortable routine. She could not imagine how she had ever done without the car. Some months later, while Gwen was in a meeting in Jackson, Mississippi, someone (she suspected Cleveland Sellers) hot-wired the car and stole it. Unfortunately for Gwen, the car had some of her personal possessions in it, including her clothes. She clearly remembers her reaction: "I was a mad black woman." Gwen was not only mad; she was determined as well. She decided she would get the car back—by herself. When she eventually located the car, Cleveland Sellers was driving it. Gwen pulled a gun on him and threatened to shoot if he did not get out and give her the keys. Gwen Robinson got her car back.[51]

The increasingly confrontational nature of some interactions between members of the SNCC staff shows just how much the group's thinking had changed. Many refused to continue their support of the nonviolent principles that had shaped the organization since its beginning in 1960. In fact, at one point Ruby Doris even recommended that "[the staff] should have training in judo and karate and gun firing." It seemed that desperate times called for desperate measures. Stokely Carmichael explained the group's new position: "We are not [Dr. Martin Luther] King or SCLC. They don't ride the highways at night. To King and SCLC nonviolence is everything. To us, we use it as a form of tactic and in demonstrations we are nonviolent."[52] In this volatile atmosphere, Ruby tried as hard as she could to make sure that all the projects and their staffs got a fair share of SNCC's resources. But it was not easy. It took all of her determination and her assertiveness to convince her colleagues to respect the organization's administrative authority.

As SNCC's vision changed, the criticism from outside the organization increased sharply. This outside criticism, coupled with the continuing and worsening discipline problems inside SNCC, made it more difficult than ever for the group's administrators. As things got more chaotic, Ruby Doris spent more and more time in the office. Stanley Wise characterizes Ruby's role at this point as that of a problem solver. And at this stage in its development, SNCC had a lot of problems to solve. While many of her colleagues expressed distrust of authority, it seemed that most in SNCC recognized and respected Ruby's commitment, and this seemed to legitimize her authority. Because of this respect, whenever anybody needed anything, "everybody in the organization went to Ruby." She carefully considered each request, and she tried to support her colleagues as much as she could. These efforts endeared her to the field staff.[53]

While it seemed that Ruby Doris tried to take care of everything, she did have certain priorities. One of her main interests was helping local people in Deep South areas who were faced with economic reprisals because of their assistance to the SNCC field staff operating in their communities. In many instances, plantation owners quickly evicted any of their sharecroppers who attempted to register to vote or provided any support or sympathy for SNCC organizers. Quite often these people became destitute because nobody else would hire them. Similarly, when black homeowners sympathized with SNCC activities, they were often threatened with foreclosure by an irate white business community determined to keep their local black citizens in a subordinate position. Ruby felt a huge debt of gratitude to these people. She knew that they were the backbone of the struggle, and she was determined to help them.

SNCC solicited donated items for these people. The items were stored in a fifty-two-thousand square-foot, three-story warehouse that SNCC leased at the corner of Simpson and Marietta Streets near downtown Atlanta. Inside the cavernous warehouse, on the top floor, stood boxes and boxes of adult clothes, their sixties-style colors contrasting sharply with the gloominess of that floor. The middle floor held a happy clutter of children's toys and clothes. On the ground floor, SNCC stored books. Periodically, the Atlanta staff would pack some of these items and send them to project directors to be distributed among the local people. Stanley Wise claims that Ruby's "idea of a good party was to bring a twelve-pack of beer and . . . sit over there and pack these boxes and these books."[54]

Increasingly, Ruby had less time for such pet projects. Instead, she spent more and more hours in the SNCC office because of the volume of the work confronting her. She became increasingly frustrated. She could not attend to all of the tasks demanding her attention, and it bothered Ruby to leave things undone. Mildred Page Forman noticed Ruby's frustration taking its toll:

> There were moments when I . . . had to talk to her, you know, and Jim [Forman] had to talk to her and say "Well Ruby, you need to rest, you need to relax, you're under too much pressure." 'Cause . . . she would spend hours—about 27 hours a day in that office. And it's just too much.[55]

Occasionally, Mildred was able to persuade Ruby to rest. But after only a few minutes, Ruby would be right back at her desk, on the phone, giving orders, solving problems, and generally conducting business.

The stress and frustration sometimes affected Ruby's personality. She could be "very moody sometimes." When she got this way, Mildred insists, it was best to leave her alone.[56] Ruby had her own coping methods. One of them, Stanley Wise remembers, was to keep a collection of Coca-Cola bottles in her office. When the pressure mounted and the frustration became unbearable, Ruby would close both of her office doors. Then she would proceed to throw the bottles against the wall and break them. After she had finished working off the frustration, or run out of bottles, Ruby Doris would open her office doors, go get the broom and sweep up the glass, and return to business as usual.[57]

In 1966, just as major philosophical changes were affecting SNCC, the organization held an election that signaled a momentous shift in its public position. Up to this point, even though it had become more militant, the Student Nonviolent Coordinating Committee had publicly continued to support the goal of interracial democracy and the belief in interracial activism to achieve that goal. As a result of the May 1966 election of officers, however, SNCC became widely perceived as a separatist organization that was becoming increasingly militant and increasingly hostile toward white people. Through this election, which was held in Kingston Springs, Tennessee, Ruby Doris was chosen for the post of executive secretary, the powerful position that Jim Forman had held since 1961. She was the only woman ever elected to such a high office in SNCC. At the same meeting, Stokely Carmichael was elected chairman, and Cleveland Sellers was chosen to fill the newly created position of program secretary.

This was an historic election. It was also a very difficult one. Previously the election of officers had been only a formality because titles meant little in SNCC. When the Kingston Springs meeting started, nobody had any reason to expect that this election would be any different, and initially it was not. As the group was called to order, everyone was completely relaxed. Many of those who had come in from the field were mentally and physically exhausted, and they sat there savoring the chance to feel completely safe for a change, far from the threats and violence that were their constant companions out in the field. Others were only half listening. In that relaxed and partially apathetic atmosphere, John Lewis, who had been SNCC's chairman since 1963, was easily reelected. At the same time, Ruby Doris was elected executive secretary and Cleveland Sellers program secretary. It happened very quickly. But just when everyone thought that the question of officers had been settled, one staff member stood up and declared in a very emotional voice that the election had occurred without adequate discussion. That staff member, Worth Long, insisted that many people had voted to reelect John Lewis only because of their loyalty to a man who had been chairman for so long.[58]

Worth Long's words hit the group like a collective cold slap in the face. The field secretaries who had been savoring the relative safety of the meeting snapped to attention. Long advised his colleagues that before they could elect new officers, they had to decide, "What was SNCC to do in a liberation period? How [was it] to guide the people?"[59] He had no doubt that John Lewis's policies were incompatible with the organization's new direction. After Long had raised the issue, the group narrowly passed a motion to set aside the election results. As the confusion reached a crescendo, uncertainty, resentment, disillusionment, and divisiveness began to surface. SNCC's fractured vision became painfully apparent. Following a good deal of heated and emotional debate, the group voted once again. This time Stokely Carmichael was elected chairman; Ruby Doris and Cleveland Sellers were again elected executive secretary and program secretary respectively.

Carmichael's election sent shock waves through the civil rights community because of the general belief that he was militant and antiwhite. His militant reputation stemmed largely from his organizing activities in Lowndes County, Alabama, in 1965. With Carmichael's help, local residents had founded the Lowndes County Freedom Organization. The emblem that the organization had chosen, a snarling black panther, had sent a militant message, even though the new group was only intended to be an independent political party. Carmichael had clearly stated the group's purpose: "This is a party, it's like the Democratic party and the Republican party. We want power, that's all we want."[60] Regardless of Carmichael's attempts to explain, the national press had linked him, the party's message, and its emblem to the increasingly popular notion of militant black nationalism.

Since SNCC's new chairman was viewed as a symbol of this militancy, many saw Lewis's defeat as a signal that SNCC's days of interracial cooperation were over. Moreover, because they had been elected along with Carmichael, both Ruby Doris Smith Robinson and Cleveland Sellers were viewed as militant and antiwhite as well. There is no record of Ruby's feelings about her election, and her SNCC colleagues have conflicting memories of how actively she had sought it. Outgoing executive secretary Jim Forman recounts that after he decided not to run again, he approached Ruby with the suggestion that she should run for the post. According to his recollection, Ruby was not very receptive to the idea initially: "Ruby was very reluctant. I mean, as a matter of fact, I had probably [to try] and really convince her, you know, that she should do that."[61] Yet coworker Curtis Hayes insists that Ruby wanted the nomination because of her relationship with field organizers: a group that clearly supported her. Consequently, he reasons, "by the time she was elected, she had a tremendous power base. . . . her allies were grassroots organizers—what we call field organizers" who recognized that meeting their needs "was [Ruby's] priority. And that's why she was elected, 'cause [field organizers] wanted somebody in there like that, that [they] could depend on, that [they] could communicate with."[62]

In the opinion of some field organizers, the strength of Ruby's commitment to them was unique among members of the central office staff. Dorie Ladner remembers that the field staff could always depend on Ruby Doris: "She was very reliable in terms of making sure we got our money . . . and she would take care of everything for us."[63] Curtis Hayes even goes so far as to charge that other members of the central office staff, seduced by power and publicity, became virtually indifferent to the needs of the field staff. He angrily exclaims, "They'd [central office staff] be flying all over the goddamned country, and we'd be sitting up on a project with not gas money to take you to the courthouse." Furthermore, Hayes insists that even though people in the field were the ones doing the critical and dangerous work of mass organizing, certain members of the office staff were the ones "who you'd see on TV, and when you'd read the paper, that's who was making the statements." Hayes is sure that Ruby was upset by this imbalance of power and emphasis on publicity. Up to this point, Ruby had demonstrated a personal abhorrence of publicity and a real fear of its potential to corrupt the organization and the movement that is completely consistent with Hayes's assessment. Prompted by this concern, Hayes remembers, "Ruby said, 'Put me in and I'll take care of it.' "[64]

Worth Long describes Ruby's demeanor during the first election as quite matter of fact. Once the first election was over, he says, Ruby Doris left the room and did not return until some time the next day.[65] At one point during the election meeting, Joanne Grant recalls, Ruby Doris took a pistol and went outside to engage in some target practice. Ruby displayed a "jolly" attitude while she was doing this even though she knew that some of her colleagues—particularly Jim Forman—might find her actions disturbing: "Jim Forman was always trying to cool that aspect, so he was a little disturbed."[66]

While Ruby's title changed after the election, her responsibilities did not. She had already been performing most of the duties of the executive secretary long before she was elected to that post, and she had already earned the reputation of being an efficient manager. Most were convinced that her emphasis on discipline and efficiency was exactly what the organization desperately needed at that time. Jack Minnis, a member of the SNCC research staff, even asserts:

> The organization would have been a hell of a lot better off if she had been in such a position [executive secretary] much sooner than she was. Up until that time, there hadn't really been the degree of administrative organization and responsibility that I thought would have made SNCC a much more effective organization.[67]

Minnis goes on to point out that by the time of Ruby's election, SNCC was much different than it had been in the Forman years. By this later period, the organization's staff and assets had grown so much that "it really required an administrative head just to keep all the balls in the air."[68]

One of the major administrative challenges confronting Ruby Doris soon after the election was the problem of reorganizing the Sojourner Motor Fleet.

There had been complaints about the administration of the fleet for some time. In the middle of May 1966, the organization issued a written directive to their new executive secretary: "Mandate; The executive secretary will sit down with those responsible for cars and work out the problems such as location of the cars, the type of insurance, servicing, etc. The staff must understand that SNCC and Sojourner are responsible for the cars and can pull them in and send them to other areas."[69] Since decisions regarding the assignment of cars could sometimes provoke anger from staff members who felt that their projects had been unfairly denied a car, this resentment accounted for many of the complaints about the fleet. But Ruby also had to contend with complaints from some of those who worked on the cars:

> During the time that we have been here, we have heard a lot of comments about the transportation problems. But we honestly feel that the only thing wrong with the SNCC transportation is the policies which direct it. *The policies are aimed at keeping the motor fleet unorganized and impoverished.* [Emphasis in original][70]

The fleet staff clearly explained just how much these policies frustrated them: "We have a lot of things in the garage that should be sold, but who can sell them? We have cars which should be pulled in, who can pull them in? What is the sense in having a garage run by a secretary?"[71] In the midst of these complaints from the fleet staff and other members of the SNCC staff, Ruby Doris began the task of reorganizing the motor fleet.

Another difficult task that confronted Ruby soon after she assumed her new office was the problem of dealing with the Internal Revenue Service. In the summer of 1966, the IRS had begun to demand that SNCC file an organizational tax return. Previously, the group had only been required to pay personal income tax on the salaries of its staff members. Jim Forman was convinced that the IRS's demand for this additional tax return was motivated by an intent to harass SNCC because of the group's newly acquired militant anti-white image. In addition to its demand for the organizational tax return, the IRS also required the group to furnish a list of all its contributors.

Most had little doubt that the Internal Revenue Service intended to use such information to scare SNCC's donors into withdrawing their support. Consequently, the organization adamantly refused to provide the list even though they did file the additional tax return. Ruby Doris spearheaded the battle against the IRS that summer, and her determination to protect SNCC's benefactors never wavered. As Jim Forman recalls:

Ruby Doris never relented in her absolute refusal to reveal those names. Many of us were prepared to go to jail on this point. We would do anything necessary to protect the right of a person to make a contribution to SNCC without his or her name winding up in the files of the FBI, the Senate Internal Security Committee, the House Un-American Activities Committee, or any other repressive agency of the U.S. Government.[72]

In the meantime, SNCC's struggle with the IRS was waged against the backdrop of a very public split in the civil rights movement. Just that spring, SNCC had made the fateful decision to participate in a march that would accelerate interorganizational conflict. Out of this march, which was conceived by James Meredith and intended as a symbolic march against fear through Mississippi, would come a slogan that stirred pride in some, and consternation in others. James Meredith began the march on 5 June 1966. A short time later he was shot by a sniper and had to be hospitalized. Such a cowardly attack angered leaders of the major civil rights groups, and they vowed to continue the march. Although Stokely Carmichael strongly urged SNCC to participate, many were reluctant because they remembered the sense of betrayal they had felt after the March on Washington. Also, many were keenly aware of how critical the more conservative civil rights groups were of the recent changes in SNCC's philosophy and goals. After fierce and emotional debate, Carmichael was just barely able to convince the Executive Committee that the organization should participate. Because of the Executive Committee's strong reservations, Carmichael recalls, he "got a very, very reluctant okay. . . . [He] thought several times about the Committee's words . . . : 'We don't want to hear anything more about this march. Don't call us for help!' "[73]

Regardless of their organization's reluctance, however, a number of SNCC staffers went to Mississippi to join representatives of CORE and SCLC on the march. Day after weary day, the hot Mississippi sun beat down on the marchers' heads, and the heat reflected up off the pavement, making them hotter than most thought possible. In this sweltering atmosphere, the marchers' fatigue was magnified, their patience wore thin, and ultimately their tempers flared. All of this contributed to a feeling of tension and a heightened sense of expectancy as the march dragged on. When the marchers moved into Greenwood on 16 June, that militancy publicly exploded. At a rally that evening, Stokely Carmichael expressed an impatience that excited the crowd's sympathy. Progress was too slow, Carmichael charged: "What we gonna start saying now is 'black power.' " His words electrified the crowd.

They roared back, "Black Power!" Adding to the excitement, Willie Ricks recalls, were members of the SNCC staff among the crowd who enthusiastically echoed Carmichael's black power exhortation. One of those was Ruby Doris Smith Robinson.[74]

The black power slogan was exciting for some, frightening for others, and confusing to many. Those words meant different things to different people. What they meant to Ruby depends on whom one asks. According to her husband Clifford, Ruby's acceptance of black power prompted her to reconsider her views on integration and to embrace a certain amount of black separatism. John Lewis recalls another part of Ruby's ideas about black power, however: "She accepted the idea of black consciousness and the need of black people to be proud and have an appreciation for blackness."[75] Worth Long insists that Ruby's notions of black power transcended national boundaries; she felt that all people of African descent should unite in their efforts to battle racist oppression.[76] What Stokely Carmichael remembers is that Ruby Doris supported notions of black power "150 percent."[77] She even taught her young son to say "black power" when he was only a year old. Regardless of Ruby's enthusiasm though, she refused to let her support for black power circumscribe her vision on the basis of race. Jim Forman recalls, "Ruby was one of the people who consistently upheld the position, as I did, . . . that the problem was not just racial." On the contrary, she reasoned, racism spawned economic oppression, which, in turn, reinforced African-American powerlessness.[78]

Just two months after black power's historic introduction, an exhausted Ruby granted an interview to *Ebony* magazine. Her observations about the direction of the movement and the role of women in the struggle are quite revealing. She argued that even though African-American women were uniquely assertive and had been effective leaders in the civil rights struggle so far, black men should be given even more leadership responsibility than they had already assumed. She went on to suggest that the crusade for racial justice was really men's work after all. Since black men had been so victimized by American society, however, they were not yet ready to shoulder the whole burden. Ruby observed that increasing numbers of black men were becoming involved. She optimistically predicted that in the future, women would not be needed for movement work anymore but that change would come very slowly: "I don't believe the Negro man will be able to assume his full role until the struggle has progressed to a point that can't even be foreseen—maybe in the next century or so."[79]

The views Ruby expressed in this interview are quite curious in light of her unique position as a powerful female administrator in SNCC. Yet her views are remarkably similar to the perceptions of the other black female civil rights veterans featured in the *Ebony* article. For example, SNCC staffer Jennifer Lawson observed, "Often women might prefer *not* to lead, but there's a responsibility to black people at this time that must be met, and it overshadows this business of being a man or a woman." Carolyn Rivers, a New Yorker working in the Alabama Black Belt, agreed and went further: "If Negro men were able to assert themselves fully, they'd be willing to send all the women back home." Rivers did not say whether she thought the women would be willing to go. Finally, Fannie Lou Hamer explained, "But as women, we feel we have done many things that have enabled us to open doors for our men and to show them that when they get their chance, we will be there to back them up all the way."[80]

This advocacy of male leadership by Ruby and the other women is quite curious, since it seems to contradict the example that each of them set. Any attempt to explain the apparent contradiction must examine the difficult reality these women faced. As a result of trying to juggle their traditional female family responsibilities with their leadership commitments, Ruby and the others were undoubtedly suffering from exhaustion and frustration. Moreover, both the popular press and scholars of the black experience were popularizing the notion that because black men had somehow been more victimized than black women, the women were obligated to support male assertiveness. Above all, race loyalty undoubtedly overshadowed gender issues in the minds of most African-American female civil rights activists of this era. They wanted to lead, but they did not wish to assert themselves at the expense of their men. Such a position was fraught with contradictions.

As Ruby and her colleagues wrestled with the issue of gender roles in the later years of the civil rights movement, their views were filtered through the prism of male chauvinism that accompanied the rise of black power. One of the distinctive tenets of the black power philosophy was the belief in black male dominance. For so long, black power advocates argued, black men had been virtually emasculated by white American society. Thus, they must assume leadership roles and reclaim their masculinity as a prerequisite to the empowerment of all black people. Some reasoned that men could only assume their rightful place if women would step aside and stop interfering. Such a negative judgment of black female leadership was inextricably bound to a twisted assessment of the tradition of black female self-reliance. This fallacious assessment blamed black women for emasculating their men through their willingness to assume dominant roles.

As this attitude became increasingly prevalent among black power and black nationalist advocates, black women leaders were subjected to tremendous and often unpleasant pressures. Well-known activist Angela Davis experienced some of those pressures when she organized a rally in San Diego, California, in 1967:

> I ran headlong into a situation which was to become a constant problem in my political life. I was criticized very heavily, especially by male members of [Ron] Karenga's [US] organization, for doing a "man's job." Women should not play leadership roles, they insisted. A woman was to "inspire" her man and educate his children.[81]

Davis found this male attitude particularly ironic, since "much of what [she] was doing had fallen to [her] by default." This was only the beginning of such problems. By 1968, Davis was obliged to confront similar male attitudes in the Los Angeles Chapter of SNCC, where both men and women served on the central office staff:

> Some of the brothers came around only for staff meetings (sometimes), and whenever we women were involved in something important, they began to talk about "women taking over the organization"—calling it a matriarchal coup d'etat. All the myths about black women surfaced. [We] were too domineering; we were trying to control everything, including the men—which meant by extension that we wanted to rob them of their manhood. By playing such a leading role in the organization, some of them insisted, we were aiding and abetting the enemy, who wanted to see black men weak and unable to hold their own.[82]

Other strong African-American women leaders experienced similar problems. Kathleen Cleaver, an officer in the Black Panther Party, was particularly frustrated by male refusal to respect her ideas: "If I suggested them, the suggestion might be rejected; if they were suggested by a man, the suggestion would be implemented." Gloria Richardson, the undisputed leader of the Cambridge, Maryland, movement, faced a forceful show of male chauvinism at a Cambridge rally in the late 1960s. When Richardson attempted to address the crowd, male members of CORE shouted her down and called her a "castrator."[83]

This blatant sexism also became an integral part of the emerging cultural black nationalism of the era. Cultural nationalists sought to define and popularize a black value system that would promote a positive self-image—at least for some. An important part of this value system was an emphasis on black male strength, which was defined in the context of an idealized image of a submissive black woman. In the words of Imamu Amiri Baraka, noted author and activist: "Nature . . . made woman submissive, she must submit to man's creation in order for it to exist." Fellow cultural nationalist Ron Karenga agreed: "What makes a woman appealing is femininity and she can't be feminine without being submissive." The teachings of these cultural nationalists implied that black women who refused to submit to male authority could prevent their men from properly developing a strong male personality. With this in mind, cultural black nationalists demanded that women conform to certain standards of behavior. For example, they thought black women should not use birth control devices, since having more children was the most strategically important service to the struggle that women could perform. They reasoned, "For us to speak in favor of birth control for Afro-Americans would be comparable to speaking in favor of genocide."[84]

Even as many of the cultural black nationalists were calling for black women to have more children, there were some in the scholarly establishment who claimed that black mothers were crippling their sons. For example, psychiatrists William Grier and Price Cobbs insisted that black mothers did this through both example and direct interaction:

> Black men develop considerable hostility toward black women as the inhibiting instruments of an oppressive system. The woman has more power, more accessibility into the system, and therefore she is more feared, while at the same time envied. And it is her lot in life to suppress masculine assertiveness in her sons.[85]

It seems, then, that black women were being blamed and chastised by many, both inside and outside the movement. The debate was sharp, emotional, and exhausting. Strength and self-reliance had been part of the black female role and persona for generations stretching all the way back into slavery. More recently, African-American women had been the leaders and the backbone of the civil rights movement. But now they were being told that they had stepped out of bounds and that the black freedom struggle could not succeed until they returned to their "proper places."

During these unsettling and uncertain times in the latter years of the civil rights struggle, Ruby Doris remained the practical strategist who refused to be persuaded by concepts she thought were impractical or slogans without substance. She always tried to take the most workable ideas and incorporate them into her thinking. In fact, Ruby's practical approach prompted her to offer her opinion to advocates of cultural nationalism who became enthralled with the romantic rhetoric of blackness popular during that era. Stanley Wise describes her reaction to his "conversion": "I remember I became very, very nationalistic . . . and was lauding the praises of why we ought to become Africans and had to go back to Africa for our roots, and she said, 'Stanley [is] just walking on the deep end. Don't worry about him. He'll be all right next week.' "[86] There were others besides Wise whose declarations of blackness she closely scrutinized. Freddie Greene Biddle explains the basis of that scrutiny:

> As far as Ruby was concerned, . . . she had always been black first. . . . And that's basically the issue that she had raised with all the people—with the Johnny-come-latelies who . . . [had] their strong black power thing. . . . That was probably one of the real strong splits with the people . . . what Ruby used to define as the northern blacks who had been so white until all of sudden they became so black conscious.[87]

Despite her attempts to navigate between all the new strains of thought in SNCC, Ruby Doris came to be closely identified with the advocates of black nationalism. Along with this identification, Ruby gained the reputation among some of being antiwhite. Regardless of how widely accepted that notion was, a number of Ruby's close friends and colleagues dispute it. John Lewis points out that like a lot of her black SNCC colleagues, Ruby Doris had to sort out her feelings about her white coworkers.[88]

Her attempt to grapple with these feelings was influenced by both her upbringing in the segregated South and the racial tensions that permeated SNCC. In particular, this attempt forced her to confront difficult and painful realities resulting from a tradition of black oppression and white suppression. Among those realities was the issue of black deference patterns in the South. Generations of African Americans had been socialized to defer automatically to white people. According to some black SNCC staff, their white coworkers expected and accepted this deference from black southerners, especially those in the rural areas. Michael Simmons was one of the black activists who found these behavioral patterns both hurtful and distressing: "I was always struck, you know, when I was in the rural areas, in Arkansas, how when it was time to go home . . . how [much] more grateful the black people were of the white people coming than us, even though . . . , you know, I gave up a lot to go down there." Equally disturbing to Simmons was what he considered white lack of respect for southern black people. One of the signs of that disrespect was "white folks calling black folks three times their age by their first name."[89]

Gwen Robinson also remembers how effusively the local black people praised the efforts of the white civil rights workers. In contrast, the efforts of black activists were almost taken for granted. For example, at the dinner table southern black hosts would routinely serve their white visitors first and treat them to the choicest dishes available. Then they would tell the black activists, "You can come get yours." Such occasions, Gwen remembers, almost always sparked heated discussions among the staff:

> And then when we'd get back to SNCC . . . headquarters, we would, I mean, we would have almost knock-down-drag-outs between the black staff and the white staff. [The black staff would say,] "Why did you sit there and let them fawn over you, treat you like you were some kind of royalty. You enjoyed it." And they would be saying, "No, I didn't. I was just trying to be polite." [And then the black staff would charge,] "You a lie; you weren't trying to be polite. You think you Miss Ann, you know; you think you Mr. Charlie."[90]

Fay Bellamy also witnessed the deferential treatment accorded to white SNCC staff on occasion. She, too, recognizes the existence of black deference patterns, but she suggests that perhaps the white staff were not at fault. Nevertheless, their presence could cause serious problems: "Some people felt that white people, because they were white, were a disruptive influence in the movement. Because African people in the South, because of the nature of their environment, felt beholden." Thus, the dilemma confronting Ruby and her African-American colleagues had less to do with the question of white sincerity than with the effect of a white presence. Fay Bellamy articulates what a difficult dilemma it was:

> You're trying to empower people, and, uh, so what do you do? You can't empower people and then confuse them at the same time by bringing in what . . . might be the enemy in their way of thinking. Even though they [white people] were nice people; they meant well. A lot of people felt concerned with the impact that they had on the black community as a result of being white—which was, of course, not their fault.[91]

Along with their concern about the impact of a white presence in the field, some black staff became alarmed about what they perceived as too much white influence in the central office. SNCC researcher Jack Minnis was one of many white staff members who were clearly disconcerted by such perceptions: "I couldn't see any reason for it. . . . It was not based in reality. Now it may have been a real perception that those people had, but if so, it was a misperception." The reality, as Minnis saw it, was unambiguous:

> I had been with SNCC since '63. Had been intimately involved in its affairs since late '62. And there had never been any question in my mind but that black people ran the organization. I didn't see white people who had any influence at all. Not in finances, not in determining program, nothing.[92]

Regardless of the reality, serious strains and resentment developed between black and white staff. Bobbi Yancy recalls that such resentment prompted a number of the black staff to hold impromptu and informal "venting" sessions, where Ruby was a frequent participant: Ruby "was one of those who felt that we [African Americans] were the people who should be controlling [the organization]."[93]

For a time, Ruby, just like the others, had wrestled with the feelings and perceptions about white people that resulted from a combination of her segregated southern upbringing and her SNCC experiences. But by 1966, when she reached the height of her power, Ruby had finally come to terms with the issue of white activists in the movement. As John Lewis puts it,

> SNCC people go through what they may call their "black nationalist" thing, and then get out of it. Because I know one person who went through it, she was all caught up in it, very early, but no one else was on this "black nationalist" kick . . . that was Ruby Doris back in the early days. She went through this whole period of . . . and she became . . . her closest friend, I guess, happened to be white. But then later . . . she became very close and very friendly with whites, you see, and she tried to convert others.[94]

Worth Long succinctly explains how Ruby could comfortably embrace parts of the black nationalist agenda even as she maintained close relationships with some of her white coworkers: "She wasn't antiwhite, she was pro-black."[95] The evidence suggests, then, that Ruby Doris did not hate white people. Rather, all of her SNCC colleagues insist that she looked beyond race and judged people largely by their degree of dedication to the crusade for social justice. Despite all these declarations to the contrary, however, the association of Ruby's memory with antiwhite sentiments persists. Undoubtedly, part of the reason for this association is rooted in the obvious sympathy Ruby displayed for parts of the black nationalist philosophy. But the other part of the reason is directly rooted in the politics of appearance.

In the mid-1960s, when notions of black consciousness and black power were becoming increasingly important, a rapidly expanding number of young black people began to insist that one's appearance should reflect one's mindset. Consequently, many made a conscious choice to reject middle-class notions of proper dress and hairstyles; they donned African garments and wore their hair in an Afro. While Ruby Doris continued to dress in a very traditional middle-class manner throughout this period, 1964–1966, she did wear an Afro. In fact, she had worn her hair this way long before the mid-1960s. Was Ruby's adoption of this hairstyle truly an accurate barometer of her political position? Or was there more to it than this?

One of the few written references that Ruby Doris made to her hair is contained in a letter she wrote while she was serving a prison sentence in the York County Jail in early 1961. Ruby lamented, "My hair is awful!" Since she was wearing her hair straightened at that time, she probably meant that she was unable to keep it straight because of the conditions she faced in jail. Her cell was very hot, and Ruby undoubtedly perspired a great deal which would have caused her hair to revert to its natural state. In that era, most black women straightened their hair with a metal straightening comb that had to be heated and then combed through the hair to remove the kinks. It is highly unlikely that jailers permitted black female prisoners to keep in their cells all the tools they needed for this procedure. In view of the difficulties of keeping one's hair straight in jail, it is reasonable to assume that when Ruby Doris first started to wear an Afro, she did so because of practical necessity, not political position.

In fact, many black women in the movement wore their hair in a natural, at least initially, out of practical considerations. Dorie Ladner found it necessary to adopt an Afro in 1962. She was attending a SNCC meeting in a rural area outside of Jackson, Mississippi. It was hot, and her hair needed to be washed and straightened, but she did not know where the closest beauty shop was located. She relates what happened when she voiced her concerns:

> Bob [Moses] said, "Dorie, wear it natural, wear it natural." I said, "*Wear what natural?* I can't wear my hair like that." I'd never heard the word natural being used in reference to hair. And all I could think of was my hair being very kinky—we called it nappy—and standing on my head. And I said, "Oh Lord, what's

wrong with you? You must be crazy. I'm not going to wear my hair that way." So I said . . . "I want to go and get my hair straightened." But there was nowhere for me to go. When he said wear it natural, I started screaming and yelling. [Emphasis added][96]

Other black women in SNCC recall that finances often played a role in their decision. According to Mildred Page Forman, SNCC staff made so little money that it was difficult for them to afford regular visits to the beauty parlor to get their hair straightened.[97]

Regardless of the reason, those women who decided to wear their hair in a natural, especially in the early days, were often the objects of curiosity. Black women who had been socialized all their lives to believe that they should always make sure their hair was straightened—no matter what— could not understand women who matter-of-factly wore their hair kinky in public. When Mildred accompanied Ruby Doris to Chicago for a SNCC fund-raiser, Ruby's hair caused quite a stir. As Mildred puts it, "A lot of my friends did not understand this short, natural look, and they would ask me, 'Why does she have her hair cut so short?' "[98] At the time, Ruby had just finished serving her jail sentence for participation in the freedom rides in 1961. When she had first entered jail her hair was straightened, but by the time she was released she was wearing a natural again.

Sometimes, those who were curious about the new hairstyle were also politely critical. "One time we were shopping," Mildred Page Forman recalls: "and a lady came up to another girl, who wore a natural, and gave her a card for a beauty shop and told her, 'I can make your hair grow.' And we laughed."[99] There were other times when the criticism could be blunt and painful, as Gwen Robinson learned after she decided to wear a natural at Spelman in the early sixties, before Afros became common or popular:

Well, first of all, I got called into the dean's office. And her thing . . . her first question was, "What is wrong with your hair?" And, of course, at that point, I had become a little sophisticated, and I said, "To my knowledge, there's nothing wrong with my hair. What do you mean?" And she said, "Don't get smart with me, you know what I mean. What have you done to your hair?" And I said, "I washed it." And she said, "And left it like that?" And I said, "Yes [it's] called a natural or an Afro," you know, and she said, ". . . it's a disgrace. . . ."[100]

174

The dean also told Gwen that as long as she wore an Afro, she would never "get a man." Ruby Doris's sister Catherine remembers that she did not think the Afro hairstyle was very flattering to Ruby. She also remembers that she was not about to offer Ruby her opinion.[101]

Even as they faced quiet disapproval and sometimes vocal criticism, those women who, like Ruby, decided to wear an Afro during the early days ran into an additional problem: they sometimes had trouble finding hairstylists or barbers who understood what to do with their hair. When Freddie Greene Biddle decided on an Afro, she asked a SNCC friend of hers, Jennifer Lawson, to cut her hair. Once Lawson finished, Biddle still did not have an Afro—exactly. Just previous to this, Biddle had had a permanent put in her hair to straighten it. Since the permanent had only partially grown out by the time Lawson cut it, when Biddle washed her hair, parts of it remained straight. Biddle had what she calls "pinpoint ends" that stuck out. This was not the effect she wanted.

After this experience, when one of Biddle's friends came to her for advice about Afros, she suggested that they consult a professional barber. That friend, Ethel Miner, had hair that was quite different from Biddle's; it was naturally much straighter. Such hair presented a real challenge to any barber who attempted to style it in an Afro. Unfortunately, the barber that Miner and Biddle chose was not up to the challenge.

> So we pick[ed] out this guy who had a barber shop. So he turn[ed] out to know as little about cutting hair as Jennifer, 'cause he whack[ed Ethel's] hair up something terrible. So he [told] her . . . "when you wash yours tonight it's going to look like hers"— meaning me. Then we knew . . . he didn't know what he was doing. Because anybody could look at Ethel and [me] and tell that we didn't have the same grade of hair and that she could wash hers for a hundred years [and it wouldn't look like mine].[102]

Trying to wear an Afro in the early sixties could be quite a frustrating experience indeed.

By the middle of the decade, and especially after the popularization of black power, Afros for both women and men became accepted and expected. In fact, the bigger the Afro the better, since by this time hair had become a politically sensitive issue. Many of those who wore their hair in a natural insisted that this was a critical outward symbol of their inner commitment to the cause of black freedom. Conversely, those women in the movement who continued to straighten their hair sometimes had their sincerity ques-

175

tioned and their motives attacked. Freddie Biddle recalls the defensive pos-
ture assumed by some who refused to wear an Afro:

> There were the people who were changing their hair and the
> people who wouldn't change their hair, and all the stories people
> would tell, you know. Somebody would say, "Oh, I would wear
> an Afro, but my hair just won't get like that . . . my hair is just
> naturally straight. . . ." I definitely think a lot of people who
> didn't in those days change their hair felt self-conscious, and they
> did make up myths about the fact . . . "my hair won't curl up like
> yours. Ooh, I would wear my hair just like yours *if I could*." [Em-
> phasis added][103]

Was Ruby Doris influenced by the political rhetoric attached to hairstyles
by the mid-1960s? This woman, who had begun wearing an Afro in 1961,
long before hair was viewed as a political symbol, apparently had no qualms
about straightening her hair for brief periods from time to time after this. A
number of Ruby's friends and family members recall intervals when she wore
her hair straightened as late as the mid-1960s. For instance, in 1965 when
Mary Ann got married, Ruby Doris straightened her hair for the wedding.

According to Mary Ann, Ruby became quite impatient with those who
were determined to attach so much significance to hair. There were times
when she protested that she should not even have to comb her hair if she
chose not to.[104] In view of her casual and practical attitude about hair, it is
doubtful that Ruby Doris's choice of hairstyle reflected her political beliefs.
Rather, it appears that this choice indicated her refusal to allow anyone—
either black or white—to define proper appearance standards for her as a
black woman.

Regardless of the importance of the debate about hair and other outward
symbols, it is clear that a profound shift in SNCC's thinking had occurred
by the mid-1960s; most of the group's members were much more militant. In
the face of this increasing militancy, SNCC began a systematic attempt to
formulate an organizational position on black power. That position started
to crystallize when the group had to reply to a White House invitation to a
civil rights conference in late 1966. Although they had not yet finished
formulating a group policy, their response to the White House invitation
was very revealing. At a SNCC Central Committee meeting in October
1966, Ruby Doris introduced a motion stipulating that SNCC should not
attend the conference. It passed. Ruby further suggested that the organization issue, to all SNCC offices and to the "ghetto," a statement explaining

its refusal to attend. She did not think that this statement should be made available to the press, however. After some deliberation, the group decided to assign Charlie Cobb and Ruby Doris to draft it.

Once she and Cobb had finished, Ruby issued the following statement:

> The Student Nonviolent Coordinating Committee believes the White House Conference entitled, "To Fulfill These Rights," is absolutely unnecessary and rejects its invitation to participate in this useless endeavor for the following reasons: (1) The founda-tion and consequences of racism are not rooted in the behavior of black Americans, yesterday or today. They are rooted in an attempt by Europeans and white Americans to exploit and dehu-manize the descendants of Africa for monetary gain.[105]

The statement went on to cite, among other reasons for not participating in the conference, SNCC's certainty that the federal government was not truly committed to ensuring black constitutional rights. Furthermore, Ruby ar-gued, SNCC refused to meet with a president it viewed as "the chief policy maker of the Vietnam War." She ended the statement by asserting:

> We reaffirm our belief that people who suffer must make the deci-sions about how to change and direct their lives. We therefore call upon all black Americans to begin building independent po-litical, economic, and cultural institutions that they will control and use as instruments of social change in this country.[106]

In addition to their consideration of the civil rights conference, the Cen-tral Committee faced a number of other difficult issues at their October meeting. One of the most difficult was the question of limitation of freedom of speech by SNCC staff members. In the early days, the organization had always prided itself on its celebration of democracy and individual rights. As philosophical differences among SNCC members became more apparent, however, many began to express their alarm about the prospect of individuals who claimed to speak for the organization issuing conflicting statements. This alarm reached the crisis stage after Stokely Carmichael was elected chairman. Carmichael was an exceptionally charismatic figure who received a lot of attention from the press. There were some who complained that Carmichael's views were quite provocative and often inconsistent with the majority opinion in SNCC. Many, including Ruby, were particularly trou-bled by Carmichael's advocacy of the destruction of Western civilization.

The amount of media coverage Carmichael was able to command finally made Ruby demand in frustration, "How could one individual make such a tremendous impression on so many people in such a short period of time . . . so much so that to some people SNCC is only the organization that Carmichael has at his disposal to do what he wants to get done?"[107]

As far as Ruby Doris was concerned, Carmichael's instant media access could be dangerous, since "at his best, he ha[d] said what [the masses of black people] wanted to hear," but "cliche after cliche ha[d] filled his orations."[108] Ruby's fear of the consequences of Carmichael's statements provoked her to action during that October Central Committee meeting. She insisted that Carmichael be stopped from holding a press conference to express his views about the draft. Accordingly,

> Ruby . . . called for the organization to silence Stokely on the grounds that what he was saying was contrary, which it was, to what the organization had been putting forward. And that she felt that if we didn't silence him that the organization ran the risk of not being in existence.[109]

Ruby further advised her colleagues to issue a fact sheet explaining the organization's position. Although there was a great deal of discussion on Ruby's proposal to silence Carmichael, the group never took any official action.

In the aftermath of this latest disagreement, it was becoming more and more obvious that serious splits were threatening to choke the life out of SNCC. But the worst was yet to come. Finally, at the end of 1966, the crisis that clearly meant the beginning of the end for SNCC erupted with a vengeance. It had been smoldering since the end of Freedom Summer, and it was rooted in the question of the proper role for white people in the movement. While that disagreement had been an emotional one all along, it took on added passion when a group of SNCC staff members established a project in Atlanta. The initial motivation for the establishment of that project came from the Georgia legislature's refusal to seat Julian Bond. Even though Bond had received a clear majority of the vote in an election for a seat in the Georgia House of Representatives, the legislature refused to seat him because of his anti-Vietnam War statements. In response to the legislature's decision, SNCC staffer Bill Ware requested and received Jim Forman's permission to start a SNCC project in Bond's district to build support for him.

During the project's earliest days, an interracial staff worked to improve living conditions for the residents of Bond's mostly black and poor district.

Within a short time, however, the black members of the Atlanta Project staff broadened their goals to include community empowerment. Their organizing appeal to residents included their advocacy of racial separatism. As far as they were concerned, only black people should be involved in any programs designed to liberate and empower African Americans. They reasoned that such a strategy would create "a sense of pride in their [African Americans'] beauty, strength, and resourcefulness; and also a meaningful sense of self-respect that they can only gain when they see Black people working together accomplishing worthwhile programs—without the guidance and/or direction and control of non-Blacks."[110] Because of their belief in black separatism, however, the Atlanta Project staff soon found themselves in serious conflict with the Atlanta central office staff. The conflict was quite emotional and sometimes even nasty. Gwen Robinson, a member of the Atlanta Project staff, remembers shouting matches that erupted between the two groups. She also recalls that even though Ruby Doris sided with the central office staff, she still managed to maintain cordial relations with members of the Atlanta Project staff.[111]

Continued pressure from members of the Atlanta Project would soon force SNCC to make a decision about the few remaining white staff members in the organization. To watch this controversy sap SNCC's strength was exceedingly painful for Ruby Doris. All summer she had been battling with issues of discipline inside the organization, and with the IRS on the outside. Throughout the fall, as the continued grumbling and bickering over the race issue practically paralyzed SNCC, an increasing number of members—both black and white—left the organization. As she watched SNCC's life ebb away, Ruby reacted angrily to the racial focus. Freddie Greene Biddle recalls that even though Ruby Doris expressed support for some black nationalist ideas at this time, she was quick to criticize those who did not want to work but would rather "sit around talking about white people."[112]

The conflict finally came to a head when SNCC met on 1 December 1966, in upstate New York at a camp owned by the black comedian Peg Leg Bates. Amid much bitterness and divisiveness, the staff began to discuss the issues that troubled them. But Jim Forman noticed that "some of the leadership were so high from smoking pot that they could not participate in any meaningful discussion." By this time, the drug culture of the 1960s had caught up with some members of SNCC. Some, like Forman and Ruby Doris, saw such behavior as another indicator of the breakdown of discipline in the organization. Forman was incensed. He was so angry that he "wanted to knock 'the shit' physically out of one leading personality for [Forman] felt that he encouraged this corruption of the organization."[113] Forman later introduced a motion stipulating that SNCC be dissolved and its funds be sent to Guinea to support African liberation movements. The motion was defeated.

No matter what issue the staff began debating at the Peg Leg Bates meeting, it seemed that the discussion always turned back to race. Even though there were only seven white people left on the SNCC staff, the Atlanta separatists and their supporters insisted that all white people should be removed. The emotional and intense debate on this issue lasted several days. Even those who were philosophically opposed to the separatist position had to admit that a white presence in the black freedom struggle did cause problems. On the other hand, a number of these white activists had proved the strength of their commitment, and black SNCC staff, including Ruby Doris, had developed very close relationships with some of them. Listening to the debate, Ruby struggled with the paradoxical view of SNCC's white members as both a problem and an asset to the organization.

During the course of the discussion, it became apparent that the black–white rift was accompanied by an old–new rift. The majority of those demanding the expulsion of white staff were relative newcomers to the organization, while the majority of those, like Ruby, who had been there from the beginning were reluctant to take this drastic and final step. Jim Forman recounts that many of the more recent recruits even began attacking those black old-timers in the organization who disagreed with their stand against white people.[114] As the angry shouting and emotional testifying continued, many fondly and sadly remembered the "band of brothers, circle of trust" that had characterized early SNCC. They knew that that SNCC was gone forever. Likewise, Ruby Doris heard the charges, countercharges, and ugly accusations, and knew that the organization she had given her life to build and administer was falling apart. She felt the anger in the air. But she also felt an overwhelming sadness and a sense of emptiness.

When the vote on the question of white expulsion finally came, it was very close. Nineteen voted in favor of expulsion, eighteen voted against, and twenty-four abstained. The large number of abstentions is indicative of the ambivalence many felt on the question. There is no record of how Ruby voted, but Freddie Green Biddle recalls: "The split that came in SNCC in terms of the black–white thing, [Ruby] definitely was not pushing that. She was not pushing kicking [white people] out."[115] Still another of Ruby's coworkers, Jack Minnis, argues that Ruby's practical nature would have prevented her from supporting white expulsion. Ruby Doris would have understood that such a move would destroy the organization's fund-raising base, which still depended on white support.[116] Thus, it is probable that Ruby Doris either voted against white expulsion or abstained.

Once the vote was taken and white expulsion became official, everyone was forced to confront the emotional pain. SNCC had been more than just a group of civil rights workers for some time; it had been more like family: "a band of brothers, circle of trust." As the meeting adjourned, the anger, hurt, and raw emotions were exposed. Freddie Greene Biddle describes the emotional turmoil that enveloped the gathering:

> There were certain things that were really very, very hurtful. I mean, the Zellners, who I had known a long time, I mean I had really known a long time . . . and I felt real bad about them personally.[117]

Despite Biddle's sympathy for white SNCC staff, she concludes that "in the end it was very clear—it was something SNCC had to do because it was splitting up the organization."[118]

It had been a distressing and turbulent year for both Ruby and her organization. She left the Peg Leg Bates meeting sick at heart, and also physically ill. Shortly after this, Ruby would enter the hospital and begin the final phase of her life. It would be a difficult and painful phase for her. It is more than a little ironic that during her months of suffering and sickness, SNCC was passing through the final phase of its life too.

CHAPTER SEVEN

Liberation

THE BITTERNESS AND ACRIMONY OF THAT PEG LEG BATES MEETING WERE like a cloud hanging over what was left of the Student Nonviolent Coordinating Committee. The organization's members left New York with heavy hearts. They felt an overwhelming sense of grief and loss for the organization that had been such an important part of their lives. They wondered where they should go from here—or even where they could go from here. Yet Ruby Doris was as determined as ever. In January 1967 soon after the Bates meeting, she flew to New York City to attend a fund-raiser. Because she had not been feeling well just prior to her departure, both her mother and her husband advised her against making the trip. Ruby would not be dissuaded.

She managed to sit through the program, but later when Ruby was in the airport waiting to board her return flight to Atlanta, the friends who had brought her there became alarmed by her appearance. Her color did not look normal, "and then they started feeling her all over, and they said, 'Dee you don't look good. . . . You're too hot. We can't let you catch that flight.' "[1] Even though she was quite ill, Ruby protested, "Oh, I'll be all right." She was so sick, though, that her friends prevailed. They took her to Beth Israel Hospital, where she was admitted immediately. Doctors ran test after test, but they had trouble making a diagnosis. Ruby Doris's condition continued to worsen. Her sister Mary Ann, who had a master's degree in biology, brought in a hematologist to consult on the case. Upon the hematologist's recommendation, Ruby's spleen was removed. Surgery resulted in complications, however; Ruby almost bled to death.[2] A short time later, she contracted infectious hepatitis from a blood transfusion. Visitors had to wear robes when they went to see Ruby to minimize their risk of infection until she recovered from the hepatitis. Finally, in April the doctors made a dreaded diagnosis. Ruby Doris Smith Robinson had terminal cancer. As the doctors broke the news, Ruby's family could not believe what they were hearing. Ruby was young; she was strong; she was determined. She simply could not be dying. The doctors talked on about Ruby's prognosis and her care, but her family could only stare uncomprehendingly as the shock, horror, and disbelief settled over them.

Ruby remained in Beth Israel Hospital until June 1967, when her family took her to Grady Hospital in Atlanta. Spending all those months in the hospital was incredibly difficult for Ruby Doris. Her anger at the confinement was so overwhelming that it threatened to suffocate her. She desperately wanted to get back to work, since there was so much unfinished business in her life—family business and movement business. Because of her dedication to both, she tried to carry on as much as possible. Bob Zellner recalls, "She wouldn't slow down, and she wouldn't . . . she didn't give up until the very end."[3]

As Ruby was particularly concerned about maintaining contact with her son, Toure, she asked her family to bring him to the hospital for frequent visits. Catherine recalls the pain and frustration that Ruby felt every time she looked at Toure and realized she would not be around to raise him. Inside her head Ruby kept saying to herself, "I will not leave him; I cannot leave him." Her desperation mounted as she lay in the hospital day after day and tried to banish her illness through sheer force of will. During these difficult months, she continued to discuss movement business with SNCC colleagues who came to visit. On one of Willie Ricks's visits to the hospital, Ruby Doris chastised him for failing to complete some SNCC business: "She was still raising hell. She still was, you know, very strong."[4]

Through the pain of the illness that had her so firmly in its grip, Ruby Doris was clearly aware of the decline of her beloved Student Nonviolent Coordinating Committee. She desperately wanted to use her influence to reverse that decline, but her physical condition prevented her, and she fretted over this. In May 1967, in the midst of Ruby's hospital stay, the organization elected a new chairman: H. Rap Brown. At the same time, the group declared itself a "human rights organization" that was shifting a large part of its focus to support Third World freedom struggles.[5] One international crisis in particular attracted SNCC's attention. That crisis, the Arab-Israeli conflict, had already stirred a great deal of emotional debate among many in the country. Clearly, SNCC entered a political minefield when members began choosing sides.

A vocal faction within the organization unequivocally favored the Palestinians and this angered many of SNCC's remaining white and Jewish supporters. Without the organization's official sanction, some of the pro-Palestinian SNCC members publicized their view in an article in the July

1967 edition of the SNCC newsletter. The article caused serious problems within the group because most in SNCC, while sympathetic to the Palestinian position, had no wish to publicize this. Many were afraid that their involvement in such an emotional conflict could generate "external pressures" that would have a disastrous effect on their already weakened organization. In fact, just as they predicted, the article touched off a storm of protest among many of SNCC's white former allies.[6] Had she been in the office, Ruby Doris would have deplored her colleagues' acting without official organizational sanction.

As SNCC wrestled with the fallout from the July article, an irreconcilable split that revealed deep philosophical differences became increasingly obvious. Members of one faction which coalesced around Stokely Carmichael, supported racial separatism and became increasingly hostile to the idea of black–white coalitions. The other faction believed that many of the ills suffered by African Americans were rooted in class oppression as well as racial oppression; this group was drawn to Jim Forman. It was much more open to the idea of forming alliances with white radicals. This latest split only served to weaken further the already wounded organization. Through the summer of 1967, as SNCC's factions fought with each other, some of the nation's cities again erupted in racial violence. The biggest riot of the summer began on 25 July 1967 in Detroit, Michigan. Before the riot ended forty-three people died and millions of dollars worth of property was destroyed.[7] It seemed that racial polarization and strife had reached a new high.

It was against this volatile background that Ruby Doris attempted to make her peace and come to terms with her condition during the last months of her life. Because she had always been such an active and forceful woman, it was very difficult for her to sit on the sidelines. She was frustrated, she was resentful, and she was angry. During those painful summer months in 1967, her emotions were complicated and sometimes wildly unpredictable, but flashes of the old tough, uncompromising, and demanding Ruby Doris shone through from time to time. Joanne Grant, one of her SNCC colleagues who visited her frequently in Beth Israel Hospital, witnessed a brief return of the old Ruby. Because Ruby did not like hospital food, Grant would often prepare meals at home and bring them to the hospital. While Ruby was grateful, she was still quite particular as Grant illustrates:

> Sometimes I'd ask her what she wanted and she'd say spaghetti. I made it and I had this hot thermal bag that I'd pack everything up in, you know, and jump in a cab and dash over there. And she'd say "there's not enough sauce on this."[8]

Grant remembers that Ruby enjoyed "down home" southern food. She was especially fond of catfish.

Ruby Doris was equally particular about the kind of care she received. There were times when she questioned the quality of her care and openly expressed her displeasure. Joanne Grant was present on one of those occasions: "Even there, as sick as she was, she was tough. She . . . broke her IV bottle—smashed it against the wall. She said it was not dripping right. And she smashed it."[9] In the midst of all her frustrations, Ruby Doris was plagued by financial problems that only added to her sense of helplessness and impotence. Both she and Clifford were wholly dependent on their SNCC salaries, which can be described as modest at best. Once Ruby was incapacitated, the family budget was in serious jeopardy. But because members of the SNCC administration were sensitive to Ruby's plight, they continued to provide financial support.

Stanley Wise, who was appointed SNCC's executive secretary after Ruby became ill, tried to reassure her that the organization would not abandon her financially. Wise's written assurances reveal just how stressful the financial issue became: "I also wanted to write you because after you called the other day, Freddie came to me in tears about how she had upset you. It seems that Cliff says that we are not meeting our responsibilities. I have here four checks for the month of April—three of which were given to Cliff. On April 7th a check #2421 for $85 was sent to Thelwell and Yalding Realty. That was the only check which Cliff did not get because it was sent directly to your realtor here in Atlanta." Wise went on to give Ruby the details of other payments that SNCC had sent to her husband. At the end of his note, Wise included one final reassurance: "I shall always henceforth send you a copy of each returned check and irregardless [sic] of our financial situation Cliff will have a check."[10] Despite SNCC's efforts, Ruby's financial situation steadily worsened. Even after she died, the financial woes continued.

Three of SNCC's administrators, H. Rap Brown, Ralph Featherstone, and Stanley Wise, appealed for funds in her behalf after her death: "Because of Ruby's extended illness, bills were incurred in the amount of $30,000. Of that figure $20,000 is being paid by the insurance company; therefore, it is most necessary that we ask for your financial support."[11] Others in the organization were concerned, too. They established a memorial fund to pay Ruby's medical bills and provide some support for Toure: "I will send money for Ruby's Memorial Fund. I wish every person Ruby touched would do likewise. We would have enough to pay her hospital bills and educate her son."[12]

Ruby Doris Smith Robinson was a proud and independent woman. The loss of financial and physical independence that resulted from her illness was an incredibly painful burden for her to bear. Those closest to Ruby who witnessed her rapid physical decline remember their own pain as they struggled to accept the permanence of her condition. Joyce Ladner remembers telephoning Ruby in the hospital. Ruby did not say much; in a matter of only forty seconds or so, she drifted off to sleep and her sister took the phone. That was the last time Joyce would ever talk to her. Gwen Robinson describes her shock at seeing Ruby:

> It wasn't until I went to the hospital to see her that, I mean—I was not prepared for what I saw. Because it was—first of all, her voice never changed. It was very . . . she had a strong voice. And when I went in, she said, "Hi Gwen," and it was her voice. But the person in the bed was like, I mean—I don't know what my reaction might have been to her. But she had wasted away. It was like a skeleton in the bed. . . . I wasn't prepared.[13]

Courtland Cox, who visited Ruby in the hospital in New York, confirms Gwen's memory: "She literally wasted away."[14] During the earliest part of Ruby's hospital stay, Willie Ricks used to "joke and clown with her" when he visited. As the illness continued to take its toll, however, Ricks began to see things differently: "One day I went there and just realized it wasn't a joking matter—it was serious."[15]

While her friends and SNCC colleagues witnessed some of Ruby's suffering, it was her family, particularly her sisters, who were closest to her pain during those last months. Mary Ann spent a great deal of time with Ruby during the early weeks of her confinement at Beth Israel Hospital in New York. Once Ruby returned to Atlanta, her doctors at Grady Hospital decided that there was little they could do for her. Consequently, they agreed to discharge her if the family could arrange twenty-four hour supervision. At this point, Catherine readily agreed to stay with Ruby.

Caring for Ruby as her condition deteriorated was physically demanding and emotionally draining. But Catherine soon realized that coping with Ruby's partial loss of memory during those final weeks was particularly difficult. On one occasion, Ruby could not remember what she had asked Catherine to cook for breakfast.

> Like, she would tell me to fix her some pancakes and sausage, and after I fixed that she would cry and say, "Oh, I don't want that. I told you [to] fix me some grits and eggs." She couldn't remember.[16]

187

On another occasion, Ruby's memory loss caused her to accuse Catherine of refusing to help her. It all started when Ruby began suffering from a great deal of pain and she asked Catherine, "Call the doctor. I need a shot, I'm in so much pain." Catherine quickly arranged for the doctor to come by the house and give Ruby an injection. A few minutes after the doctor left, however, Ruby started crying and charged, "You won't even help me."[17] Although Catherine realized that Ruby's accusations were a result of her memory loss, it was still difficult for her to cope with her sister's angry words.

During this trying time, Catherine took Ruby to the hospital every two weeks for blood transfusions. Because the cancer had weakened Ruby so much, Catherine put her in a wheelchair for these hospital visits. At the same time, the cancer had aged Ruby dramatically. While Catherine was painfully aware of her sister's deteriorating condition, the extent of Ruby's weakness was still very difficult to accept. After all, she was still Catherine's older sister who had always been the strong one; she was still the powerful woman who had run the Student Nonviolent Coordinating Committee. But, one day, as Catherine was pushing Ruby's wheelchair down the hall in the hospital, a woman approached them and congratulated Catherine for being conscientious enough to care for her grandmother.[18]

This incident served to emphasize in a profoundly dramatic way the loss of strength and control that was so very difficult for Ruby to bear. She was particularly sensitive about her SNCC colleagues and acquaintances seeing her in her weakened state. Because of her importance, however, this proved to be very difficult. Ruby had a lot of visitors, as she had touched so many lives during her movement work. Once she was discharged from the hospital, colleagues and friends would often come by her house on Sundays after church. While they talked in the living room, Ruby Doris, who was in the bedroom, would hear them and become frustrated. She would often demand, "Catherine, get those people out of my house."[19]

Yet, as Ruby Doris faced the premature end of her life, her old strength did not desert her completely. She found at least part of the source of that strength in her religious background. Ruby had been raised in the church, and she called on some of her religious beliefs now. Catherine recalls:

> I began to sense from being there with her all the time, and cooking her meals, that she knew it wasn't going to be very long before she was leaving. And she would tell me to sing Christian songs for her. And . . . she would try to sing along with me, and I would pray with her.[20]

188

During her final days, Ruby would often ask Catherine to read the Psalms to her, along with some of the other scriptures.

While she struggled to make peace and hold on to her dignity, Ruby became increasingly stoic despite the ravages of her illness—especially at the very end. There were still times when the pain caused her to cry out, but increasingly, Ruby suffered through incredible physical discomfort in silence.

> Two weeks before she died . . . I [Catherine] had her in a wheelchair, sitting up looking at TV. And I think I was looking at *Backstreet* [with] Susan Hayward. And I started talking about it and everything, and I said "Dee, did you see"—I called her Dee—"Dee, did you see that?" And . . . she said, "Catherine, you know I'm blind." I said, "blind? When did you go blind?" She said, "I've been blind." I said, "Why . . . didn't [you] tell us?"[21]

Catherine is not sure how long before this incident Ruby Doris had lost her sight. She never mentioned it to the family, her friends, or the doctors.

As the cancer increasingly robbed Ruby of control over her body, she tried to exert some control over what was left of her life. The doctors prescribed a number of different drugs to ease her pain and make her last days more comfortable. Ruby dutifully took them for a while, but about two weeks before her death, she made the decision to stop taking all medicine. That morning, Catherine measured out the medicine as she always did, but Ruby refused to take it. She clamped her jaws shut and said, "No more." From then on, Catherine recalls, "she never took another pill." Ruby knew the end was near, and she wanted a clear head so that she could arrange things as much as possible. The morning of her death, Ruby "gave up her son"; she asked her mother to care for him. That same morning, Ruby's anguished husband, Clifford, looked at her, and he knew this was the end. He told the rest of the family that they would only have to make up her bed that one last time.[22]

And then it was over. Ruby Doris Smith Robinson was gone. A rare form of cancer, lymphosarcoma, had killed her. Before she died, her physical pain was excruciating, and her emotional pain was overwhelming too. She was leaving behind the things she loved most; someone else would have to raise her son, and others would have to direct her organization. In the end, Ruby Doris Smith Robinson, the most powerful woman in SNCC, had been powerless to change her fate. Clifford recalls that she had once said she would probably be in the movement for the rest of her life. She was. But even though death won this final round, Ruby Doris had still achieved a victory of monumental proportions. She had defied all of society's efforts to categorize her and circumscribe her ambitions. Ruby Doris Smith Robinson had made her own decisions, charted her own course, and ultimately invented herself. This triumphant and irrepressible spirit was the Ruby Doris Smith Robinson that all those mourners at her funeral remembered that fall day in Atlanta. They could never forget her.

Yet in the period since her death, Ruby Doris Smith Robinson has received very little scholarly attention. Even though there has been an explosion of interest in the civil rights movement in recent years, scholarly neglect of Ruby Doris still continues. While she is mentioned in many works on the movement, scholars have treated her only sparingly and sporadically. For example, Robert Brisbane's *Black Activism* summarizes Ruby's participation in the freedom rides, voter registration in McComb, Mississippi, and events in Rock Hill in one paragraph.[23] Jim Forman's *The Making of Black Revolutionaries* contains a few more references to Ruby. It concludes "Ruby Doris was one of the few genuine revolutionaries in the black liberation movement."[24]

Even in more recent movement scholarship, little attention is focused on Ruby Doris. Taylor Branch's Pulitzer Prize winning work *Parting the Waters* devotes a good deal of space to certain SNCC activities and leaders. But it only mentions Ruby's name in discussions of Rock Hill, the freedom rides, and voter registration in McComb.[25] In his lengthy movement study, *Free At Last? The Civil Rights Movement and the People Who Made it*, Fred Powledge refers to Ruby Doris only once in connection with events in Rock Hill.[26] Clayborne Carson's biography of SNCC, *In Struggle*, includes a number of references to Ruby. However, none of them provides enough detail to give readers a clear sense of the complexity of her existence.[27] Ruby also appears briefly in the pages of Vincent Fort's essay "The Atlanta Sit-in Movement, 1960–1961: An Oral Study," Paula Giddings's book *When and Where I Enter*, Sara Evans's book *Personal Politics*, and Mary King's memoir *Freedom Song*. All of these authors acknowledge Ruby's importance, and they agree that she was a complicated woman who could sometimes be difficult to work with and to understand.

But regardless of their perspectives, colleagues inside and scholars outside the movement all agree that she was a critical part of the SNCC leadership. In view of such widespread agreement about her importance, the scholarly silence surrounding Ruby's life and movement role raises an important question: Why has so little been written about her? The easiest and most obvious answer suggests that Ruby's gender has consigned her to obscurity. Undoubtedly, this is part of the answer. Yet there is much more to it. Ruby's own vision of her proper role seems to provide another part of the answer. Yes, she was powerful. Yes, she had no qualms about using that power. But Ruby never wanted to call attention to herself and her power. As early as her Rock Hill experience, Ruby made it clear that she did not want any special recognition. She was sometimes critical of colleagues who seemed to enjoy the limelight, an attitude that prompted her to refer to Stokely Carmichael as Stokely Starmichael.[28] Above all, Ruby was convinced that the interests of the movement could best be advanced by dedicated workers who would not allow themselves to be singled out for media attention. To personalize movement issues, she believed, would be tantamount to trivializing them, or worse.

There were others who expressed similar concerns. One of those was prominent militant activist Angela Davis. Her flirtation with communism and her connection to the flamboyant Black Panthers attracted widespread media attention. Because of her high visibility, friends and coworkers pressed Davis to write about her life. Her reply to this encouragement is revealing: "When I expressed my initial hesitancy to begin working on an autobiography, it was not because I did not wish to write about the events of that time and generally in my lifetime, but rather because I did not want to contribute to the already widespread tendency to personalize and individualize history."[29] Davis, like Ruby, believed that movement concerns and events were bigger than any single individual. Thus, Ruby Doris shunned publicity throughout her activist career. This course of action has consigned her to virtual anonymity outside the movement, causing her memory to remain in the shadow of the movement leaders who received media attention.

Regardless of outsiders' views, early members of the Student Nonviolent Coordinating Committee were guided by a vision of a beloved community. Because of its idealism, early SNCC remained fluid. All things were truly possible. It was in this early SNCC that Ruby Doris began her journey to leadership. After the disappointing summer of 1964, however, SNCC became less fluid and flexible; battle lines were drawn on issues of race and gender. When everyone began to choose sides, Ruby became a critical component of SNCC's leadership. During the months following Freedom Summer, she further consolidated her power; Ruby Doris was a strong voice for unity even as divisive and destructive forces sought to rip the organization apart. She continued to work—often quietly, always in the background—and through it all, displayed a remarkable consistency. Because her involvement spanned both the early and the late SNCC, Ruby Doris Smith Robinson became a very potent symbol for continuity within an increasingly unstable organization.

Concomitantly, Ruby's death, in some ways, symbolized the final breakup of the SNCC family. It is more than a little ironic that the organization unraveled during the nine months that Ruby Doris lay dying. SNCC members lost Ruby Doris in 1967, but they were losing their organization and each other as well during that same traumatic year. Curtis Hayes recalls how pervasive the pain was: "See, by now, even though we ain't consciously admitting it, we are all in pain—about everybody. 'Cause we [are] losing people, and they [are] mad, and people are disappearing. They don't call; don't tell you where they are going . . . and we [are] really going through a lot of pain."[30]

The losses were so traumatic that many former SNCC staffers have yet to come to terms with the loss of their comrades or their organization. In fact, the memory of the loss is still so fresh and immediate for Dottie Zellner that she was recently moved to write a poem. When Zellner viewed an episode of the civil rights documentary *Eyes on the Prize*, the memories came flooding back. The result was "A Poem for Ruby Doris Robinson."

> *Ruby Doris, I saw you on TV last night*
> *Twenty-six years ago*
> *In the police wagon*
> *On the way to the station*
> *In Jackson, Mississippi,*
> *After you got off the Greyhound bus*
> *On the Freedom Rides.*
>
> *You looked directly at the camera*
> *Completely unafraid*
> *And you nearly smiled.*
>
> *But this is a confusion of time and space and face.*
>
> *For one thing, you've been dead twenty years*
> *(That was an awful winter in New York,*
> *Snow piled high everywhere*
> *And nobody knew anything about wind-chill factors,*
> *It was just so cold,*
> *It was even cold in the hospital room at Beth Israel*
> *Where you lay for week upon week*
> *At age 26*
> *Filling the bedpans full of blood).*

My oldest daughter is older now than you were
When you first went to jail
At Rock Hill, South Carolina,
And my youngest daughter, who was named for you, Ruby,
Stares at the young black face on the screen
At your image.

Your son must be her age now,
Your age
When you went on the Freedom Rides.

But this is a confusion
Of time
And space
And face
And age.

Do you think, Ruby, that these children
Will have faces like yours
Faces full of hope
Smiling at the camera
Unafraid?[31]

Zellner and many of her SNCC colleagues knew Ruby, admired her, recognized her contributions, and still mourn her. She lives on in their memories.

Up until now, though, because of who and what Ruby was, most people outside of SNCC did not even know her name. She led a complicated life, and her activities in SNCC were fraught with complexities and contradictions. Yet those who seek a true understanding of the civil rights movement and its impact on the social, political, and economic landscape of this country must confront the reality of Ruby's life. Furthermore, those who seek to explore the complicated existence of African-American women in a racist and sexist society must also confront the reality of Ruby's life. She navigated through the stereotypes; she defied convention; she kept her eyes on the prize. And as she worked for the liberation of her people, she paid the highest price imaginable, but she ultimately liberated herself.

Chapter Notes

CHAPTER ONE

1. Cleveland Sellers and Robert Terrell, *The River of No Return: The Autobiography of a Black Militant and the Life and Death of SNCC* (New York: William Morrow, 1973), 204.

2. H. Rap Brown, Ralph Featherstone, and Stanley Wise to the SNCC membership, 8 October 1967, SNCC Papers, Martin Luther King, Jr. Center for Nonviolent Social Change, Atlanta, Georgia.

3. Clayborne Carson, *In Struggle: SNCC and the Black Awakening of the 1960's* (Cambridge, Mass.: Harvard University Press, 1981), 209–10.

4. James Forman, *The Making of Black Revolutionaries: A Personal Account* (New York: Macmillan, 1972), 457.

5. Margaret and Whitney Young to Clifford Robinson, telegram, 11 October 1967, Mary Ann Smith Wilson's private papers, Atlanta, Georgia.

6. Ahmed Sekou Toure to Clifford Robinson, in care of Stanley Wise, telegram, n.d., Mary Ann Smith Wilson papers.

7. Carson, *In Struggle*, 69–70.

8. Julian Bond, interview by author, Washington, D.C., 16 December 1988.

9. John Lewis, interview by author, Knoxville, Tennessee, 24 April 1989.

10. Joyce Ladner, interview by author, Washington, D.C., 18 December 1988.

11. Dorothy Zellner, telephone interview by author, 3 November 1991.

12. Sellers and Terrell, *The River of No Return*, 204.

13. Forman, *The Making of Black Revolutionaries*, 480.

14. Paula Giddings, *When and Where I Enter: The Impact of Black Women on Race and Sex in America* (New York: Bantam Books, 1984), 318.

15. Inez Hill, interview by author, Atlanta, Georgia, 4 April 1993.

16. Bobby Smith, Willie Smith, Mary Ann Smith Wilson, and Catherine Smith Robinson, interview by author, Atlanta, Georgia, 9 February 1991.

17. Mary Ann Smith Wilson, interview by author, Atlanta, Georgia, 19 November 1989.

18. Willie Ricks, interview by author, Atlanta, Georgia, 8 April 1990.

19. Ibid.

20. Quite often, African-American funeral programs feature a picture of the deceased on the front cover.

21. Dorothy Zellner, telephone interview.

22. Ricks, interview.

23. *The Twentieth Century: Hate Groups*, narrated by Mike Wallace with speech by Dave Dennis, video. Arts and Entertainment Network.

24. Robert Weisbrot, *Freedom Bound: A History of America's Civil Rights Movement* (New York: W. W. Norton, 1990), 136.

25. *Bay Area SNCC Liberation News*, November 1967.

26. *SNCC Newsletter*, September–October 1967.

27. Michael Simmons, interview by author, Philadelphia, Pennsylvania, 16 May 1991.

28. William Porter, telephone interview by author, 9 June 1991.

29. Brenda Jefferson Smith, interview by author, Anaheim, California, 17 April 1993.

30. Avon W. Rollins to members of SNCC, in care of Stanley Wise or Ralph Featherstone, 18 October 1967, Avon Rollins's private papers, Knoxville, Tennessee.

31. Joyce Ladner, interview.

32. Porter, telephone interview.

33. Matthew Jones, Jr., interview by author, Knoxville, Tennessee, 24 April 1989.

34. Silas Norman, interview by author, Detroit, Michigan, 24 September 1990.

35. Ricks, interview.

36. *SNCC Newsletter*, September–October 1967.

37. Forman, *The Making of Black Revolutionaries*, 480.

CHAPTER TWO

1. Mary Ann Smith Wilson, interview by author, Atlanta, Georgia, 19 November 1989.

2. Benjamin Quarles, *The Negro in the Making of America* (New York: Collier Books, 1987), 217.

3. John Hope Franklin, *From Slavery to Freedom: A History of Negro Americans* 6th edition (New York: Alfred A. Knopf, 1980), 442.

4. Numan Bartley, *The Creation of Modern Georgia* (Athens: University of Georgia Press, 1983), 133.

5. Ibid., 133–34.

6. Ibid., 139.

7. Mary Ann Smith Wilson, Catherine Smith Robinson, and Ruby Banks O'Neal, interview by author, Atlanta, Georgia, 4 April 1993.

8. Ibid.

9. Ibid.

10. Wilson, interview.

11. Wilson, Robinson, and O'Neal, interview.

12. Benjamin Brown and Mary Ann Smith Wilson, interview by author, Atlanta, Georgia, 11 November 1990.

13. Clifford M. Kuhn, Harlon E. Joye, and E. Bernard West, *Living Atlanta: An Oral History of the City, 1914–1948* (Athens: University of Georgia Press, 1990), 3–4.

14. First Annual Summerhill Reunion Booklett, n. d. (reunion held on 18 June 1988 in Atlanta, Georgia) Special Collections, Fulton County Public Library (downtown branch), Atlanta, Georgia.

15. Kuhn, Joye, and West, *Living Atlanta*, 337.

16. Wilson, Robinson, and O'Neal, interview.

17. Wilson, interview.

18. Mary Ann Smith Wilson, telephone interview by author, 27 May 1997.

19. Wilson, interview, 19 November 1989.

20. Kuhn, Joye, and West, *Living Atlanta*, 217.

21. James D. Anderson, *The Education of Blacks in the South, 1860–1935* (Chapel Hill: University of North Carolina Press, 1988), 233.

22. Kuhn, Joye, and West, *Living Atlanta*, 60, 64.

23. Ibid., 268.

24. Ibid., 37.

25. Ibid., 99.

26. Bartley, *The Creation of Modern Georgia*, 136.

27. Kuhn, Joye, and West, *Living Atlanta*, 99, 106.

28. Ibid., 115.

29. Ibid.

30. Ibid., 116.

31. Ibid., 313, 314.

32. Ibid., 316.

33. Ibid., 316–17.

34. Ibid., 337, 344.

35. Wilson interview, 19 November 1989.

36. Ibid.

37. Wilson, Robinson, and O'Neal, interview.

38. Ibid.

39. Ibid.

40. Ibid.

41. Brenda Jefferson Smith, interview by author, Anaheim, California, 17 April 1993.

42. Ibid.

43. Ibid.

44. Ibid.

45. Bobby Smith, Willie Smith, Mary Ann Smith Wilson, and Catherine Smith Robinson, interview by author, Atlanta, Georgia, 9 February 1991.

46. Brenda Jefferson Smith, interview.

47. Ruby Banks O'Neal and Catherine Smith Robinson, interview by author, Atlanta, Georgia, 3 March 1990.

48. Wilson, interview, 19 November 1989.

49. O'Neal and Robinson, interview.

50. Luther Judson Price High School Yearbook, *The Wildcat*, 1958.

51. O'Neal and Robinson, interview.

52. Vincent Franklin, *Black Self-Determination* (Westport, Conn.: Lawrence Hill, 1984), 175.

53. Brown and Wilson, interview.

54. Vincent Franklin, *Black Self-Determination*, 176.

55. Smith, Smith, Wilson, and Robinson, interview.

56. Wilson, interview, 19 November 1989.

57. Smith, Smith, Wilson, and Robinson, interview.

58. Wilson interview, 19 November 1989.

59. O'Neal and Robinson, interview.

60. Phyl Garland, "Builders of a New South," *Ebony*, August 1966, 36.

61. Smith, Smith, Wilson, and Robinson, interview.

62. Ibid.

63. Ibid.

64. Wilson, Robinson, and O'Neal, interview.

65. O'Neal and Robinson, interview.

66. Ibid.

67. Wilson telephone interview, 27 May 1997.

68. Brenda Jefferson Smith, interview.

CHAPTER THREE

1. Beverly Guy-Sheftall, *Daughters of Sorrow: Attitudes toward Black Women, 1880–1920* (New York: Carlson, 1990), 139.

2. Ibid., 142.

3. Ibid., 137.

4. Ibid., 136.

5. John Haller, *Outcasts from Evolution: Scientific Attitudes of Racial Inferiority, 1858–1900* (New York: McGraw-Hill, 1971), 46–47.

6. Ibid., 53.

7. Ibid., 52.

8. Ibid., 54.

9. Ibid., 56.

10. Ibid., 54.

11. Wilson Jeremiah Moses, *The Golden Age of Black Nationalism, 1850–1925* (New York: Oxford University Press, 1978), 115.

12. Ibid., 124.

13. Clifford M. Kuhn, Harlon E. Joye and E. Bernard West, *Living Atlanta: An Oral History of the City, 1914–1948* (Athens: University of Georgia Press, 1990), 153.

14. Ibid., 154.

15. Kathy Russell, Midge Wilson, and Ronald Hall, *The Color Complex: The Politics of Skin Color among African Americans* (New York: Harcourt Brace Jovanovich, 1992), 28.

16. Mary Ann Smith Wilson, telephone interview by author, 27 May 1997.

17. Kuhn, Joye, and West, *Living Atlanta*, 152.

18. Ibid., 158.

19. Ibid., 166.

20. Lana Taylor Sims and Norma June Davis, interview by author, Atlanta, Georgia, 11 November 1990.

21. Gwen Robinson, interview by author, Philadelphia, Pennsylvania, 17 December 1988.

22. Albert Brinson, interview by author, Atlanta, Georgia, 10 November 1990.

23. Sims and Davis, interview.

24. Gwen Robinson, interview.

25. *Spelman Messenger*, November 1957, 8–9.

26. *Spelman Messenger*, May 1960, 19.

27. *Spelman Messenger*, May 1959, 30.

28. *Spelman Messenger*, May 1960, 12–13.

29. *Spelman Messenger*, August 1960, 12.

30. *Atlanta Inquirer*, 7 June 1961.

31. *Spelman Messenger*, May 1957, 23.

32. Howard Zinn, *The Southern Mystique* (New York: Alfred A. Knopf, 1964), 115.

33. Ibid., 117.

34. Howard Zinn, *SNCC: The New Abolitionists* (Boston: Beacon Press, 1964), 17.

35. Vincent D. Fort, "The Atlanta Sit-in Movement, 1960–1961: An Oral Study," in *Atlanta, Georgia, 1960–1961: Sit-ins and Student Activism*, ed., David J. Garrow (New York: Carlson, 1989), 133.

36. Ibid.

37. Julian Bond, interview by author, Washington, D.C., 16 December 1988.

38. Benjamin Brown and Mary Ann Smith Wilson, interview by author, Atlanta, Georgia, 11 November 1990.

39. Clayborne Carson, *In Struggle: SNCC and the Black Awakening of the 1960's* (Cambridge, Mass.: Harvard University Press, 1981), 20.

40. Eric R. Burner, *And Gently He Shall Lead Them: Robert Parris Moses and Civil Rights in Mississippi* (New York: New York University Press, 1994), 25.

41. Paula Giddings, *When and Where I Enter: The Impact of Black Women on Race and Sex in America* (New York: Bantam Books, 1984), 271.

42. Charlayne Hunter-Gault, *In My Place* (New York: Farrar Straus Giroux, 1992), 144.

43. Howell Raines, *My Soul Is Rested: The Story of the Civil Rights Movement in the Deep South* (New York: Penguin Books, 1977), 98–99.

44. Diane Nash, "Inside the Sit-ins and Freedom Rides: Testimony of a Southern Student," in *The New Negro*, ed. Matthew H. Ahmann (New York: Biblo and Tannen, 1969), 60.

45. Casey Hayden, remarks during the Women's Panel at the Trinity College SNCC Conference, Hartford, Connecticut, 1988.

46. Fort, "The Atlanta Sit-in Movement," 135.

47. Vincent Fort notes on an audiotape by Lionel Newsome, Vincent Fort's private papers, Atlanta, Georgia.

48. *Atlanta Inquirer*, 14 August 1960.

49. Ibid.

50. Mary Ann Smith Wilson, interview by author, Atlanta, Georgia, 19 November 1989.

51. Brown and Wilson, interview.

52. Ibid.

53. Zinn, *SNCC: The New Abolitionists*, 39.

54. *Readers Digest*, September 1987, 150.

55. Sims and Davis, interview.

56. Brown and Wilson interview.

57. Jack M. Bloom, *Class, Race, and the Civil Rights Movement* (Bloomington: Indiana University Press, 1987), 160–61.

58. Debbie Louis, *And We Are Not Saved: A History of the Movement As People* (New York: Doubleday, 1970), 117.

59. Bloom, *Class, Race, and the Civil Rights Movement*, 161.

60. Vincent Fort, notes on an audiotape by Lionel Newsome.

61. Anne Moody, *Coming of Age in Mississippi* (New York: Dial Press, 1968), 235.

62. Albert Manley, interview by author, Washington, D.C., 16 December 1988.

63. Joyce Ladner, Womens' Panel, Trinity College SNCC Conference.

64. Wilson, interview, 19 November 1989.

65. Fort, "The Atlanta Sit-in Movement," 151.

66. Bobby Smith, Willie Smith, Mary Ann Smith Wilson and Catherine Smith Robinson, interview by author, Atlanta, Georgia, 9 February 1991.

67. Wilson, interview, 19 November 1989.

68. Ruby Doris Smith to Mary Ann Smith, 25 February 1961, Mary Ann Smith Wilson's private papers, Atlanta, Georgia.

69. Smith, Smith, Wilson, and Robinson, interview.

70. Sims and Davis, interview.

71. Joyce Ladner, interview by author, Washington, D.C., 18 December 1988.

72. Martha Prescod Norman, interview by author, Detroit, Michigan, 30 December 1988.

73. Gwen Robinson, interview.

74. Wilson, interview, 19 November 1989.

75. Gwen Robinson, interview.

76. Dorie Ladner, interview by author, Washington, D.C., 5 May 1991.

77. Joyce Ladner, interview.

78. Lois Moreland, interview by author, Atlanta, Georgia, 7 February 1991.

79. Ibid.

80. Zinn, *The Southern Mystique*, 116.

81. Fort, "The Atlanta Sit-in Movement," 149.

82. Brown and Wilson, interview.

83. Sims and Davis, interview.

84. Fort, "The Atlanta Sit-in Movement," 149.

85. Ibid.

86. *Atlanta Inquirer*, 22 April 1961.

87. Sims and Davis, interview.

88. Ibid.

89. *Atlanta Inquirer*, 15 April 1961.

90. Brown and Wilson, interview.

91. Ibid.

92. Sims and Davis, interview.

93. Casey Hayden, Womens' Panel, Trinity College SNCC Conference.

94. Wilson, interview, 19 November 1989.

CHAPTER FOUR

1. Clayborne Carson, *In Struggle: SNCC and the Black Awakening of the 1960's* (Cambridge, Mass.: Harvard University Press, 1981), 23.

2. Report of the Findings and Recommendations Committee, n.d., Student Nonviolent Coordinating Committee Papers reel 11 (microfilm).

3. Ella Baker interview by Sue Thrasher and Casey Hayden, New York, New York, 19 April 1977, Southern Historical Collection, Southern Oral History Program, collection 4007, interview G-8, 70–71.

4. Carson, *In Struggle*, 28.

5. *The Student Voice*, 1, 2 (August, 1960).

6. Taylor Branch, *Parting the Waters: America in the King Years. 1954–1963* (New York: Simon & Shuster, 1988), 351.

7. Vincent D. Fort, "The Atlanta Sit-In Movement, 1960–1961: An Oral Study," in *Atlanta Georgia 1960–1961: Sit-ins and Student Activism*, ed. David J. Garrow (New York: Carlson, 1989), 140.

8. Meeting report SNCC Papers, n.d. reel 3 (microfilm).

9. Ibid., frame 0784.

10. *Student Voice*, 2, 2 (February 1961).

11. Benjamin Brown and Mary Ann Smith Wilson, interview by author, Atlanta, Georgia, 11 November 1990.

12. Connie Curry, interview by author, Atlanta, Georgia, 10 November 1990.

13. Charles Jones and Reginald Robinson, interview by author, McComb, Mississippi, 28 June 1991.

14. Howard Zinn, *SNCC: The New Abolitionists*, 38.

15. Diane Nash, interview by author, Chicago, Illinois, 6 November 1989.

16. Curry, interview.

17. Jones and Robinson, interview.

18. *Atlanta Inquirer*, 18 March 1961.

19. Ibid.

20. Ruby Doris Smith to Mary Ann Smith, 25 February 1961.

21. Nash, interview.

22. Ruby Doris Smith to Brenda Jefferson, 8 February 1961, Brenda Jefferson Smith's private papers, Anaheim, California.

23. Nash, interview.

24. *Atlanta Inquirer*, 18 March 1961. See also Zinn, *SNCC: The New Abolitionists*. 38–39.

25. Nash, interview.

26. Ruby Doris Smith to Mary Ann Smith, 25 February 1961.

27. *Atlanta Inquirer*, 11 February 1961.

28. Fort, "The Atlanta Sit-in Movement," 135.

29. Nash, interview.

30. Diane Nash, "Inside the Sit-Ins and Freedom Rides: Testimony of a Southern Student," in *The New Negro*, ed. Mathew H. Ahmann (New York: Biblo and Tannen, 1969), 46.

31. Ruby Doris Smith to Mary Ann Smith, 25 February 1961.

32. *Atlanta Inquirer*, 18 March 1961.

33. Casper L. Jordan, "The First Freedom Rider," *Negro Digest*, August, 1961, 39, 41.

34. Jim Peck, "The First Freedom Ride," *Southern Exposure* 9, no. 1 (Spring 1981): 37.

35. Zinn, *SNCC: The New Abolitionists*, 41.

36. James Forman, "Freedom Rides: Speech by James Farmer and interview with Lucretia Collins," *Southern Exposure* 9, no. 1 (Spring 1981): 34.

37. Ibid.

38. Zinn, *SNCC: The New Abolitionists*, 42.

39. James Farmer, *Lay Bare the Heart: An Autobiography of the Civil Rights Movement* (New York: Dutton, New American Library, 1985), 202–3.

40. Zinn, *SNCC: The New Abolitionists*, 43–44.

41. Farmer, *Lay Bare the Heart*, 203.

42. Zinn, *SNCC: The New Abolitionists*, 45.

43. Ibid.

44. Ibid., 45–46.

45. Ibid., 44.

46. Pete Seeger and Bob Reiser, *Everybody Say Freedom: A History of the Civil Rights Movement in Songs and Pictures* (New York: W. W. Norton, 1989), 62.

47. Zinn, *SNCC: The New Abolitionists*, 47.

48. Ibid., 47–48.

49. *Atlanta Inquirer*, 27 May 1961.

50. Farmer, *Lay Bare the Heart*, 2–4.

51. Howell Raines, *My Soul Is Rested: The Story of the Civil Rights Movement in the Deep South* (New York: Penguin Books, 1983), 277.

52. John Lewis, interview by author, Knoxville, Tennessee, 24 April 1989.

53. Raines, *My Soul Is Rested*, 125.

54. Ibid.

55. Zinn, *SNCC: The New Abolitionists*, 54.

56. Ruby Doris Smith to Alice Smith, 10 June 1961, Mary Ann Smith Wilson papers.

57. Zinn, *SNCC: The New Abolitionists*, 54.

58. Ruby Doris Smith to Alice Smith, 10 June 1961.

59. Zinn, *SNCC: The New Abolitionists*, 54.

60. Seeger and Reiser, *Everybody Say Freedom*, 61.

61. Zinn, *SNCC: The New Abolitionists*, 54.

62. Seeger and Reiser, *Everybody Say Freedom*, 63.

63. Zinn, *SNCC: The New Abolitionists*, 55.

64. Seeger and Reiser, *Everybody Say Freedom*, 65.

65. Carson, *In Struggle*, 41.

66. Stokely Carmichael, interview by author, Knoxville, Tennessee, 14 March 1990.

67. Ibid.

68. Constancia Romilly, interview by author, Atlanta, Georgia, 14 June 1991.

69. Charles McDew, interview by author, McComb, Mississippi, 28 June 1991.

70. Carmichael, interview.

71. Carson, *In Struggle*, 42.

72. Ibid., 47–48.

73. Jones and Robinson, interview.

74. C. C. Bryant, interview by author, McComb, Mississippi, 28 June 1991.

75. Jack L. Walker, "Sit-Ins in Atlanta: A Study in the Negro Revolt," in *Atlanta Georgia 1960–1961: Sit-ins and Student Activism*, ed. David J. Garrow (New York: Carlson, 1989), 90.

76. Jacqueline Jones Royster, "A Heartbeat for Liberation: The Reclamation of Ruby Doris Smith," *Sage: A Scholarly Journal on Black Women—Student Supplement* (1988): 64.

77. Ibid., 64–65.

78. Julian Bond, interview by author, Washington, D.C., 16 December 1988.

79. *Atlanta Constitution*, 14 February 1962.

80. Jones and Robinson, interview. See also Carson, *In Struggle*, 59.

81. *New York Times*, 14 August 1962.

82. James Forman, *The Making of Black Revolutionaries: A Personal Account* (New York: Macmillan, 1972), 221.

83. Ibid., 220.

84. Ibid., 234.

85. Ibid., 235–36.

86. James Forman, interview by author, Washington, D.C., 15 May 1991.

87. Jones and Robinson, interview.

88. Carson, *In Struggle*, 82.

89. James Forman, interview.

90. Staff meeting minutes, 29 December 1963, SNCC Papers, reel 3 (microfilm).

91. Stanley Wise, interview by author, Atlanta, Georgia, 11 November 1988.

92. Matthew Jones, Jr., interview by author, Knoxville, Tennessee, 24 April 1989.

93. Jones and Robinson, interview.

94. Jack Minnis, interview by author, New Orleans, Louisiana, 24 November 1990.

95. Worth Long, interview by author, Atlanta, Georgia, 8 February 1991.

96. Curtis Hayes, interview by author, McComb, Mississippi, 29 June 1991.

97. Minnis, interview.

98. Long, interview.

99. Dorothy Zellner, telephone interview by author, 3 November 1991.

100. Jones and Robinson, interview.

101. Michael Simmons, interview by author, Philadelphia, Pennsylvania, 16 May 1991.

102. Diamond, interview.

103. Michael Simmons, interview.

104. Hayes, interview.

105. Bob Zellner, interview by author, New Orleans, Louisiana, 4 November 1990.

106. Hayes, interview.

107. Long, interview.

108. Ruby Doris Smith to Avon Rollins, 30 July 1963, Avon Rollins papers.

109. Ibid.

110. Long, interview.

111. Ruby Doris Smith to Avon Rollins, 2 August 1963, Avon Rollins papers.

112. Joanne Grant, ed., *Black Protest: History, Documents, and Analyses—1619 to the Present* (Greenwich, Conn.: Fawcett, 1968), 377.

113. Ruby Doris Smith to Avon Rollins, n.d., Avon Rollins papers.

CHAPTER FIVE

1. Charles Jones and Reginald Robinson, interview by author, McComb, Mississippi, 28 June 1991.

2. Dorothy Zellner, telephone interview by author, 3 November 1991.

3. Jones and Robinson, interview.

4. Sara Evans, *Personal Politics: The Roots of Women's Liberation in the Civil Rights Movement and the New Left* (New York: Vintage Books, 1979), 84.

5. Jean Wheeler Smith, remarks during Women's Panel at the Trinity College SNCC Conference, Hartford, Connecticut, 1988.

6. Jones and Robinson, interview.

7. Bobbi Yancy, interview by author, New York, New York, 16 May 1991.

8. Freddie Greene Biddle, interview by author, McComb, Mississippi, 29 June 1991.

9. Ruby Banks O'Neal and Catherine Smith Robinson, interview by author, Atlanta, Georgia, 3 March 1990.

10. Stanley Wise, interview by author, Atlanta, Georgia, 11 November 1988.

11. Yancy, interview.

12. Bob Zellner, interview by author, New Orleans, Louisiana, 4 November 1990.

13. Jones and Robinson, interview.

14. Wise, interview.

15. Ricks, interview.

16. Biddle, interview.

17. Ibid.

18. Joyce Ladner, interview by author, Washington, D.C., 18 December 1988.

19. Dorie Ladner, interview by author, Washington, D.C., 18 May 1991.

20. Ibid.

21. Biddle, interview.

22. Emma Bell Moses, interview by author, McComb, Mississippi, 29 June 1991.

23. Gwen Robinson, interview by author, Philadelphia, Pennsylvania, 17 December 1988.

24. Clifford Robinson, interview by author, Atlanta, Georgia, 17 March 1989.

25. Biddle, interview.

26. Wise, interview.

27. Bobby Smith, Willie Smith, Mary Ann Smith Wilson, and Catherine Smith Robinson, interview by author, Atlanta, Georgia, 9 February 1991.

28. Wise, interview.

29. Smith, Smith, Wilson, and Robinson, interview.

30. Ibid.

31. Biddle, interview.

32. Ibid.

33. Mildred Page Forman, interview by author, Chicago, Illinois, 6 November 1989.

34. Biddle, interview.

35. Paula Giddings, *When and Where I Enter: The Impact of Black Women on Race and Sex in America* (New York: Bantam Books, 1984), 315.

36. Clayborne Carson, *In Struggle: SNCC and the Black Awakening of the 1960's* (Cambridge, Mass.: Harvard University Press, 1981), 97–98.

37. Hollis Watkins, interview by author, New Market, Tennessee, 5 May 1990.

38. Constancia Romilly, interview by author, Atlanta, Georgia, 14 June 1991.

39. Worth Long, interview by author, Atlanta, Georgia, 8 February 1991.

40. Minutes of the Atlanta office staff meeting, 2 February 1964, p. 3, Student Nonviolent Coordinating Committee Papers, reel 3 (microfilm).

41. Staff meeting minutes, 9–11 June 1964, pp. 3–4, SNCC Papers, reel 2, (microfilm).

42. Romilly, interview.

43. Minutes of the Executive Committee, 11 June 1964, SNCC Papers, reel 3, frame 0889 (microfilm).

44. Staff meeting minutes, 9–11 June 1964.

45. Joyce Ladner, Women's Panel, Trinity College SNCC Conference.

46. Staughton Lynd to H Z [Howard Zinn] 12 June 1964, SNCC Papers, reel 2, frame 442 (microfilm).

47. Staff meeting minutes, 10 June 1964, p. 13, SNCC Papers, reel 2, frame 421 (microfilm).

48. Ibid., 14.

49. Casey Hayden, Womens' Panel, Trinity College SNCC Conference.

50. "General Thought Processes" from the office staff meeting, 2 February 1964, SNCC Papers, reel 3 (microfilm).

51. Staff meeting minutes, 29 December 1963, p. 17, SNCC Papers, reel 3 (microfilm).

52. C. C. Bryant, interview by author, McComb, Mississisppi, 28 June 1991.

53. "General Thought Processes" from the office staff meeting, 2 February 1964.

54. John Dittmer, *Local People, The Struggle for Civil Rights in Mississippi* (Chicago: University of Illinois Press, 1994), 237.

55. Carson, *In Struggle*, 109.

56. Staff meeting minutes, 9–11 June 1964, p. 4.

57. Carson, *In Struggle*, 105.

58. Staff meeting minutes, 9–11 June 1964, p. 6.

59. Ibid., pp. 4, 14.

60. Staff meeting minutes, 5 May 1964, SNCC Papers, reel 3, frame 0914 (microfilm).

61. Mary Aicken Rothschild, *A Case of Black and White: Northern Volunteers and the Southern Freedom Summers, 1964–65* (Westport, Conn: Greenwood Press, 1982), 138.

62. Ibid., 147.

63. Evans, *Personal Politics*, 81.

64. Cynthia Washington, "We Started From Different Ends of the Spectrum," *Southern Exposure*, 5 (Winter, 1977), 14.

65. Ibid., 14.

66. Evans, *Personal Politics*, 88.

67. Gwen Robinson, interview.

68. Jones and Robinson, interview.

69. See the discussion of black female morality in chapter 3.

70. Gwen Robinson, interview.

71. Ibid.

72. Josephine Carson, *Silent Voices: The Southern Negro Woman Today* (New York: Delacorte Press, 1969), 160.

73. Ibid., 159.

74. Dorothy Zellner, telephone interview.

75. Curtis Hayes, interview by author, McComb, Mississippi, 29 June 1991.

76. Stokely Carmichael, interview by author, Knoxville, Tennessee, 14 March 1990.

77. Michael Simmons, interview by author, Philadelphia, Pennsylvania, 16 May 1991.

78. Jones and Robinson, interview.

79. Carmichael, interview.

80. Dion Diamond, interview by author, McComb, Mississippi, 28 June 1991.

81. Michael Simmons, interview.

82. Casey Hayden, Womens' Panel, Trinity College SNCC Conference.

83. Angela Davis, *Women, Race, and Class* (New York: Vintage Books, 1983), 5.

84. Beverly Guy-Sheftall, *Daughters of Sorrow: Attitudes toward Black Women, 1880–1920* (New York: Carlson, 1990), 78.

85. Ibid., 41.

86. Donald Bogle, *Toms, Coons, Mulattoes, Mammies, and Bucks*, (New York: Bantam Books, 1974), 10.

87. Ibid., 9–10.

88. Guy-Sheftall, *Daughters of Sorrow*, 104.

89. Courtland Cox, interview by author, Washington, D.C., 16 December 1988.

90. Joanne Grant, interview by author, New Orleans, Louisiana, 4 November 1990.

91. Joyce Ladner, interview.

92. Ricks, interview.

93. Romilly, interview.

94. Hayes, interview.

95. Dorothy Zellner, telephone interview.

96. Ricks, interview.

97. James Bond, interview by author, Atlanta, Georgia, 9 February 1991.

98. Giddings, *When and Where I Enter*, 290.

99. Ibid., 292.

100. Charles McDew, interview by author, McComb, Mississippi, 28 June 1991.

101. Giddings, *When and Where I Enter*, 242–43.

102. Washington, "We Started From Different Ends of the Spectrum," 14.

103. Dorothy Zellner, telephone interview.

104. Gwen Robinson, interview.

105. Alvin Poussaint, "The Stresses of the White Female Worker in the Civil Rights Movement in the South," *Journal of American Psychiatry* 123 (October 1966), 404.

106. Casey Hayden, interview by author, 17 March 1989, Atlanta, Georgia.

107. Connie Curry, interview by author, Altanta, Georgia, 10 November 1990.

108. Yancy, interview.

109. Dorie Ladner, interview.

110. Romilly, interview.

111. Joyce Ladner, interview.

112. Ann Romaine, interview by author, Knoxville, Tennessee, 8 August 1990.

113. Hayden, interview.

114. Doug McAdam, *Freedom Summer* (New York: Oxford University Press, 1988), 104 quoted from Elizabeth Sutherland, ed., *Letters From Mississippi* (New York: McGraw-Hill, 1965), 202.

115. Ibid.

116. McDew, interview.

117. Biddle, interview.

118. Dorie Ladner, interview.

119. McDew, interview.

120. Watkins, interview.

121. McDew, interview.

122. Ibid.

123. Biddle, interview.

124. Fay Bellamy, interview by author, Atlanta, Georgia, 12 November 1990.

125. McAdam, *Freedom Summer*, 59.

126. Cleveland Sellers and Robert Terrell, *The River of No Return: The Autobiography of a Black Militant and the Life and Death of SNCC* (New York: William Morrow, 1973), 96.

127. Michael Simmons, interview.

128. Bellamy, interview.

129. Evans, *Personal Politics*, 78–79.

130. Romilly, interview.

131. Diamond, interview.

132. Romaine, interview.

133. Gwen Robinson, interview.

134. Bellamy, interview.

135. Martha Prescod Norman, interview by author, Detroit, Michigan, 30 December 1988.

136. McAdam, *Freedom Summer*, 124.

137. Giddings, *When and Where I Enter*, 302.

138. Jones and Robinson, interview.

139. Dorie Ladner, interview.

140. William Porter, telephone interview by author, 9 June 1991.

141. Dorie Ladner, interview.

142. Romilly, interview.

143. Michael Simmons, interview.

144. Curry, interview.

145. John Lewis, interview by author, Knoxville, Tennessee, 24 April 1989.

146. Hayden, interview.

147. Romaine, interview.

148. Poussaint, "The Stresses of the White Female Worker in the Civil Rights Movement in the South," 403.

149. McAdam, *Freedom Summer*, 124.

150. Wise, interview.

CHAPTER SIX

1. SNCC staff meeting minutes, 5 September 1964, p. 8, Mary Ann Smith Wilson's private papers, Atlanta, Georgia.

2. "African President Visits the South," *Ebony*, December 1960, 144.

3. David Lamb, *The Africans* (New York: Vintage Books, 1983), 222.

4. Ibid.

5. *Ebony*, February 1960, 26.

6. SNCC Executive Committee meeting minutes, 4 September 1964, p. 10, Mary Ann Smith Wilson's papers.

7. Julian Bond, interview.

8. Clayborne Carson, *In Struggle: SNCC and the Black Awakening of the 1960's* (Cambridge, Mass.: Harvard University Press, 1981), 134.

9. Stanley Wise, interview by author, Atlanta, Georgia, 11 November 1988.

10. Bond, interview.

11. Matthew Jones, Jr., interview by author, Knoxville, Tennessee, 24 April 1989.

12. Ruby Doris Smith Robinson, typescript of Guinea diary, p. 5, Mary Ann Smith Wilson's papers.

13. Worth Long, interview by author, Atlanta, Georgia, 8 February 1991.

14. Kay Mills, *This Little Light of Mine: The Life of Fannie Lou Hamer* (New York: Dutton, New American Library, 1993), 136.

15. Carson, *In Struggle*, 135.

16. Stokely Carmichael, interview by author, Knoxville, Tennessee, 8 February 1991.

17. Lewis, interview.

18. Long, interview.

19. Wise, interview.

20. Rowland Evans and Robert Novak, "Inside Report," *Washington Post*, 2 December 1964.

21. James Forman, *The Making of Black Revolutionaries: A Personal Account* (New York: Macmillan, 1972), 427.

22. Ibid., 415.

23. Ibid., 420.

24. Carson, *In Struggle*, 139.

25. Ibid., 141.

26. Memo, n.d., Student Nonviolent Coordinating Committee Papers, reel 11, frame 951 (microfilm).

27. Forman, *The Making of Black Revolutionaries*, 436.

28. Mary King, *Freedom Song: A Personal Story of the 1960's Civil Rights Movement* (New York: William Morrow, 1987), 453.

29. Ibid.

30. Bobbi Yancy, interview by author, New York, New York, 16 May 1991.

31. Wise, interview.

32. Ibid.

33. Yancy, interview.

34. King, *Freedom Song*, 568–69.

35. Ibid., 453.

36. Wise, interview.

37. Michael Simmons, interview by author, Philadelphia, Pennsylvania, 16 May 1991.

38. Gwen Robinson, interview by author, Philadelphia, Pennsylvania, 17 December 1988.

39. Fay Bellamy, interview by author, Atlanta, Georgia, 12 November 1990.

40. Hollis Watkins, interview by author, New Market, Tennessee, 5 May 1990.

41. Martha Prescod Norman, interview by author, Detroit, Michigan, 30 December 1988.

42. Dorie Ladner, interview by author, Washington, D.C., 18 May 1991.

43. Michael Sayer, interview by author, New Market, Tennessee, 5 May 1990.

44. Jean Wheeler Smith and Joyce Ladner, remarks during Women's Panel at the Trinity College SNCC Conference, Hartford, Connecticut, 1988.

45. Ibid.

46. Bellamy, interview.

47. Sara Evans, *Personal Politics: The Roots of Women's Liberation in the Civil Rights Movement and the New Left* (New York: Vintage Books, 1979), 41.

48. Dorothy Zellner, telephone interview by author, 3 November 1991.

49. Sayer, interview.

50. Minutes of the Holly Springs, Mississippi Executive Committee meeting, 12–14 April 1964, pp. 4, 15, SNCC Papers, reel 3, (microfilm).

51. Gwen Robinson, interview.

52. Minutes of the Holly Springs, Mississippi Executive Committee meeting 12–14 April 1964, pp. 9–10.

53. Wise, interview.

54. Ibid.

55. Mildred Page Forman, interview by author, Chicago, Illinois, 6 November 1989.

56. Ibid.

57. Wise, interview.

58. Long, interview.

59. Ibid.

60. Carson, *In Struggle*, 166.

61. James Forman, interview by author, Washington, D.C., 15 May 1991.

62. Curtis Hayes, interview by author, McComb, Mississippi, 29 June 1991.

63. Dorie Ladner, interview.

64. Hayes, interview.

65. Long, interview.

66. Joanne Grant, interview by author, New Orleans, Louisiana, 4 November 1990.

67. Jack Minnis, interview by author, New Orleans, Lousiana, 4 November 1990.

68. Ibid.

69. Recommendations and mandates of the SNCC Central Committee to mem-

bers of the secretariat and other staff members, 14 May 1966, SNCC Papers, reel 3, frame 0587 (microfilm).

70. Memo to the Coordinating Committee from the Sojourner Motor Fleet, n.d., SNCC Papers, reel 3 (microfilm).

71. Ibid.

72. Forman, *The Making of Black Revolutionaries*, 474.

73. Carson, *In Struggle*, 207.

74. Ricks, interview. See also Forman, *The Making of Black Revolutionaries*, 457.

75. John Lewis interview, by author, Knoxville, Tennessee, 24 April 1989.

76. Long, interview.

77. Carmichael, interview.

78. James Forman, interview.

79. Phyl Garland, "Builders of a New South," *Ebony*, August 1966, 36.

80. Ibid., 37.

81. Paula Giddings, *When and Where I Enter: The Impact of Black Women on Race and Sex in America* (New York: Bantam Books, 1984), 316.

82. Ibid.

83. Ibid., 317.

84. Ibid., 318.

85. William Grier and Price Cobbs, *Black Rage* (New York: Basic Books, 1968), 63.

86. Wise, interview.

87. Freddie Biddle, interview by author, McComb, Mississippi, 29 June 1991.

88. Lewis, interview.

89. Michael Simmons, interview.

90. Gwen Robinson, interview.

91. Bellamy, interview.

92. Minnis, interview.

93. Yancy, interview.

94. Emily Stoper, *The Student Nonviolent Coordinating Committee: The Growth of Radicalism in a Civil Rights Organization* (New York: Carlson 1989), 217.

95. Long, interview.

96. Dorie Ladner, interview.

97. Mildred Page Forman, interview.

98. Ibid.

99. Ibid.

100. Gwen Robinson, interview.

101. O'Neal and Robinson, interview.

102. Biddle, interview.

103. Ibid.

104. Wilson, interview 19 November 1989.

105. Copy of a typescript from the University of Wisconsin Civil Rights Collection, n.d., Vincent Fort's private papers, Atlanta, Georgia.

106. Ibid.

107. Carson, *In Struggle*, 230.

108. Ibid.

109. James Forman, interview.

110. Carson, *In Struggle*, 194.

111. Gwen Robinson, interview.

112. Biddle, interview.

113. Forman, *The Making of Black Revolutionaries*, 476.

114. Ibid.

115. Biddle, interview.

116. Minnis, interview.

117. Biddle, interview.

118. Ibid.

CHAPTER SEVEN

1. Ruby Banks O'Neal and Catherine Smith Robinson, interview by author, Atlanta, Georgia, 3 March 1990.

2. Mary Ann Smith Wilson, interview by author, Atlanta, Georgia, 19 November 1989.

3. Bob Zellner, interview by author, New Orleans, Louisiana, 4 November 1990.

4. Willie Ricks, interview by author, Atlanta, Georgia, 8 April 1990.

5. Clayborne Carson, *In Struggle: SNCC and the Black Awakening of the 1960's* (Cambridge, Mass.: Harvard University Press, 1981), 266.

6. Ibid., 267–68.

7. John Hope Franklin and Alfred A. Moss, Jr., *From Slavery to Freedom: A History of Negro Americans* 6th ed. (New York: McGraw-Hill, 1988), 403.

8. Joanne Grant, interview by author, New Orleans, Louisiana, 4 November 1990.

9. Ibid.

10. Stanley Wise to Ruby Doris Robinson, 9 June 1967, Student Nonviolent Coordinating Committee Papers, reel 3, frame 0085 (microfilm).

11. Rap Brown, Ralph Featherstone, and Stanley Wise to the SNCC membership, 8 October 1967, SNCC Papers.

12. Avon W. Rollins to the SNCC membership, 18 October 1967, Avon Rollins's private papers, Knoxville, Tennessee.

13. Gwen Robinson, interview by author, Philadelphia, Pennsylvania, 17 December 1988.

14. Coutland Cox, interview by author, Washington, D.C., 16 December 1988.

15. Ricks, interview.

16. O'Neal and Robinson, interview.

17. Ibid.

18. Ibid.

19. Ibid.

20. Ibid.

21. Ibid.

22. Ibid.

23. Robert Brisbane, *Black Activism: Racial Revolution in the United States, 1954–1970* (Valley Forge, Pa.: Judson Press, 1974), 130.

24. James Forman, *The Making of Black Revolutionaries: A Personal Account* (New York: Macmillan, 1972), 475.

25. Taylor Branch, *Parting the Waters: America in the King Years, 1954–63* (New York: Simon & Schuster Inc.), 392, 440, 496.

26. Fred Powledge, *Free at Last? The Civil Rights Movement and the People Who Made It* (New York: Harper Collins, 1992).

27. Carson, *In Struggle*, 204.

28. Worth Long, interview by author, Atlanta, Georgia, 8 February 1991.

29. Angela Davis, *Angela Davis: An Autobiography* (New York: Random House, 1974), viii.

30. Curtis Hayes, interview by author, McComb, Mississippi, 29 June 1991.

31. Dorothy M. Zellner, "A Poem for Ruby Doris Robinson," Dorothy M. Zellner's private papers, New York, New York.

Index

Nonviolent High, McComb, Mississippi, 90

Norman, Martha Prescod, 60–61, 136, 155

Oppression, 118, 128

Packard, Sophia, 39–40
Palestinian support, 184–85
Pan-Africanism, 148
Pan American Airways, 145–46
Parchman State Penitentiary, Mississippi, 86–87
Parenting, 27–28, 35–37
Parks, Rosa, 36
Patch, Penelope, 92
Patriotism, 36
Peck, Jim, 78–79, 80
Person, Charles, 80
Personality characteristics, 48, 104, 124–26, 130, 160
Physical appearance, 31, 74, 77, 119–22, 173–76, 183
Picket lines, 56, 67, 76, 132
"A Poem for Ruby Doris Robinson," 192–93
Police officers, mob control, 84
Political system, distrust for, 114–15
Ponder, Annelle, 125
Porter, William, 10, 11, 137–38
Poussaint, Alvin, 127–28, 139
Powledge, Fred, 190
Pregnancy, 106
Price High School, Atlanta, Georgia, 30–32, 38, 46
Protest demonstrations, 51–53, 55–56, 57; Atlanta businesses, 55–58; disapproval of by faculty, 64; effect on protestor's life, 67–68; family pressures on, 59–60; Georgia, 71–72; hospitals, 91–92; Manley endorsement of, 50; participants' views of, 58–59; South Carolina, 72, 76; support for by faculty, 62–64; views of leaders, 60–61; see also Sit-ins
Purdue, Amanda, 158

Race relations, 46–47, 177; black females/white females, 116–18, 127–28; black-white conflicts, 128–29; field staff, 172; racial separatism, 179, 185; Robinson's early reaction to, 34–35; violence and, 112–13; whites expulsion from SNCC, 180–81
Racial discrimination, 13, 14–15, 32–36
Railroad workers, 21
Randolph, A. Phillip, 13
Ransom, Cassius, 78
Reagon, Cordell, 86–87
Reeb, James, 1
Religious beliefs, 188–89
Religious persecution, 75–76
Respect issues, 170–71
Rhythm and blues music, 29–30, 66
Richardson, Gloria, 168
Richardson, Judy, 151
Rich's Department Store, Atlanta, Georgia, 71
Ricks, Willie, 2, 8, 104, 125, 166, 184, 187
Riots, 14–15, 185
Robinson, Casper, 103
Robinson, Catherine, 187–88
Robinson, Clifford, 3, 103, 104, 105–106, 108, 166, 186–87
Robinson, Gwen, 47, 105, 118–19, 137; family view of protests, 61–62; field staff relationships, 136; on gender issues, 153–54; on hairstyles, 174–75; on Robinson's health, 187; SNCC automobile incident, 158; on SNCC conflicts, 179; on treatment of white workers, 171; on white females, 127
Robinson, Kenneth Toure, 3, 106–107, 184
Robinson, Reginald, 96, 102, 104, 118
Rock Hill, South Carolina, 72–75, 80
Rollins, Avon, 10–11, 98–99
Romaine, Ann, 130, 136, 139
Romilly, Constancia, 88, 111, 124, 129, 135, 137–38
Roosevelt, Franklin, 13
Rothschild, Mary Aicken, 116–17